100 SIGNS OF THE TIMES

LEADING UP TO THE SECOND COMING OF CHRIST

FAMILY DELUXE EDITION

100 SIGNS OF THE TIMES

LEADING UP TO THE SECOND COMING OF CHRIST

DAVID J. RIDGES

CFI
AN IMPRINT OF CEDAR FORT, INC.
SPRINGVILLE, UTAH

PRESENTED
TO

_____

NAME

_____

DATE

ISBN 13: 978-1-4621-2129-8

Published by CFI, an imprint of Cedar Fort, Inc.
2373 W. 700 S., Springville, UT 84663
Distributed by Cedar Fort, Inc., www.cedarfort.com

The Library of Congress has cataloged the previous edition of this book as follows:

Ridges, David J., author
Using the signs of the times to strengthen your testimony / David J. Ridges.
    pages cm
Includes bibliographical references and index.
ISBN 978-1-4621-1325-5 (alk. paper)
1. Eschatology. 2. Second Advent. 3. Witness bearing (Christianity)--Church of Jesus Christ of Latter-day Saints. 4. Church of Jesus Christ of Latter-day Saints--Doctrines. I. Title.

BX8643.E83R53 2014
236--dc23

2013038843

Designed and typeset by Shawnda T. Craig
Cover design © 2017 Cedar Fort, Inc.
Edited by Kaitlin Barwick

Printed in the United States of America

10 9 8 7 6 5 4 3

Printed on acid-free paper

CONTENTS

CONTENTS

CONTENTS

CONTENTS

CONTENTS

BOOKS BY DAVID J. RIDGES

The Gospel Studies Series:

- *Your Study of The Book of Isaiah Made Easier, Second Edition*
- *The New Testament Made Easier, Part 1 (Second Edition)*
- *The New Testament Made Easier, Part 2 (Second Edition)*
- *Your Study of The Book of Mormon Made Easier, Part 1*
- *Your Study of The Book of Mormon Made Easier, Part 2*
- *Your Study of The Book of Mormon Made Easier, Part 3*
- *Book of Mormon Made Easier, Family Deluxe Edition, Vols. 1 and 2*
- *Your Study of The Doctrine and Covenants Made Easier, Part 1*
- *Your Study of The Doctrine and Covenants Made Easier, Part 2*
- *Your Study of The Doctrine and Covenants Made Easier, Part 3*
- *The Old Testament Made Easier, Part 1*
- *The Old Testament Made Easier—Selections from the Old Testament, Part 2*
- *The Old Testament Made Easier—Selections from the Old Testament, Part 3*
- *Your Study of the Pearl of Great Price Made Easier*
- *Your Study of Jeremiah Made Easier*
- *Your Study of The Book of Revelation Made Easier, Second Edition*

- *Our Savior, Jesus Christ: His Life and Mission to Cleanse and Heal*
- *Mormon Beliefs and Doctrines Made Easier*
- *The Proclamation on the Family: The Word of the Lord on More Than 30 Current Issues*
- *65 Signs of the Times and the Second Coming*
- *Doctrinal Details of the Plan of Salvation: From Premortality to Exaltation*
- *Using the Signs of the Times to Strengthen Your Testimony*
- *Temples: Sacred Symbolism, Eternal Blessings*
- *Priesthood Power Unlocked*
- *The Red Porsche (You're Worth It): And Other Topics for LDS Youth*
- *Gospel Questions Gospel Answers*

INTRODUCTION

SOME SAY THAT there is no such thing as proof that God exists or that the scriptures are true. If the scientific method is applied to the signs of the times, then it leads to the obvious conclusion (to an unbiased and rational mind) that God indeed does exist and that the scriptures are based on sound truth. Simply put, the scientific method states a hypothesis or idea and searches for observable evidence that the proposal holds up under scrutiny or that it does not. If it holds up under careful examination, it becomes accepted as a law or rule upon which one can rely.

So it is with the signs of the times. They are prophecies given by the Lord through His prophets since the beginning. They have been recorded in the scriptures for all to read, and refer to observable events that will take place in the last days, alerting the honest in heart that the Savior's Second Coming is drawing near. When one studies these prophecies and sees how many of them have been fulfilled and are now in process of being fulfilled, it becomes ready "proof" that the gospel is true. Coupled with the witness and teaching of the Holy Ghost, these signs build and fortify testimony.

The purpose of this book is to make it relatively easy to study several of the signs of the times listed together in one place, in order to feel the power and testimony associated with them and the accompanying fulfillment of prophecy. You will quickly see that the approach taken is that of strengthening tes-

timony, not creating fear or panic. Indeed, the Savior counseled against using these prophecies and their fulfillment to promote extreme concern and irrational panic. After speaking to His disciples about the signs of the times (Matthew 24; JS—Matthew 1), He expressly emphasized "see that ye be not troubled" (Matthew 24:6; JS—Matthew 1:23).

The format is simple. We will use **bold** for emphasis throughout this book. One hundred signs of the times (there are obviously more than this) are listed at the front of the book. You can read straight through the list for a quick overview or browse it for ones that especially interest you and then turn to the page or pages listed in chapter four to read more.

For the purposes of this book, we have assigned most of the signs to one of the following three general categories:

1. FULFILLED

2. BEING FULFILLED

3. YET TO BE FULFILLED

With some, as you will see, we have simply assigned a question mark (?) because we don't know which of the categories they belong in. With many of the signs of the times that we will consider, the lines between these categories will be rather clear. But with some, the lines will be blurry, and, in fact, the fulfillment could involve two of these categories and sometimes all three. It is particularly interesting to look at the signs that are yet to be fulfilled.

As mentioned above, for purposes of this book, we will formally consider 100 "signs of the times." They are designed, among other things, to strengthen testimonies and provide encouragement and confidence in the hearts of believers in a day when many no longer even believe in God. Hopefully, they will even persuade some skeptics or non-believers to start believing in God. Every one of these prophecies has been, is being, or will be fulfilled.

As we prepare to discuss these prophecies of the last days and their fulfillment, we will first look at a number of cautions and observations in chapter 3. Then we will list and look at the selected 100 signs themselves in chapter 4, giving brief details only from doctrinally trustworthy sources. In chapter 5, we will see a comparison between our signs of the times and the amazingly similar signs that were given to the Nephites before the coming of the Savior to them. Next, in chapter 6, we will take a quick look at what will actually happen when the Savior comes and then, in chapter 7, we will briefly talk about "how good" a person needs to be in order to have a pleasant Second Coming.

In the first edition of this book, *50 Signs of the Times and the Second Coming*, published in 2004, 50 signs of the times were included. In the second edition, *65 Signs of the Times and the Second Coming*, published in 2009, 65 of these prophecies were included. The third edition, *Using the Signs of the Times to Strengthen Your Testimony*, published in 2013,

included 31 additional signs for a total of 96 and had a number of additional comments and notes not included in the first two publications. This deluxe edition brings the number of signs to 100.

The Savior will come as prophesied. He will be right on time. It is the privilege of those who study the scriptures and heed the words of the prophets, ancient and modern, to be informed and prepared. They are "the children of light," spoken of in Doctrine and Covenants 106:5, and will be alerted and encouraged by the signs of the times as His coming draws near. Because they recognize the fulfillment of these prophecies, they can live their lives with increased stability and confidence and will not be caught off guard when He comes.

An especially deep expression of appreciation goes to my wife, Janette, who has encouraged and helped throughout the writing and organizing of this work.

DAVID J. RIDGES

COLOR CODE USED IN THIS BOOK

David Ridges Commentary

Background Commentary

Text from Scriptures

References and Quotes

AND WHOSO TREASURETH UP MY WORD, SHALL NOT BE DECEIVED, FOR THE SON OF MAN SHALL COME.

JOSEPH SMITH—MATTHEW 1:37

CHAPTER 1
"SEE THAT YE BE NOT TROUBLED"

IT IS QUITE common for people who study the signs of the times in the scriptures, attend lectures on them, or read articles or books on the subject to come away feeling fear or even panic. In many cases, authors and lecturers approach the topic in ways that promote fear in their readers. We will avoid this approach in this book. Instead, we will use the signs of the times as witnesses that the gospel is true, that the Lord is keeping us informed, and that His words will all be fulfilled, including His promise to redeem us from our sins and bring us safely back to live with the Father, as we diligently strive to live His gospel.

In the course of this book, we will indeed follow the Savior's counsel to His disciples to "see that ye be not troubled" as we review and study a goodly number of the signs of the times. This counsel to His disciples came during the last week of His mortal mission. The disciples had quietly approached Him as He sat on the Mount of Olives and asked Him to tell them the signs of the times that would precede His Second Coming and "the end of the world" (Matthew 24:3). After hearing many of these signs, we sense that there were obvious looks of fear and concern on their faces. The Master responded with simple counsel that applies to us as well. He said (bold added for emphasis):

Matthew 24:6
6 And ye shall hear of wars and rumours of wars: **see that ye be not troubled**: for all these things must come to pass, but the end is not yet.

Joseph Smith—Matthew 1:23
23 Behold, I speak these things unto you for the elect's sake; and you also shall hear of wars, and rumors of wars; **see that ye be not troubled**, for all I have told you must come to pass; but the end is not yet.

So, the next question is how can we "be not troubled" when all around us the prophesied social upheaval, turmoil, war, and savagery rage, not to mention the fact that nature is in commotion, as prophesied. The Savior went on to give His disciples some keys to having peace in their hearts. He said (bold added for emphasis):

Joseph Smith—Matthew 1:37–39, 48–50
37 And **whoso treasureth up my word, shall not be deceived**, for the Son of Man shall come, and he shall send his angels before him with the great sound of a trumpet, and they shall gather together the remainder of his elect from the four winds, from one end of heaven to the other.

38 Now learn a parable of the fig tree— When its branches are yet tender, and it begins to put forth leaves, you know that summer is nigh at hand;

39 **So likewise, mine elect, when they shall see all these things, they shall know that he is near, even at the doors**;

48 Therefore **be ye also ready**, for in such an hour as ye think not, the Son of Man cometh.

49 Who, then, is a faithful and wise servant, whom his lord hath made ruler over his household, to give them meat in due season?

50 **Blessed is that servant whom his lord, when he cometh, shall find so doing**; and verily I say unto you, he shall make him ruler over all his goods.

Verse 37 is particularly helpful. We have numerous opportunities to "treasure up" His word. A big one is to listen to the words of our modern prophets. Have you noticed that they do not preach panic? While they give serious and sobering counsel, they do not preach alarm or frenzy. Another way we "treasure up" His word is to study the scriptures. As we consistently read and study the scriptures, we invite the Holy Ghost to rest upon us. One of the functions of the Holy Ghost is to bring peace, which can significantly help us "be not troubled." Another is to guide us to avoid deception. One form of deception with respect to the signs of the times would be inordinate fear and nervousness.

Verse 39 reminds us that as we become more and more familiar with the signs of the times, we will recognize that they are being fulfilled all around us. Consequently, our testimonies will be strengthened and our confidence in the Second Coming will increase. We will "know that he is near, even at the doors" and we can look forward to it, whether it takes place during our lifetime or after we have passed away. If we have been righteous, and it takes place during our mortal life, we can look forward to being caught up to meet Him and then descending back down to earth with Him. (Bold added for emphasis:)

D&C 88:96 and 98
96 And **the saints that are upon the earth, who are alive, shall be quickened and be caught up to meet him**.

98 **They are** Christ's, the first fruits, **they who shall descend with him** first, and they who are on the earth and in their graves,

who are first caught up to meet him; and all this by the voice of the sounding of the trump of the angel of God.

If we have already passed away, and if we lived the gospel faithfully during our sojourn on earth, we will be resurrected and likewise caught up to meet Him and join Him for His descent to the earth to begin the Millennium. (Bold added for emphasis:)

D&C 88:97–98
97 And **they who have slept in their graves shall come forth**, for their graves shall be opened; and **they also shall be caught up to meet him** in the midst of the pillar of heaven—

98 **They are** Christ's, the first fruits, **they who shall descend with him** first, and they who are on the earth and in their graves, who are first caught up to meet him; and all this by the voice of the sounding of the trump of the angel of God.

Going back to Joseph Smith—Matthew 1:50, quoted before, we see that those who are righteous at the time of His coming are described as "blessed." This is a scriptural term that often means "happy." Thus, those who are striving to live in harmony with the gospel will have peace and happiness in spite of world conditions. They will successfully follow the counsel to "be not troubled."

As we treasure up His word, under the tutelage of the Holy Ghost, we gain sound knowledge. Such knowledge brings stability and testimony, which brings assurance and peace. In the Doctrine and Covenants, we are told (bold added for emphasis):

D&C 38:30
30 I tell you these things because of your prayers; wherefore, treasure up wisdom in your bosoms, lest the wickedness of men reveal these things unto you by their

wickedness, in a manner which shall speak in your ears with a voice louder than that which shall shake the earth; but **if ye are prepared ye shall not fear**.

So how does one prepare such that the prospect of the Second Coming strengthens testimony and brings confidence and inner peace rather than fear and trouble to the soul? One of the answers is found among the righteous Saints during the "war years" in the Book of Mormon that preceded the prophesied coming of the Lord to the Nephites. Many "signs of their times" were taking place all around them. About 71 BC, when righteous Captain Moroni and his armies were engaged in near continuous battle against the enemies of righteousness, the environment for the faithful Saints was one of wars, turmoil, and commotion. Yet, in the midst of all this, we are told (bold added for emphasis):

Alma 50:22–23

22 And those who were **faithful in keeping the commandments of the Lord** were delivered at all times, whilst thousands of their wicked brethren have been consigned to bondage, or to perish by the sword, or to dwindle in unbelief, and mingle with the Lamanites.

23 But behold **there never was a happier time among the people of Nephi**, since the days of Nephi, than in the days of Moroni, yea, even at this time, in the twenty and first year of the reign of the judges.

It thus becomes clear that one of the keys to inner peace and quality of life is to simply keep the commandments of the Lord.

Another key to being strengthened by the signs of the times is to recognize one of the major purposes for which they are given. As noted previously, they are given to strengthen testimony. By way of review, the signs of the times are prophecies given by the Lord through His prophets since the beginning, which refer to events that will take place during the last days leading up to the Second Coming of the Savior. They are designed to alert the honest in heart who study the scriptures that His coming is drawing near. They are designed to be a continual witness, daily before our eyes, that God exists and the scriptures are true.

Over my many years of teaching, students have occasionally expressed a wish to have lived in former times when many of the miracles recorded in scripture took place. They felt that their testimonies would have been greatly strengthened by personally witnessing such obvious evidences of the blessings of the gospel in action. On such occasions, it has been satisfying to point out to them that they do indeed live in such a time themselves! In these marvelous last days before the Second Coming, we are surrounded with testimony-building fulfillment of past prophecies. The gospel has been restored and is going forth into all the world, as prophesied. Temples are beginning to dot the earth, as prophesied. The priesthood has been restored, as prophesied, and quiet miracles of healing—physical and spiritual—take place among the faithful on a daily basis. Never before has there been a time in the history of the earth when so many prophecies are being fulfilled before our very eyes. To the spiritually alert and wise, these prophecies become a great means of strengthening and confirming personal testimony. Increased faith brings increased peace.

Examples of some of these fulfilled prophecies are:

- Ezekiel prophesied that the "stick of Joseph" (Ezekiel 37:15–19; the Book of Mormon) would come forth in the last days. It's here.

- Daniel interpreted the king's dream (Daniel 2:28–45), explaining that, in the last days, the true gospel would be restored and would go forth to fill "the whole earth." It's happening before our very eyes. And with the prophetic lowering of the ages for young men and young women to serve missions, we are watching an unprecedented jump in the number of missionaries. It is no doubt part of the dramatic fulfilling of the Lord's own prophecy in which He said, "I will hasten my work in its time" (D&C 88:73). We are watching this right now. It adds strength and endurance to our testimonies.

- The scriptures prophesy that, in the last days, there will be a great increase in natural disasters (D&C 88:88–91). The daily news is full of such things.

And the list goes on and on, as exemplified by numerous signs of the times included in this book. As you browse through the list of 100 signs provided herein (there are more), you can no doubt see how each one that has now been fulfilled or that is now being fulfilled becomes a testimony strengthener and builder for each of us. Thus, the signs of the times serve as a strong witness of the truth of the scriptures and that God's words will all be fulfilled, including His promises to each of us that through the Atonement, coupled with sincere living of the gospel, each of us can be made clean and ready to receive exaltation and live in the presence of God eternally.

Over many years, I have given more than 500 presentations on the signs of the times. The usual approach has been to give a handout listing several signs of the times, discussing them, and then having the class or audience participate in checking off the various signs as "fulfilled," "being fulfilled," or "yet to be fulfilled." As we deal with so many that have been fulfilled or are underway, people's eyes light up as a spirit of testimony and positive excitement comes

upon them. It has been very gratifying, at the end of the lectures or presentations, to have many come up and express appreciation for the "positive" approach. Up until then, they had routinely approached the topic with some dread, but now they could study the signs with great appreciation for the strong witness they provide that the gospel is indeed true.

Sometimes, misunderstandings of doctrine can lead to "being troubled," that is to say, unnecessary fear or concern when discussing the signs of the times, the Second Coming, the Millennium, etc. During an institute class some years ago, when we were discussing the signs of the times and the Millennium that would start with the arrival of the Lord (D&C 29:11), one of my students, a young man, was not showing the same enjoyment and enthusiasm for the discussion as the other students in class. Several had indicated that they were encouraged by the many signs fulfilled or underway and hoped that the Savior would soon come. Finally, he raised his hand and said, "I don't want the Second Coming to get here yet." That took us back a bit, and I invited him to share his concern with the class.

With a perplexed look on his face, he said he didn't want the Savior to come yet because he was not married. I invited him to explain further. He went on to say that once the Savior had come, there would be no more marriage. I don't know where he got that idea, but he was greatly relieved when we discussed the doctrine that there would indeed be marriage and family during the Millennium. He grinned widely when I further informed him that he could date any girl he wanted to without having to worry about her standards, because none of the wicked would still be on earth, once the thousand years of peace has begun. The big thing for him would be to make sure he was still here. He then said,

"Let it come!" The class chuckled and we went on with our exciting discussion.

In summary, it is important to use the signs of the times for their intended purpose. When studied and reasonably understood, these great prophecies and their fulfillments can provide strength and testimony. They can create righteous anticipation for every word of the Lord to be fulfilled (D&C 1:38). This can include looking forward to seeing friends and loved ones long since dead, who, hopefully, will come with the Savior. Of course, we do not know if He will come during our lifetime, and, consequently, we need to carefully avoid setting a "deadline" in our own thoughts as to when He will arrive. We need to especially avoid forming timetables in our own mind and teaching or seriously suggesting them to others. This could lead to deception. He will be here the moment He arrives.

The Lord foretold that the coming of the Lord would catch the wicked off guard, but that the righteous would not be taken by surprise. He said (bold added for emphasis):

> D&C 106:4–5
> 4 And again, verily I say unto you, **the coming of the Lord draweth nigh, and it overtaketh the world as a thief in the night** [*it will catch the worldly off guard*]—
>
> 5 Therefore, gird up your loins [*prepare*], **that you may be the children of light, and that day shall not overtake you as a thief.**

A "thief in the night" is not expected and thus catches people unawares. As faithful members listen to the Lord's servants, they are kept informed. Perhaps you have noticed that during recent general conferences of the Church, the Second Coming is being mentioned more frequently. One example is the April 2011 general conference address of Elder Neil A. Andersen, of the Quorum of the Twelve, during the priesthood session. He mentioned the

Second Coming at least twelve times, one way or another. It was mentioned with quiet calm, and by way of a call to duty to help prepare the world for the Savior's arrival. We will provide a few brief excerpts of his sermon and **bold** the words "Second Coming" and other phrases referring directly to it so you can find them more readily.

> One of your important responsibilities is to help prepare the world for the **Second Coming** of the Savior . . .
>
> Your mission will be a sacred opportunity to bring others to Christ and help prepare for the **Second Coming** of the Savior. . . .
>
> The world is being prepared for the **Second Coming** of the Savior in large measure because of the Lord's work through His missionaries . . .

Speaking to you, the First Presidency has said (bold added for emphasis):

> We pray for each of you . . . [that] you can do the great work that lies before you . . . that you will be worthy [and willing] to carry on the responsibilities of building the kingdom of God and preparing the world for the **Second Coming** of the Savior. . . .
>
> My young brethren of the priesthood, I testify of the majesty, but most of all, of **the certainty of this magnificent event**. The Savior lives. **He will return to the earth**. And whether on this side of the veil or the other, you and I will rejoice in **His coming** and thank the Lord that He sent us to earth at this time to fulfill our sacred duty of helping prepare the world for **His return**.

As "children of light," we have the opportunity to "enjoy the journey" and to "be of good cheer," as counseled often by President Thomas S. Monson. As we do our part to spread the gospel and serve others in these marvelous days of revelation and fulfillment of prophecy that precede the Second Coming of the Savior, we can readily follow the Master's instruction to "see that ye be not troubled."

"SEE THAT YE BE NOT TROUBLED"

THE COMING OF THE LORD DRAWETH NIGH, AND IT OVERTAKETH THE WORLD AS A THIEF IN THE NIGHT.

D & C   106:4

CHAPTER 2

THE LAST DAYS,
AN EXCITING TIME TO LIVE

IN HIS PREFACE to the Doctrine and Covenants (section 1), the Savior explained many benefits of living in this last dispensation when the fulness of His gospel has been restored. After briefly detailing prevailing conditions of wickedness and issuing a warning to the inhabitants of the earth (D&C 1:7–16), He proceeded to outline the great blessings that are available to those who will accept and live according to the restored gospel as it goes forth upon the earth. The personal benefits are tremendous and make this an exciting time to live! He said:

D&C 1:20–28

20 But **that every man might speak in the name of God the Lord**, even the Savior of the world;

21 **That faith also might increase** in the earth;

22 **That mine everlasting covenant might be established**;

23 **That the fulness of my gospel might be proclaimed** by the weak and the simple unto the ends of the world, and before kings and rulers.

24 Behold, I am God and have spoken it; these commandments are of me, and were given unto my servants in their weakness, after the manner of their language, that they might come to understanding.

25 And **inasmuch as they erred it might be made known**;

26 And **inasmuch as they sought wisdom they might be instructed**;

27 And **inasmuch as they sinned they might be chastened, that they might repent**;

28 And **inasmuch as they were humble they might be made strong, and blessed from on high, and receive knowledge from time to time**.

What a great introduction to the personal and collective benefits of living at a time when the gospel is so readily available! What a wonderful blessing it is to participate in His "everlasting covenant," including living as families sealed together on earth and for eternity! How satisfying it is to look forward to being instructed by living prophets every general conference and, on numerous occasions, in between! How precious it is to be able to call upon worthy priesthood holders for blessings and administrations for the sick! How humbling and nourishing it is to have authorized baptism and the gift of the Holy Ghost and to partake of the sacrament and thus have access to the full benefits of the Atonement! What wonder fills our hearts as we are taught by the Holy Ghost while reading and studying our Book of Mormon and other sacred scriptures!

How exciting it is to have the complete standard works available on personal electronic devices, along with general conferences in both audio and video format! Lesson manuals, Church magazines, and myriad other resources developed by the Church are instantly available on computers and personal devices. A few keystrokes on a computer can bring up and print out helpful resources for talks and lessons.

The ability to communicate, travel, take online courses, blog, and keep in touch with family and friends is mind boggling. Photos of family activities can be transmitted instantaneously to other family members and friends. Parents of missionaries are, for the most part, no longer dependent on postal services to stay in touch with their missionaries. The anxiousness of missed or missing letters has been replaced with scheduled instant communication.

During our most recent mission, though we were physically far away from our children and grandchildren, we seldom felt or sensed the distance. It was almost a nonissue! As senior missionaries, we were free to call as desired, and they were free to call us. When a new granddaughter was born, we first saw her via video calling. One of our daughters completed a very rigorous course of study leading to a PhD while we were away. With permission, we flew home on a weekend, attended her graduation services, and were back in our mission field the following Monday. It is an exciting time to be alive!

The culminating event, indeed the most exciting event of all during the last days, will obviously be the Lord's Second Coming. The signs of the times provide ongoing evidence, assurance, and a degree of excitement that He will come again. It is mentioned over 1,500 times in the Old Testament and some 300 times in the New Testament. It is a much-anticipated event in our day. We obviously don't know just when He will arrive, and we should steadfastly avoid serious

detailed calculations as to when it will take place. He will simply be here the moment He arrives. That is about as close as we can come to narrowing it down. Although, we can look at the signs that have already been fulfilled, study the ones that are now underway, and think about the ones that have not yet started (basically) and perhaps get a bit of a feeling of what needs to happen still. But we should avoid serious calculations and speculation on the timing of His arrival. The whole topic is exciting!

Several years ago, one of my students asked, "Wouldn't it be nice if our modern prophets had real revelations, like ancient prophets did in the scriptures?" It was a bit difficult to stifle a grin as I responded to her question. Of course, the class discussion that resulted led to the definite conclusion that they do! And it was pointed out that one of the most important revelations to the Church in these last days came through President Gordon B. Hinckley: these last days are a wonderful time to be alive! If you are old enough to personally remember him, how many times did you hear him say, in one way or another, that this is a great time to be alive? How many talks of his did you hear in which he said, in effect, "What a wonderful day to be alive"? For example, in the Saturday morning session of general conference, October 5, 2001, he said the following:

> I do not know what we did in the preexistence to merit the wonderful blessings we enjoy. We have come to earth in this great season in the long history of mankind. It is a marvelous age, the best of all. As we reflect on the plodding course of mankind, from the time of our first parents, we cannot help feeling grateful. ("Living in the Fulness of Times," *Ensign*, November 2001, 4)

More recently, President Thomas S. Monson has repeatedly counseled us to "enjoy the journey."

For example, in the October 2008 general conference of the Church, he said,

> Let us relish life as we live it, find joy in the journey, and share our love with friends and family. One day each of us will run out of tomorrows. (*Ensign*, November 2008)

To some, at first, this may not seem particularly spectacular. But it is! One of the signs of the times that is given in the scriptures is that in the last days there will be much gloom and doom, much fear, discouragement, and despair. For instance, Luke describes one of the prevailing conditions in the last days, before the Savior's coming, as follows (bold added for emphasis):

> Luke 21:25–27
> 25 And there shall be signs in the sun, and in the moon, and in the stars; and upon the earth distress of nations, with perplexity; the sea and the waves roaring;
>
> 26 **Men's hearts failing them for fear**, and for looking after those things which are coming on the earth: for the powers of heaven shall be shaken.
>
> 27 And then shall they see the Son of man coming in a cloud with power and great glory.

President Hinckley's prophetic counsel reminds us to avoid getting caught up in the prevailing pessimism and fatalism that permeates much of the thinking of our day. The word "hearts," in verse 26, above, as used in the scriptures, usually means "courage, hope, confidence," and so on. The word "failing" means "to run out of." Thus, the phrase "Men's hearts failing them for fear" can mean that there will be much depression and despair in the final days before the Second Coming. This sign of the times is very obviously being fulfilled. It has been our great blessing and privilege to follow the counsel of President Hinckley and President Monson, to do all we can to avoid this plague, including serving one another, which brings the spirit of peace and optimism.

Those of you who remember President Gordon B. Hinckley, or are familiar with his teachings and sermons, know that he was a wonderful prophet to follow. He exuded optimism and had a delightful sense of humor. At a multi-stake regional conference some years ago that I attended, during the Saturday priesthood leadership session, President Hinckley kept the priesthood brethren laughing for a solid 45 minutes. During a snack break partway through that meeting, an elders quorum president from my stake came up to me, his eyes still wide with wonder, and exclaimed, "I didn't know that a prophet was allowed by the Lord to be so funny. I mean, President Hinckley is really funny! He's good!" And so he was. What a great example of happiness and hope and optimism from the Lord's mouthpiece!

And have you noticed that President Thomas S. Monson also exemplifies, preaches, and teaches optimism? One example is his general conference talk given Sunday morning, April 5, 2009, entitled "Be of Good Cheer":

> It would be easy to become discouraged and cynical about the future—or even fearful of what might come—if we allowed ourselves to dwell only on that which is wrong in the world and in our lives. Today, however, I'd like us to turn our thoughts and our attitudes away from the troubles around us and to focus instead on our blessings as members of the Church. The Apostle Paul declared, "God hath not given us the spirit of fear; but of power, and of love, and of a sound mind."
>
> None of us makes it through this life without problems and challenges—and sometimes tragedies and misfortunes. After all, in large part we are here to learn and grow from such events in our lives. We know that there are times when we will suffer, when we

will grieve, and when we will be saddened. However, we are told, "Adam fell that men might be; and men are, that they might have joy."

How might we have joy in our lives, despite all that we may face? Again from the scriptures: "Wherefore, be of good cheer, and do not fear, for I the Lord am with you, and will stand by you."

President Monson concluded this conference address by declaring the following:

I testify to you that our promised blessings are beyond measure. Though the storm clouds may gather, though the rains may pour down upon us, our knowledge of the gospel and our love of our Heavenly Father and of our Savior will comfort and sustain us and bring joy to our hearts as we walk uprightly and keep the commandments. There will be nothing in this world that can defeat us.

My beloved brothers and sisters, fear not. Be of good cheer. The future is as bright as your faith.

I declare that God lives and that He hears and answers our prayers. His Son, Jesus Christ, is our Savior and our Redeemer. Heaven's blessings await us. In the name of Jesus Christ, amen. (*Ensign*, May 2009, 89–92)

In conclusion, these last days before the Savior's return are indeed an exciting time to be alive. There is so much fascinating technology. There are so many advances in medical science and practice. The Church is expanding, and the gospel is spreading throughout the world as never before. Unprecedented communications technology allows us to keep in touch with friends and loved ones no matter where we go or serve. We can visit exotic and faraway places without ever leaving home. Although Satan and his cunning allies use such advances to further their evil schemes, if we follow the advice and counsel of our modern prophets, we will emphasize the positives and do our best to limit the negatives, thus appreciating and enjoying the vast blessings of living in the last days.

CHAPTER 3
SOME CAUTIONS AND OBSERVATIONS

BEFORE WE STUDY the selection of 100 specific signs of the times given in chapter 4, some cautions and observations are in order. First of all, by way of observation, no doubt Satan is intensifying his efforts to deceive us in the last days. The Bible gives us an insight as to why this is the case (bold added for emphasis):

Revelation 12:12

12 Therefore rejoice, ye heavens, and ye that dwell in them. Woe to the inhabiters of the earth and of the sea! for the devil is come down unto you, having great wrath, **because he knoweth that he hath but a short time**.

Even though it can still be many years before the Savior comes, Satan's time is relatively very limited. He is obviously anxious to do as much damage as possible before his vile kingdom is put out of commission for the thousand years of the Millennium (D&C 88:110). He desires "that all men might be miserable like unto himself" (2 Nephi 2:27).

We learn from the Doctrine and Covenants that the earth has a total of 7,000 years for its "temporal" existence. This information comes from section 77. By way of background for this section, some questions had come up about "seals" spoken of in the book of Revelation. Joseph Smith was in Hiram, Ohio, at the time working on what has become known as the Joseph Smith Translation of the Bible (JST).

Joseph asked the Lord and received a revelation in which he received an explanation of the seals mentioned in Revelation 5–9. As a result, we learn that this earth has 7,000 years from the Fall of Adam and Eve to the end of the "little season" (D&C 88:111) after the Millennium—in other words, its "temporal existence." (Bold added for emphasis:)

D&C 77:6–7

6 Q. What are we to understand by the book which John saw, which was sealed on the back with **seven seals**?

A. We are to understand that it contains the revealed will, mysteries, and the works of God; the hidden things of his economy concerning **this earth** during **the seven thousand years of its continuance, or its temporal existence**.

7 Q. What are we to understand by the **seven seals** with which it was sealed?

A. We are to understand that **the first seal contains the things of the first thousand years, and the second also of the second thousand years, and so on until the seventh**.

"Temporal" has to do with time, and time has had mortal significance for us since the Fall of Adam and Eve, when their physical bodies became mortal. It will continue to have such meaning until the earth is finished up and becomes a celestial planet upon which time will no longer be significant since its celestial inhabitants will be in eternity.

From the approximate chronology given in the Bible Dictionary of our LDS edition of the scriptures, we are aware that the earth has already used up roughly 6,000 years of its allotted 7,000 "temporal" years, and we know that the Millennium will require 1,000 years. Therefore, Satan has very little time remaining before being bound at the beginning of the Millennium (Revelation 20:1–2; D&C 101:28). To reemphasize what we said above, no wonder he is mounting such an intense last-minute campaign to do as much damage as possible before his wicked kingdom falls at the Second Coming! He indeed knows that he has "but a short time"!

As we continue with some cautions and observations, it may be worthwhile at this point to look at some of Lucifer's cunning and widespread deceptions as he intensifies his efforts to lead us astray in these last days. We only have space to consider a few.

CAUTIONS AND OBSERVATIONS

DESTROYING VALID HEROES

Certainly, one of the devil's effective approaches for deceiving is to attempt to do away with decent heroes. For instance, it is sad to note how many writers and historians have joined in the effort to "dethrone" our Founding Fathers as heroes for residents of the United States of America and others. These writers and historians seem to want to rewrite history and superimpose a lack of virtue and character on these national heroes, perhaps as a means of justifying the departure from God's ways of a great many in our society.

When we encounter such tearing down of the founders of our nation, we would do well to study what the Lord says about these great individuals. There is safety and stability in holding to God's word on such issues. Staying close to the revelations of the Lord in this matter of our Founding Fathers will help us remain sound in our thinking and retain honorable heroes. In the Doctrine and Covenants, the Lord says the following (bold added for emphasis):

> D&C 101:77–80
> 77 According to the laws and constitution of the people, which I have suffered to be established, and should be maintained for the rights and protection of all flesh, according to just and holy principles;
>
> 78 That every man may act in doctrine and principle pertaining to futurity, according to the moral agency which I have given unto him, that every man may be accountable for his own sins in the day of judgment.
>
> 79 Therefore, it is not right that any man should be in bondage one to another.
>
> 80 And for this purpose have I established the Constitution of this land, by the hands of **wise men whom I raised up unto this very purpose**, and redeemed the land by the shedding of blood.

Thus we see that the framers of the Constitution were great premortal spirits who were sent to this earth by the Lord to establish the United States of America and set up its constitution. In fact, almost all of these great men now are members of the Church. How did that happen? President Wilford Woodruff tells us:

> I will here say, before closing, that two weeks before I left St. George, the spirits of the dead gathered around me, wanting to know why we did not redeem them. Said they, "You have had the use of the Endowment House for a number of years, and yet nothing has ever been done for us. We laid the foundation of the government you now enjoy, and we never apostatized from it, but we remained true to it and were faithful to God." These were the signers of the Declaration of Independence, and they waited on me for

two days and two nights. I thought it very singular, that notwithstanding so much work had been done, and yet nothing had been done for them. The thought never entered my heart, from the fact, I suppose, that heretofore our minds were reaching after our more immediate friends and relatives. I straightway went into the baptismal font and called upon brother McCallister to baptize me for the signers of the Declaration of Independence, and fifty other eminent men, making one hundred in all, including John Wesley, Columbus, and others; I then baptized him for every President of the United States, except three; and when their cause is just, somebody will do the work for them. (*Journal of Discourses,* 26 vols. [London: Latter-day Saints' Book Depot, 1854–86], 19:229–30, September 16, 1877)

A few weeks before his death, President Woodruff again bore witness of this and, furthermore, mentioned that endowments had also been performed for these men:

> I am going to bear my testimony to this assembly, if I never do it again in my life, that those men who laid the foundation of this American government and signed the Declaration of Independence were the best spirits the God of heaven could find on the face of the earth. They were choice spirits, not wicked men. General Washington and all the men that labored for the purpose were inspired of the Lord.
>
> Another thing I am going to say here, because I have a right to say it. Every one of those men that signed the Declaration of Independence, with General Washington, called upon me, as an Apostle of the Lord Jesus Christ, in the Temple at St. George, two consecutive nights, and demanded at my hands that I should go forth and attend to the ordinances of the House of God for them . . . I told these brethren that it was their duty to go into the Temple and labor until they had got endowments for all of

them. They did it. Would those spirits have called upon me, as an Elder in Israel, to perform that work if they had not been noble spirits before God? They would not. (Wilford Woodruff, in Conference Report, April 1898, 89–90)

It is significant that these great men were permitted by the Lord to come to His holy temple and personally request that their temple work be done. It is conclusive evidence that they were taught the gospel in the postmortal spirit world and exercised the faith and repentance necessary to overcome their sins and mortal frailties and thus qualify for baptism, the gift of the Holy Ghost, and membership in the Lord's true church. It is a fitting finale to their dedicating their all to the cause of freedom during their mortal lives. To say that we all benefit from their sacrifices in our behalf is a significant understatement.

It is interesting to note that among the "other eminent men" mentioned by Wilford Woodruff, who appeared in the St. George temple, were Daniel Webster, Henry Clay, and Benito Juarez who was the "Abraham Lincoln" of Mexico. Also, after Brother McCallister had baptized Wilford Woodruff for those 100 men, Sister Lucy Bigelow Young was then baptized for 70 prominent women, including Martha Washington and Elizabeth Barrett Browning. For your information, we will include the names of these men and women here.

CAUTIONS AND OBSERVATIONS

OTHER "EMINENT MEN"

(Taken by permission from *The Other Eminent Men of Wilford Woodruff*, Second Edition, revised 2000, by Vicki Jo Anderson, Nelson Book, Malta, Idaho.)

1. Agassiz, Louis
    (Swiss-American Naturalist)

2. Bonaparte, Charles Louis Napoleon
    (Emperor of France)

3. Brougham, Lord Henry
    (Statesman/Lord Chancellor of
    England)

4. Bulwer-Lytton, Baron Edward George
    (English novelist, politician)

5. Burke, Edmund
    (Irish/English statesman, political
    author)

6. Burns, Robert
    (Scottish poet)

7. Byron, Lord George Gordon
    (English poet)

8. Calhoun, John C.
    (American statesman)

9. Cavour, Count Camillo Benso de
    (Italian statesman, diplomat)

10. Chalmers, Thomas
    (Scottish religious reformer)

11. Clay, Henry
    (U.S. Statesman, "The Great
    Compromiser")

12. Cobden, Richard
    (English leader of free trade)

13. Columbus, Christopher
    (Discoverer of the New World)

14. Curran, John Philpot
    (Irish statesman)

15. Faraday, Michael
    (English scientist, father of
    electromagnetism)

16. Farragut, Admiral David Glasgow
    (American naval officer)

17. Frederick the Great
    (King of Prussia)

18. Garrick, David
    (English actor and director)

19. Gibbon, Sir Edward
    (English historian)

20. Goethe, Johann Wolfgang von
    (Writer and philosopher, father of
    German literature)

21. Goldsmith, Oliver
    (Irish/English poet, playwright,
    novelist)

22. Grattan, Henry
    (Irish statesman)

23. Humboldt, Alexander von
    (Father of physical geography)

24. Irving, Washington
    (Father of American literature)

25. Jackson, Thomas Jonathan "Stonewall"
    (American Confederate general)

26. Johnson, Samuel
    (English moralist, writer, lexicographer)

27. Juarez, Benito Pablo
    (Mexican president, statesman; the
    "Abraham Lincoln of Mexico")

28. Kemble, John Philip
    (English Shakespearean actor, director)

29. Liebig, Baron Justus von
    (Father of organic chemistry)

30. Livingstone, David
    (Scottish missionary, physician)

31. Macaulay, Thomas Babington
    (English historian, essayist, politician)

32. Nelson, Lord Horatio
    (British naval hero)

33. O'Connell, Daniel
    (Irish statesman)

34. Peabody, George
    (American philanthropist)

35. Powers, Hiram
    (American sculptor)

36. Reynolds, Sir Joshua
    (English painter)

37. Shiller, Johann Christoph Friedrich
    von (German poet, dramatist,
    historian)

38. Scott, Sir Walter
    (Scottish poet, novelist)

39. Seward, William Henry
    (American statesman)

40. Stephenson, George
    (English father of the railway)

41. Thackeray, William Makepeace
    (English humorist, satirist, novelist)

42. Vespucci, Amerigo
    (Italian navigator and mapmaker,
    established the fact that America was a
    new continent rather than a part of
    Asia)

43. Webster, Daniel
    (American senator, legislator, secretary
    of state, strong defender of the
    Constitution)

44. Wesley, John
    (English religious reformer, founder of
    Methodism)

45. Wordsworth, William
    (English poet)

46. Parepa, Count Dimitrius
    (Romanian baron, lived in England for
    a time. His daughter became a famous
    opera singer in Europe and America.)

The 46 men listed above are the only 46 names mentioned in the ordinance records of the temple. We are thus left to wonder if the "fifty other eminent men" mentioned by President Wilford Woodruff (Journal of Discourses 19:229) was an approximation or if our records are missing four names. We await further research to provide an answer. It is interesting to note that George Washington, John Wesley, Benjamin Franklin, and Christopher Columbus were ordained high priests, according to Wilford Woodruff's journal (*Teachings of Ezra Taft Benson*, 603–4).

WOMEN WHOSE BAPTISMS WERE ALSO PERFORMED

1. Armour, Jean, of Scotland
   (Wife of Robert Burns)

2. Austen, Jane, of England
   (Author)

3. Ball, Mary, of America
   (Mother of George Washington,
   second wife of Augustine Washington
   whose first wife, Jane Butler, died in
   1728)

4. Barnard, Sarah, of England
   (Wife of Michael Faraday)

5. Brontë, Charlotte, of England
   (Novelist)

6. Browne, Felicia Dorothea, of England
   (Poet)

7. Browning, Elizabeth Barrett, of
   England (Poet; wife of Robert
   Browning)

8. Burney, Francis, of England
   [Madame d'Arblay]

9. Butler, Jane, of America
   (First wife of Augustine Washington,
   father of George Washington; she died
   in 1728. Augustine Washington
   remarried and George Washington
   was born to his second wife, Mary Ball
   Washington, in 1732.)

10. Caldwell, Martha, of America
    (Mother of John C. Calhoun)

11. Calvert, Eleanor, of America
    (Step-granddaughter of George
    Washington)

CAUTIONS
AND
OBSERVATIONS

12. Carpenter, Charlotte Margaret, of
    England (Wife of Sir Walter Scott)

13. Christina, Elizabeth, of Prussia
    (Wife of Frederick the Great of Prussia)

14. Corday, Charlotte, of Normandy
    (French patriot)

15. Creagh, Sarah, of Ireland
    (Wife of John Philpot Curran)

16. Custis, Martha Parke, of America
    (Daughter of Martha Washington)

17. Dandridge, Martha, of America
    (Wife of George Washington)

18. Donelson, Rachel, of America
    (Wife of Andrew Jackson)

19. Dykes, Elizabeth, of Ireland
    (Wife of Thomas Moore)

20. Eastman, Abigail, of America
    (Mother of Daniel Webster)

21. Eden, Mary Anne, of England
    (Wife of Lord Henry Brougham)

22. Edgeworth, Maria, of England
    (Novelist)

23. Fairfax, Anne, of America
    (Wife of Lawrence Washington,
    George Washington's half-brother)

24. Fitzgerald, Henrietta, of Ireland
    (Wife of Henry Grattan)

25. Fletcher, Grace, of America
    (Wife of Daniel Webster)

26. Ford, Sarah, of England
    (Mother of Samuel Johnson)

27. Fuller, Sarah Margaret, of America
    (Social reformer)

28. Gurney, Elizabeth, of England
    (Religious social reformer)

29. Henderson, Frances, of England
    (Wife of George Stephenson)

30. Herbert, Frances, of England
    (Wife of Lord Horatio Nelson)

31. Hoffman, Matilda, of America
    (Betrothed of Washington Irving)

32. Hopkins, Priscilla, of England
    (Wife of John Philip Kemble)

33. Huntley, Lydia, of America
    (Author)

34. Hutchinson, Mary, of England
    (Wife of William Wordsworth)

35. Junkins, Elinor, of America
    (Wife of "Stonewall" Jackson)

36. Judson, Emily Chubboch, of America
    (Author—pen name "Fanny Forester")

37. Landon, Letitia Elizabeth, of England
    (Poet and novelist)

38. Lingefeld, Charlotte Von, of Prussia
    (Wife of Frederick Schiller)

39. Livingston, Sarah Van Brugh, of
    America (Wife of John Jay)

40. Locke, Frances, of America
    (Poet)

41. Marie Antoinette, of France
    (Queen)

42. Maria Theresa, of Austria
    (Empress, Mother of Marie Antoinette)

43. Mazza, Margarita, of Mexico
    (Wife of Benito Juarez)

44. Melbourne, Emily Lamb, of England
    (Wife of Lord Palmerston of England)

45. Milbanke, Anna Isabella, of England
    (Wife of Lord Byron)

46. Mitford, Mary Russell, of England
    (Playwright/Novelist)

47. More, Hannah, of England
    (Religious author)

48. Morgan, Lady Sydney, of Ireland
    (Novelist)

49. Murphy, Anna, of Ireland (Author/Archaeologist)

50. Nugent, Jane, of England (Wife of Edmund Burke)

51. O'Connell, Mary, of Ireland (Wife of Daniel O'Connell)

52. Pakenham, Lady Catherine, of England (Wife of Arthur Wellesley [the Duke of Wellington])

53. Parepa, Countess Demetrius, of England (Mother of Euphrosyne Parepa; wife of Baron Georgiades de Boyesku)

54. Parepa, Euphrosyne, of England (Opera singer)

55. Payne, Dorothy ["Dolley"], of America (Wife of James Madison)

56. Philipse, Mary, of America (English patriot; friend of George Washington)

57. Sedgwick, Catherine Maria, of America (Novelist)

58. Shawe, Isabella, of England (Wife of William Makepeace Thackeray)

59. Siddons, Sarah Kemble, of Wales (English Actress; sister of John Philip Kemble)

60. Smith, Abigail, of America (Wife of John Adams)

61. Somerville, Mary Fairfax, of Scotland (Mathematician/Scientist)

62. Veigel, Eva Maria, of England (Wife of David Garrick)

63. Vulpius, Christiane, of Prussia (Wife of Johann Wolfgang von Goethe)

64. Warner, Mildred, of America (Mother of Augustine Washington; paternal grandmother of George Washington; wife of Lawrence Washington)

65. Wayles, Martha, of America (Wife of Thomas Jefferson)

66. Wife of John Washington, of America (her name is unknown)

67. Wife of Henry Washington, of America (her name is unknown)

68. Wife of Lawrence Washington, of America (her name is unknown—not the same person as 23 or 64 above.)

As you can see, two names of the seventy women are missing from the records. We await further research to learn their names. Also, did you notice that a number of these women were related to George Washington? Much of this work contributed toward making eternal families. You may wish to learn more about these men and women by looking them up on the Internet.

PITTING MEN AGAINST WOMEN

Another all-out effort on Lucifer's part to deceive and destroy in our last days is his evil effort to pit men against women. This is an obvious and overt attempt at the destruction of families, which, according to "The Family: A Proclamation to the World" given September 23, 1995, is the "fundamental unit of society." Pitting men against women and women against men destroys unity and teamwork. It destroys the very finest of feelings and relationships. The debate rages on as to who is most important, man or woman. The battle for equality continues and often turns into a battle for supremacy. And what is the truth? Are men and women truly equal? This is a place where correct doctrine provides a clear answer and comes to the rescue. In fact, one of the ways to avoid deception and gloom and trouble in the last days is to understand correct doctrine and conform our behaviors and thought processes to it. It brings peace.

CAUTIONS AND OBSERVATIONS

What has the Lord said about the equality of husbands and wives? What is correct doctrine? A recent revelation from the Lord on this matter came in "The Family: A Proclamation To The World," as mentioned above. Given by the First Presidency and the Council of the Twelve Apostles on September 23, 1995, the word of the Lord is (bold added for emphasis):

> Fathers and mothers are obligated to help one another as **equal partners**.

This is correct doctrine. Men and women are to be equal partners now as well as in eternity. If our attitudes and behaviors do not reflect this eternal truth, then we need to change, repent, and conform genuinely to the truth.

It is significant to note that this eternal truth about the equality of husbands and wives is taught very clearly in the Doctrine and Covenants. Pay close attention to the use of plural pronouns in what the Lord tells us here (bold added for emphasis):

D&C 132:19–20
19 And again, verily I say unto you, **if a man marry a wife** by my word, which is my law, and by the new and everlasting covenant, and it is sealed unto **them** by the Holy Spirit of promise, by him who is anointed, unto whom I have appointed this power and the keys of this priesthood; and it shall be said unto **them**—Ye shall come forth in the first resurrection; and if it be after the first resurrection, in the next resurrection; and shall inherit thrones, kingdoms, principalities, and powers, dominions, all heights and depths—then shall it be written in the Lamb's Book of Life, that he shall commit no murder whereby to shed innocent blood, and if ye abide in my covenant, and commit no murder whereby to shed innocent blood, it shall be done unto **them** in all things whatsoever my servant hath put upon **them**, in time, and through all eternity; and shall be of full force when **they** are out of the world; and **they** shall pass by the angels, and

the gods, which are set there, to **their** exaltation and glory in all things, as hath been sealed upon **their** heads, which glory shall be a fulness and a continuation of the seeds forever and ever.

20 Then shall **they** be gods, because **they** have no end; therefore shall **they** be from everlasting to everlasting, because **they** continue; then shall **they** be above all, because all things are subject unto **them**. Then shall **they** be gods, because they have all power, and the angels are subject unto **them**.

If anyone has trouble still in understanding this truth, the teaching of Bruce R. McConkie can help:

> If righteous men have power through the gospel and its crowning ordinance of celestial marriage to become kings and priests to rule in exaltation forever, it follows that the women by their side (without whom they cannot attain exaltation) will be queens and priestesses. (Rev. 1:6; 5:10.) Exaltation grows out of the eternal union of a man and his wife. Of those whose marriage endures in eternity, the Lord says, "Then shall they be gods." (D&C 132:20); that is, each of them, the man and the woman, will be a god. As such they will rule over their dominions forever. (Bruce R. McConkie, *Mormon Doctrine*, 2nd ed. [Salt Lake City: Bookcraft, 1966], 613)

Understanding correct doctrine has great power to change and mold thought processes and behaviors, to bring peace and stability. Thus, understanding correct doctrine is essential for our progression toward becoming like our Father in Heaven. You may wish to take time to study Alma, chapters 39–42, and pay attention to how Alma skillfully used correct doctrines to help his wayward son, Corianton, change his thinking on vital issues in order to have genuine change take place within his soul. Alma 48:18 and Alma 49:30 inform us that the efforts were successful.

In general conference, October 1986, Elder Boyd K. Packer said the following:

> True doctrine, understood, changes attitudes and behavior. The study of the doctrines of the gospel will improve behavior quicker than a study of behavior will improve behavior. ("Little Children," *Ensign*, November 1986, 16)

Understanding correct doctrine on the equality of men and women can keep us from getting embroiled in Satan's deceptions on this very significant issue. Indeed, understanding and applying correct doctrine blesses our lives with respect to many other matters calculated by the adversary to keep things stirred up so that peace and righteous satisfaction will elude many during the final scenes before the Lord's coming.

We will continue with a few more cautions:

AVOID USING THE SIGNS OF THE TIMES TO FRIGHTEN OR SPREAD PANIC

Unfortunately, whether intentional or not, many who teach and discuss the signs of the times seem to end up causing fear and panic in the hearts and minds of their listeners. Let's see what the Savior says about this. By way of repetition, we will again refer to Joseph Smith—Matthew in the Pearl of Great Price and repeat for emphasis some observations made earlier in this work. There, the Master answers questions asked by His disciples concerning the signs of the times that will precede the Second Coming. As His disciples listen intently, it appears that fear and concern enter their hearts. In response, Jesus tells them (bold added for emphasis):

Joseph Smith—Matthew 1:23
23 Behold, I speak these things unto you for the elect's sake; and you also shall hear of wars, and rumors of wars; **see that ye be not troubled**, for all I have told you must come to pass; but the end is not yet.

It is very significant that the Savior instructed His loyal followers not to allow the signs of the times to promote fear and trouble in their own hearts. We should follow that counsel too. In that same chapter, Christ continues to emphasize the value of preparation as well as the fact that the signs of the times are designed to strengthen people's testimonies (bold added for emphasis):

Joseph Smith—Matthew 1:35, 37, 39, 46, 48
35 Although, the days will come, that heaven and earth shall pass away; yet **my words** shall not pass away, but **all shall be fulfilled**.

37 And **whoso treasureth up my word, shall not be deceived**, for the Son of Man shall come, and he shall send his angels before him with the great sound of a trumpet, and they shall gather together the remainder of his elect from the four winds, from one end of heaven to the other.

39 So likewise, mine elect, **when they shall see all these things, they shall know** that he is near, even at the doors;

46 And what I say unto one, I say unto all men; **watch, therefore, for you know not at what hour your Lord doth come**.

48 Therefore **be ye also ready**, for in such an hour as ye think not, the Son of Man cometh.

Thus, the Savior emphasizes that the signs of the times are given to help faithful Saints "know" that His coming is close. This "knowing," which comes from obvious, observable fulfillment of prophecy, is a powerful testimony strengthener. These signs, then, are given to inform, bear witness to us, and reassure.

It is as if the Lord were saying, "In the last days, there will be many who do not believe in God. Therefore, I will place many prophecies in the scriptures that will be fulfilled prior to

SEE THAT YE BE NOT TROUBLED, FOR ALL I HAVE TOLD YOU MUST COME TO PASS; BUT THE END IS NOT YET.

JOSEPH SMITH— MATTHEW 1:23

the Second Coming. There will be so many of these "signs of the times' that anyone who is honest in heart will be able to consider them as proof that I do exist." In the world of science, so many "coincidences" or "lucky guesses" would not be considered "coincidences." The signs of the times are not coincidences. They are obvious proof that God exists and that His Son will come again.

President Gordon B. Hinckley gave the following counsel about fear in the last days (bold added for emphasis):

> I need not remind you that we live in perilous times, . . . [but] **there is no need to fear**. We can have peace in our hearts and peace in our homes. We can be an influence for good in this world, every one of us. ("Report of the 171st Semiannual General Conference of The Church of Jesus Christ of Latter-day Saints," *Ensign*, November 2001, 1)

THE "MARK OF THE BEAST"

One of the most often quoted scriptural references used inappropriately in our day to spread fear among people comes from Revelation, chapter 13. In this tremendous chapter, John the Revelator warns against many of Satan's ploys and deceptions in the last days. Among other things, John refers to what is now commonly known as the "mark of the beast" (Revelation 13:16–17). Unfortunately, many people misread verses 15 through 17 and come to believe that all people in the last days will come under the domination and evil control of the "beast."

According to the heading for chapter 13, in our LDS edition of the scriptures, the "beasts" referred to in the chapter "represent degenerate earthly kingdoms controlled by Satan." Let's look at some verses in this chapter, and then discuss them. First, we will bold words and phrases that seem to lead to misinterpretation.

Revelation 13:15–17

15 And he had power to give life unto the image of the beast, that the image of the beast should both speak, and cause that **as many as would not worship the image of the beast should be killed.**

16 And he causeth **all**, both small and great, rich and poor, free and bond, to **receive a mark in their right hand, or in their foreheads**:

17 And that **no man** might buy or sell, save he that had the mark, or the name of the beast, or the number of his name.

If we were to use these verses exclusively, and pay attention especially to the bolded portions of the verses above, we would, as do many others, conclude that Satan will gain such a stranglehold and such awful power in the final days before the Second Coming that everyone including the righteous Saints will ultimately come under his power and control. This is not the case. The problem with this approach, which leads to gloom and despair and hopelessness, is that it ignores other verses in the book of Revelation. It also ignores President Hinckley's counsel to look at the bright side. It ignores President Monson's counsel to "enjoy the journey" and to "be of good cheer" referred to elsewhere in this book. If we joined others in their misinterpretation of the above verses, there would be no bright side.

Other verses within the book of Revelation itself show that everyone does not come under the grasp and power of the "beast." Some of these verses follow (bold added for emphasis):

Revelation 14:9

9 And the third angel followed them, saying with a loud voice, **If** any man worship the beast and his image, and receive *his* mark in his forehead, or in his hand,

Revelation 20:4

4 And I saw thrones, and they sat upon them, and judgment was given unto them: and *I saw* the souls of them that were beheaded for the witness of Jesus, and for the word of God, and which **had not worshipped the beast**, neither his image, **neither had received *his* mark upon their foreheads**, or in their hands; and they lived and reigned with Christ a thousand years.

Revelation 22:3–4

3 And there shall be no more curse: but the throne of God and of **the Lamb** shall be in it; and **his servants shall serve him**:

4 And they shall see his face; and **his name *shall be* in their foreheads**.

"Context" is key in interpreting and understanding verses such as Revelation 13:15–17. When seen in the context of the whole book of Revelation—indeed, in the context of the whole standard works and the words of modern prophets—such misunderstanding and discomfort attending chapter 13 is removed. We conclude that only the wicked and those who foolishly ignore the counsel of the prophets to live the gospel, to live within their means, and so forth, will fall under the control of the "beast" in the last days before the coming of the Lord. This, indeed, is one of the signs of the times and is being fulfilled rather dramatically as we speak.

Elder L. Tom Perry, of the Quorum of the Twelve Apostles, spoke of avoiding unnecessary debt in the October 1995 general conference of the Church. He counseled:

> Avoid excessive debt. Necessary debt should be incurred only after careful, thoughtful prayer and after obtaining the best possible advice. We need the discipline to stay well within our ability to pay. Wisely we have been counseled to avoid debt as we would avoid the plague. President J. Reuben Clark

fearlessly and repeatedly counseled members of the Church to take action.

> "Live within your means. Get out of debt. Keep out of debt. Lay by for a rainy day which has always come and will come again. Practice and increase your habits of thrift, industry, economy, and frugality" (in Conference Report, Oct. 1937, 107). . . .

> Incurrence of debt is such an enticement. Accompanying the ease with which we can obtain debt should be the great caution of avoidance. Take the opportunity to compute how much you would add to your personal net worth if your home mortgage was only for ten or fifteen years instead of thirty. Compute the value of sweat equity if your time and your talents are invested in adding to the size and comfort of your home.

> It is so easy to allow consumer debt to get out of hand. If you do not have the discipline to control the use of credit cards, it is better not to have them.

An interesting question comes up as we study the verses in Revelation quoted above, concerning the "mark of the beast" in one's forehead. What does forehead symbolize? Answer: In Jewish culture, forehead symbolizes loyalty. Thus, the mark of the beast in people's foreheads would symbolize that they are loyal to Satan and his front organizations. Whereas, in Revelation 14:1, we see 144,000 who are loyal to the Father. In other words, they are righteous (bold added for emphasis):

Revelation 14:1

1 And I looked, and, lo, a Lamb stood on the mount Sion, and with him an hundred forty *and* four thousand, having his **Father's name written in their foreheads.**

Elsewhere in Revelation, we see servants who are loyal to God (bold added for emphasis):

Revelation 7:2–4

2 And I saw another angel ascending from the east, having the seal of the living God:

and he cried with a loud voice to the four angels, to whom it was given to hurt the earth and the sea,

3 Saying, Hurt not the earth, neither the sea, nor the trees, **till we have sealed the servants of our God in their foreheads.**

4 And I heard the number of them which were sealed: *and there were* sealed an hundred *and* forty *and* four thousand of all the tribes of the children of Israel.

Joseph Smith asked the Lord what the meaning of verse 4, above, is and received the following answer (bold added for emphasis):

D&C 77:11
11 Q. What are we to understand by sealing the one hundred and forty-four thousand, out of all the tribes of Israel—twelve thousand out of every tribe?

A. We are to understand that **those who are sealed are high priests**, ordained unto the holy order of God, to administer the everlasting gospel; for they are they who are ordained **out of every nation**, kindred, tongue, and people, by the angels **to whom is given power over the nations of the earth, to bring as many as will come to the church of the Firstborn**.

Thus, those who were "sealed . . . in their foreheads," in verse 3, above, are righteous high priests who will assist with a great missionary effort in the last days.

Simply put, symbolically, those who are loyal to wickedness, financial greed, and so forth, are depicted as having the mark of the beast on their foreheads. Whereas, those who are loyal to God and to righteousness, are depicted in the revelation, according to the Jewish cultural symbolism of John's day, as having the name of God on their foreheads. A similar image is found in Alma, where the righteous are seen as having the image of Christ in their countenance (bold

added for emphasis). This, of course, is literal (bold added for emphasis):

Alma 5:14
14 And now behold, I ask of you, my brethren of the church, have ye spiritually been born of God? **Have ye received his image in your countenances**? Have ye experienced this mighty change in your hearts?

In conclusion, those who insist on taking Revelation 13:15–17 out of context and misinterpreting it come up with some rather fascinating, frightening, and widespread false rumors. For example, many people have come to believe incorrectly that the "mark of the beast in their foreheads" will turn out to be a bar code, tattooed upon people's foreheads in the last days. And those who do not join in corrupt financial institutions, controlled by secret combinations, and thus qualify to have such a bar code tattooed on their foreheads, will not be allowed to "buy or sell" (Revelation 13:17) and will perish.

Another variation of the false rumors about the "mark of the beast" is the idea that people who desire to buy and sell in the last days will have a computer chip implanted in their right hand or forehead or whatever. Without this chip, they will be unable to purchase what they need in order to survive and thus will perish. In earlier but still recent days, plastic credit cards were considered by some to represent the mark of the beast.

Such rumors do little to help and much to harm. Let us remain true to God and, as a result, see the wisdom of having the name of God, in effect, "engraved" upon our features and our souls.

THE EXACT TIMING OF THE SECOND COMING

The scriptures are very clear in explaining that no one knows the exact timing of the Second Coming of the Savior. We will use two references to emphasize this point (bold added for emphasis):

> Matthew 24:36
>
> 36 But of **that day and hour knoweth no man**, no, **not the angels** of heaven, but **my Father only.**

> Mark 13:32
>
> 32 But of that day and *that* hour knoweth no man, no, not the angels which are in heaven, **neither the Son**, but the Father.

In spite of such scriptures as above quoted, some people still insist on trying to pin down the timing of the Second Coming to a rather specific date or narrow period of time. For example, some have been heard to say that even though we can't know the day and hour, we can know the month and year. Some make elaborate calculations, based on personal interpretation of scriptures combined with the statements of prophets to narrow down the timing. When others refuse to accept their calculations as being inspired, they respond by saying that those who are truly in tune with the Spirit will gain a witness that what they claim is true. Still others claim that our prophets and apostles today do indeed know the exact day and hour, but have been instructed not to tell us.

Elder M. Russell Ballard, of the Quorum of the Twelve, spoke to a devotional audience in the Brigham Young University Marriott Center about the last days and signs of the times on March 12, 1996. After some brief introductory remarks, he continued by saying the following (bold added for emphasis):

> Now with the Lord's help I would like to speak to you about a subject that is on a lot of people's minds. **My intention is not to alarm or to frighten, but to discuss the significant and interesting times in which we are now living**, to consider some of the events and circumstances we can anticipate in the future and to suggest a few things we can all do to fortify ourselves and our families for the challenges and trials that will surely come into all of our lives at one time or another.

Elder Ballard continued, reading from Matthew 24:3–7, and commenting as he went along.

> Matthew 24:3–7
>
> 3 And as he sat upon the mount of Olives, the disciples came unto him privately, saying, Tell us, when shall these things be? and what shall be the sign of thy coming, and of the end of the world?
>
> 4 And Jesus answered and said unto them, Take heed that no man deceive you.
>
> 5 For many shall come in my name, saying, I am Christ; and shall deceive many.
>
> 6 And ye shall hear of wars and rumours of wars: see that ye be not troubled: for all these things must come to pass, but the end is not yet.
>
> 7 For nation shall rise against nation, and kingdom against kingdom: and there shall be famines, and pestilences, and earthquakes, in divers places.

He then paused, cautioning those in attendance to avoid trying to narrow the Lord's coming to a specific period of time.

> I want to pause here for a moment and suggest to you, if you haven't been aware, that some of these things seem to be occurring with ever-increasing regularity. If you measured the natural disasters that have occurred in the world during the last ten years and plotted that year-by-year, you would see an acceleration. The earth is rumbling, and earthquakes are occurring in "divers places." Human nature being what it is, we don't normally pay much attention to these natural phenomena until they happen close to where we are living. But when we contemplate what has happened during the past decade, not only with earthquakes but also with regard

to hurricanes, floods, tornadoes, volcanic eruptions, and the like, you would see an accelerating pattern.

So can we use this scientific data to extrapolate that the Second Coming is likely to occur during the next few years, or the next decade, or the next century? Not really. I am called as one of the apostles to be a special witness of Christ in these exciting, trying times, and **I do not know when He is going to come again. As far as I know, none of my brethren in the Council of the Twelve or even in the First Presidency know. And I would humbly suggest to you, my young brothers and sisters, that if we do not know, then nobody knows**, no matter how compelling their arguments or how reasonable their calculations. The Savior said that "of that day and hour knoweth no man, no, not the angels of heaven, but my Father only" (Matthew 24:36).

I believe when the Lord says "no man" knows, it really means that no man knows. You should be extremely wary of anyone who claims to be an exception to divine decree. But while the exact timing of the Second Coming remains in doubt, there is no question that scriptural prophecy relative to that momentous and sacred event is being fulfilled, sometimes in remarkable ways.

Some years ago, at the conclusion of a Know Your Religion lecture that I gave for BYU Continuing Education on the signs of the times, an elderly brother came up to the stand and corrected me by saying, in effect, that Matthew 24:36 ("But of that day and hour knoweth no man . . .") does not apply to the First Presidency and the Twelve, and thus, those Brethren do know. In support of his thinking, he went on to quote Amos:

Amos 3:7
Surely the Lord God will do nothing, but he revealeth his secret unto his servants the prophets.

He was well intentioned, and when I quoted Elder Ballard's statement to him, as quoted above, he thanked me, saying, "I didn't realize Elder Ballard had said that."

As far as I am concerned, such thinking that the Brethren do know the day and even the hour is neither evil nor sinful. It merely expresses a sincere testimony that the Brethren are guided and directed by the Lord. But it could cause trouble and become apostasy if pushed as a "gospel hobby" or if preached as doctrine. It may even be that the Lord will tell the Brethren just before He comes, or it may be that it will pleasantly surprise them just as it will other righteous and prepared people. We simply don't know. In fact, in Mark 13:32 as quoted previously, the Savior seems to emphasize "neither the Son, but the Father." We are wise to hold tightly to the scriptures on this one.

It is even interesting to note that Revelation 14:15, if we understand it correctly, reinforces the thought that the Father will tell the Son when it is time for the Second Coming. In this verse, John the Revelator describes seeing an angel come out of the temple (where the Father rules upon His throne of power—see Revelation 7:15) with a message from the Father. The angel instructs the Savior that it is "harvest" time, or in other words, time for the Second Coming. As stated above, we are wise to stick closely to the scriptures and avoid speculation.

CAUTIONS AND OBSERVATIONS

Revelation 14:15
15 And another angel came out of the temple [*where Heavenly Father is; Revelation 3:12; 7:15*], crying with a loud voice to him [*Christ*] that sat on the cloud [*giving instructions to the Savior from the Father*], Thrust in thy sickle, and reap: for the time is come for thee to reap; for the harvest of the earth is ripe [*it is time for the Second Coming*]; for the harvest of the earth is ripe [*in iniquity*].

DO NOT PUT YOUR LIFE ON HOLD BECAUSE OF THE CLOSENESS OF THE SECOND COMING

Some years ago, a stalwart member of the Church came into my office and expressed concern that her husband, a faithful high priest, had decided that since the Savior's coming is getting so close, they would no longer put additional money into their savings account nor contribute toward their retirement plan with their employer. His thinking was that since the Millennium would obviously be starting soon, they would no longer need money, so he wanted to use their savings and retirement funds now for a boat and other things to go along with it. Such thinking is obviously way off the mark!

Occasionally, over the years, students have indicated that they are not sure that it is necessary for them to be pursuing any further education, since the Second Coming is getting so close, and thus their financial needs will all be taken care of as the Millennium arrives. That thinking is also way off base. Ours is a Church that constantly emphasizes preparation for emergencies and long-term preparation for the future. Our prophets encourage education and planning financially for the future. Simply following the Brethren does away with any notion of putting life on hold because of the proximity of the Second Coming.

It is interesting to note that in the Book of Mormon, Mosiah 3:5, King Benjamin tells his people that the time "is not far distant" when the Savior will be born. "Not far distant," in this case, turns out to be 124 years. The Lord's expression of time is not necessarily the same as ours. Thus, we realize, based on the rapid fulfilling of signs of the times all around us that the coming of Christ is indeed getting close. However, "getting close"

could still mean many, many years. Or, it could mean "just around the corner." Neither of these statements helps to really pin it down. Therefore, we are left to decide which group of "five virgins" we want to be like, the five wise or the five foolish. Both groups started out with oil in their lamps (see Matthew 25:8, footnote a) but the five wise virgins took extra oil in containers along with their lamps (see verses 3 and 4). For both groups, it took longer than they expected for the Bridegroom (Christ) to come (see verse 5), and so they slept while He "tarried," meaning that life went on normally right up until the Bridegroom came. The point we are making here is that in the parable, it took longer than expected for the Bridegroom to come. Therefore, we would be foolish to put our lives on hold while waiting for the Lord's arrival.

WILL EVERYONE BE CAUGHT OFF GUARD, AS IN THE SCRIPTURAL "THIEF IN THE NIGHT" IMAGERY?

In the Doctrine and Covenants, we are taught by the Lord that not everyone will be caught off guard by His Second Coming; rather, those who are caught up in the ways of the world will be taken by surprise (bold added for emphasis).

> D&C 106:4–5
> 4 And again, verily I say unto you, the coming of the Lord draweth nigh, and **it overtaketh the world as a thief in the night**—
> 5 Therefore, gird up your loins, that you may be the **children of light**, and **that day shall not overtake you as a thief**.

The phrase "the world" as used in verse 4, above, means the worldly, the wicked, the foolish, and so forth, who ignore the scriptures and the words of the prophets and thus, like the people in the days of Noah, are caught off guard by the prophesied destructions. On the other hand, the "children of light" have the light of the gospel and are aware of the signs of the times. Thus, they know that the Second Coming is getting close, and when it actually takes place, they are not surprised. The Parable of the Fig Tree, as given in the Pearl of Great Price, confirms this as follows (bold added for emphasis):

Joseph Smith—Matthew 1:38–40

38 Now learn a parable of the fig tree—When its branches are yet tender, and it begins to put forth leaves, **you know that summer is nigh at hand;**

39 **So likewise, mine elect, when they shall see all these things, they shall know that he is near, even at the doors;**

40 But of that day, and hour, no one knoweth; no, not the angels of God in heaven, but my Father only.

AVOID TRYING TO DEVELOP AN EXACT SEQUENCE FOR THE FINAL SIGNS OF THE TIMES

It is rather fascinating to view the signs of the times as a general sequence of events leading up to the actual coming of the Lord. However, it is wise to avoid attempting to develop an exact sequence for the final few events before the Second Coming. It seems that the Lord does not want us to know the exact sequence of these final fulfillments of prophecy.

For example, by reading a few scripture references, including Zechariah 14:1–9, which deals with the appearance of the Savior to the Jews in Jerusalem (when the Mount of Olives splits open), one might begin to think that the last days appearance of Christ in battle-torn Jerusalem would signal His immediate coming to the rest of the world. These verses in Zechariah are as follows (bold added for emphasis):

Zechariah 14:1–9

1 Behold, **the day of the Lord cometh**, and thy spoil shall be divided in the midst of thee.

2 For I will gather **all nations against Jerusalem** to battle; and **the city shall be taken**, and the houses rifled, and the women ravished; and half of the city shall go forth into captivity, and the residue of the people shall not be cut off from the city.

3 **Then shall the Lord go forth, and fight against those nations, as when he fought in the day of battle.**

4 And **his feet shall stand in that day upon the mount of Olives**, which is before Jerusalem on the east, and the mount of Olives shall cleave in the midst thereof toward the east and toward the west, and there shall be a very great valley; and half of the mountain shall remove toward the north, and half of it toward the south.

5 And ye shall flee to the valley of the mountains; for the valley of the mountains shall reach unto Azal: yea, ye shall flee, like as ye fled from before the earthquake in the days of Uzziah king of Judah: and **the Lord my God shall come**, *and* **all the saints with thee.**

6 And it shall come to pass in that day, that the light shall not be clear, nor dark:

7 But it shall be one day which shall be known to the Lord, not day, nor night: but it shall come to pass, that at evening time it shall be light.

8 And it shall be in that day, that living waters shall go out from Jerusalem; half of them toward the former sea, and half of them toward the hinder sea: in summer and in winter shall it be.

9 And **the Lord shall be king over all the earth**: in that day shall there be one Lord, and his name one.

CAUTIONS AND OBSERVATIONS

Thus, in reading these verses, especially verse 9, a person would perhaps decide that the final major prophesied event before the actual Second

Coming would be this appearance of the Savior to the Jews, followed immediately by His coming.

However, suppose that during another personal scripture reading session, he or she ends up reading the following verses in Ezekiel and begins to realize that there may still be considerable time between the appearance of the Lord to the Jews and His final coming. Note that these verses deal primarily with the cleanup that will take place after the Lord rescues the Jews from their enemies in the Holy Land in the last days (bold added for emphasis):

Ezekiel 39:8–16

8 Behold, it is come, and it is done, saith the Lord God; **this *is* the day whereof I have spoken**.

9 And they that dwell in the cities of Israel shall go forth, and shall set on fire and burn the weapons, both the shields and the bucklers, the bows and the arrows, and the handstaves, and the spears, and they shall burn them with fire **seven years**:

10 So that they shall take no wood out of the field, neither cut down any out of the forests; for they shall burn the weapons with fire: and they shall spoil those that spoiled them, and rob those that robbed them, saith the Lord God.

11 And it shall come to pass in that day, that I will give unto Gog [*Israel's enemies who were destroyed by the Lord*] a place there of graves in Israel, the valley of the passengers on the east of the sea: and it shall stop the *noses* of the passengers: and there shall they bury Gog and all his multitude: and they shall call it The valley of Hamon-gog.

12 And **seven months** shall the house of Israel be burying of them, that they may cleanse the land.

13 Yea, all the people of the land shall bury them; and it shall be to them a renown the day that I shall be glorified, saith the Lord God.

14 And they shall sever out men of continual employment, passing through the land to bury with the passengers those that remain upon the face of the earth, to cleanse it: **after the end of seven months** shall they search.

15 And the passengers that pass through the land, **when *any* seeth a man's bone, then shall he set up a sign by it**, till the buriers have buried it in the valley of Hamon-gog.

16 And also the name of the city shall be Hamonah. Thus shall they cleanse the land.

There are many more examples of such situations that make it impossible for us to calculate with exactness the timing or sequencing of the final events before the Advent of the Lord. If it were possible to do so, perhaps some would be inclined to calculate how much time they have before the Second Coming and then live out of harmony with the commandments up to a certain time, then begin to become "active" in the Church again, pay tithing, and so forth, supposedly thereby getting ready for the arrival of the Savior. We know from Matthew 24:36, as previously quoted in this book, that no one knows the exact time of His coming.

MANY THOUGHT THE SAVIOR WOULD COME BY THE YEAR 2000

If you are old enough to remember back to the years and months prior to the turn of the century, you will probably recall that there was considerable anxiety. Some thought and taught that the world would end. Some who didn't necessarily even believe in God or the scriptures were fearful about what might happen to the computer world, as computer clocks had trouble making the transition to a new century. Many who believed on the Bible were quite certain that Christ would come before 11:59 p.m. on the last day of 1999. They based this belief on the "six seals" spoken of in Revelation, chapter 6. As explained in Doctrine and Covenants

77:6–7, these six "seals" represent the first 6,000 years of the earth's history after the fall of Adam. We will include the sixth chapter of Revelation here, with explanatory notes provided within the verses. We will also include some changes provided by the Joseph Smith Translation of the Bible (the JST).

Revelation 6:1–17

1 And I saw when the Lamb [*Christ*] opened one of the seals [*the first one, representing the first thousand years of the earth's temporal existence, i.e., approximately 4,000–3,000 BC; (D&C 77:7)*], and I heard, as it were the noise of thunder, one of the four beasts saying, Come and see.

JST Revelation 6:1

1 And I saw when the Lamb opened one of the seals, one of the four beasts, and I heard, as it were, the noise of thunder, saying, Come and see.

2 And I [*John*] saw, and behold a white horse [*symbolically, white can mean righteousness and horse represents victory*]: and he that sat on him had a bow; and a crown [*authority*] was given unto him: and he went forth conquering, and to conquer [*one possible interpretation could be Adam. Another, Enoch and his victories with the City of Enoch*].

3 And when he [*Christ*] had opened the second seal [*3,000–2,000 BC*], I heard the second beast say, Come and see.

4 And there went out another horse that was red [*bloodshed, war*]: and power was given to him [*perhaps Satan and wicked worldly leaders during the days of Noah*] that sat thereon to take peace from the earth, and that they should kill one another: and there was given unto him a great sword [*representing terrible destruction*].

5 And when he [*Christ*] had opened the third seal [*2,000–1,000 BC*], I heard the third beast say, Come and see. And I beheld [*I looked*], and lo a black horse [*evil, darkness, despair*]; and he that sat on him had a pair of balances [*representing famine; food had to be carefully measured and meted out*] in his hand. [*During this seal, Abraham went to Egypt because of famine; Joseph's brothers later came to him in Egypt because of famine; also, the Israelites were held as slaves in Egypt during this period.*]

6 And I heard a voice in the midst of the four beasts say, A measure [*two US pints*] of wheat for a penny [*a day's wages*], and three measures of barley for a penny; and see thou hurt not [*don't waste*] the oil and the wine [*i.e., terrible famine*].

JST Revelation 6:6

6 And I heard a voice in the midst of the four beasts say, A measure of wheat for a penny, and three measures of barley for a penny; and hurt not thou the oil and the wine.

7 And when he [*Christ*] had opened the fourth seal [*1,000–0 BC; Assyrian captivity, Ten Tribes lost about 722 BC; Babylonian captivity about 588 BC; Daniel in lion's den; Romans take over prior to Christ's birth*], I heard the voice of the fourth beast say, Come and see.

8 And I looked, and behold a pale horse [*not much left of Israel, few righteous people, terrible conditions among the wicked, etc.*]: and his name that sat on him was Death, and Hell followed with him. And power was given unto them over the fourth part [*perhaps meaning not quite as severe destruction as in the windup scenes of the world in Revelation 9:15*] of the earth, to kill with sword [*military destruction*], and with hunger, and with death [*pestilence, plagues*], and with the beasts of the earth.

9 And when he [*Christ*] had opened the fifth seal [*AD 0–1,000*], I saw under the altar [*altar represents sacrifice*] the souls of them that were slain for the word of God [*for the gospel*], and for the testimony which they held [*i.e., those who gave their lives for the gospel's sake*]:

10 And they [*the people who had given their lives for the gospel*] cried with a loud voice,

saying, How long, O Lord, holy and true, dost thou not judge and avenge our blood on them [*the wicked*] that dwell on the earth? [*When will the wicked get what's coming to them? The same question is asked by Joseph Smith in Doctrine and Covenants 121 and by Habakkuk in Habakkuk 1.*]

11 And white robes [*exaltation; see Revelation 3:5*] were given unto every one of them [*the righteous martyrs in verse 9*]; and it was said unto them, that they should rest yet for a little season, until their fellowservants also and their brethren, that should be killed as they were, should be fulfilled [*i.e., others would have similar fates throughout earth's remaining history*].

12 And I beheld when he [*Christ*] had opened the sixth seal [*roughly AD 1,000–2,000*], and, lo, there was a great earthquake; and the sun became black as sackcloth of hair [*perhaps meaning black goat's hair, used in weaving fabric*], and the moon became as blood [*i.e., great signs in heaven and earth during this period of time*];

13 And the stars of heaven [*perhaps including satellites, airplanes, etc., in our day*] fell unto the earth, even as a fig tree casteth her untimely figs, when she is shaken of a mighty wind.

John now jumps ahead to the Second Coming for a few verses. Caution, do not put the Second Coming in the sixth seal. See headings to Revelation 8 and 9 and Doctrine and Covenants 77:13.

14 And the heaven departed as a scroll when it is rolled together; and every mountain and island were moved out of their places [*one continent, one ocean again; D&C 133:22–24, Genesis 10:25*].

JST Revelation 6:14
14 And the heavens opened as a scroll is opened when it is rolled together; and every mountain, and island, was moved out of its place.

15 And the kings [*wicked political leaders*] of the earth, and the great men, and the rich men, and the chief captains, and the mighty men, and every bondman, and every free man [*i.e., all the wicked*], hid themselves in the dens [*caves*] and in the rocks of the mountains [*like Isaiah said the wicked would do at the Second Coming; see Isaiah 2:19, and 2 Nephi 12:10, 19, 21*];

16 And said to the mountains and rocks, Fall on us, and hide us from the face of him [*the Father; Revelation 5:1, 7, 13*] that sitteth on the throne, and from the wrath [*anger*] of the Lamb [*Christ*]:

17 For the great day of his [*the Savior's*] wrath is come; and who shall be able to stand [*i.e., who will be able to survive the Second Coming*]? [*Answer: those living a terrestrial or celestial lifestyle. D&C 5:19 plus 76:81–85 and 88:100–101 tell us that those who live the wicked lifestyle of telestials, which includes lying, stealing, sexual immorality, and murder (and of course, sons of perdition) will be destroyed by the Savior's glory at the Second Coming and will not be resurrected until after the Millennium is over.*]

As stated above, many interpreted these verses in Revelation to mean that the Savior would come at the end of the sixth "seal." They believed this to be by or before the last day of AD 1999, the beginning of the year AD 2000 or at the end of the year AD 2000. Because of this mistaken idea, derived from a misunderstanding of the "seals," some in recent years have predicted the exact day of the Lord's coming. They have gathered others around them who abandoned homes and property, resigned their employment, and joined together as groups to await the Lord's coming. Needless to say, they have been disappointed.

What such individuals do not understand is that the Savior will not come at the end of the six thousand years. He will come sometime in the beginning of the "seventh seal," in other words, sometime in the beginning of the seventh thousand years. This is clearly stated in the Doctrine and Covenants, where the Lord answered specific questions about the book of Revelation through the Prophet Joseph Smith.

D&C 77:6–7, 12–13.

6 Q. What are we to understand by the book which John saw, which was sealed on the back with **seven seals**?

A. We are to understand that it contains the revealed will, mysteries, and the works of God; the hidden things of his economy concerning **this earth** during the **seven thousand years** of its continuance, or its **temporal existence**.

7 Q. What are we to understand by the **seven seals** with which it was sealed?

A. We are to understand that **the first seal contains the things of the first thousand years, and the second also of the second thousand years, and so on until the seventh.**

12 Q. What are we to understand by the sounding of the trumpets, mentioned in the 8th chapter of Revelation?

A. We are to understand that as God made the world in six days, and on the seventh day he finished his work, and sanctified it, and also formed man out of the dust of the earth, even so, in the beginning of the seventh thousand years will the Lord God sanctify the earth, and complete the salvation of man, and judge all things, and shall redeem all things, except that which he hath not put into his power, when he shall have sealed all things, unto the end of all things; and the sounding of the trumpets of the seven angels are the preparing and **finishing of his work, in the beginning of the seventh thousand years—the preparing of the way before the time of his coming**.

13 Q. When are the things to be accomplished, which are written in the 9th chapter of Revelation?

A. They are to be **accomplished after the opening of the seventh seal, before the coming of Christ**.

The fact that the Lord will come sometime in the beginning of the seventh thousand year period of the earth's temporal existence certainly eliminates the possibility that anyone could calculate the exact time of His coming!

Just one more note here. We are led by prophets, seers, and revelators in these momentous last days. As many of you will recall, there was indeed much concern some years ago, as the world approached the beginning of the year 2000, about how computers would react to the switch to a new century. This great worry was referred to as "Y2K." Amid the hype and concern, which approached panic on some fronts, President James E. Faust of the First Presidency said the following about Y2K (bold added for emphasis).

CAUTIONS AND OBSERVATIONS

Today many people are obsessed with the Y2K problem and worry about the date coming up right because of the way computers measure time. As someone once said about time: "[It] changes with time: in youth, time marches on; in middle age, time flies; and in old age, time runs out." We have come to rely on electronics for much of our daily work, and we are naturally concerned about the need to reprogram computers to move into the next century. **While some glitches may occur, I am optimistic that no great catastrophic computer breakdown will disrupt society as we move into the next century.** I have a far greater fear of the disruption of the traditional values of society.

When I heard this prophetic statement from President Faust, any concerns that I had previously entertained about Y2K dissolved away to mere curiosity as to what little "glitches," if any, might occur. As some of you remember, there were hardly any at all. What a great blessing to be led by true prophets of God! It brings peace and stability and allows us to use our strength and energy in worthwhile pursuits. Confidence and faith in such guidance from the Lord's servants empowers us to follow the Savior's counsel, to which we have already referred several times (bold added for emphasis):

Joseph Smith—Matthew 1:23

23 Behold, I speak these things unto you for the elect's sake; and you also shall hear of wars, and rumors of wars; **see that ye be not troubled**, for all I have told you must come to pass; but the end is not yet.

CAUTIONS
AND
OBSERVATIONS

CHAPTER 4
100 SIGNS OF THE TIMES

A S STATED EARLIER in this book, "signs of the times" are prophecies of events and conditions that will bear witness to people who live in the last days that the Second Coming of the Savior is getting close (Joseph Smith—Matthew 1:39). From the beginning, the Lord has placed these prophecies in the scriptures. Then, by fulfilling them in such open and obvious ways, He provides those who live in the last days with assurance and evidence that He exists and that the scriptures contain His word. In addition, any who are honest in heart and some who are not can be drawn toward God by observing the fulfillment of these prophecies.

In this chapter, we will consider 100 signs of the times. We will not intentionally place them in any particular chronological order. We will "treasure them up" in our hearts as counseled in the Pearl of Great Price, and use them as the Lord intended we should, namely, to bear witness to us that the gospel is true, thus strengthening our testimonies (bold added for emphasis):

Joseph Smith—Matthew 1:37–39

37 And **whoso treasureth up my word, shall not be deceived**, for the Son of Man shall come, and he shall send his angels before him with the great sound of a trumpet, and they shall gather together the remainder of his elect from the four winds, from one end of heaven to the other.

38 Now learn a parable of the fig tree—When its branches are yet tender, and it begins to put forth leaves, you know that summer is nigh at hand;

39 So likewise, **mine elect, when they shall see all these things [*the signs of the times being fulfilled*], they shall know** that he is near, even at the doors;

We will number these prophecies for convenience in referring back to them in this book as well as for the convenience of readers who may be studying them in groups or individually in their own books and then discussing them together. Other than this, **the numbering of these signs of the times in this book has no significance**. As previously noted, there are many more than 100 such signs.

Also, we will assign most of the 100 signs of the times we consider in this book to a general category as follows:

General Categories:
1. **Already Fulfilled**—these signs have already taken place in significant measure.
2. **Being Fulfilled**—that is to say, these signs are currently underway.
3. **Yet to Be Fulfilled**—in other words, for all intents and purposes, these signs have not yet begun to be fulfilled.

While these are general categories only (and obviously some fulfillment of prophecies may span all three), it is at least interesting to look at most signs in this way in order to feel the marvelous testimony being born to us from the heavens by way of the fulfillment of these prophecies in our times.

SIGN 1

A MAN NAMED "DAVID" WILL LEAD THE CHURCH

CATEGORY: ?

Misinterpretation of Ezekiel 34:23 and other scriptures has given rise to a false sign of the times among some members of the Church to the effect that the Savior will come when a prophet named David is the president of the Church. I'm including this false sign, in this context, here for clarification and warning. Let's read this verse in its context and setting. Ezekiel prophesied of the last days, including the gathering of Israel (see heading to Ezekiel 34, in your LDS Bible; bold added for emphasis):

Ezekiel 34:13, 16, 20–24
13 **And I will bring them out from the people, and gather them from the countries**, and will bring them to their own land, and feed them upon the mountains of Israel by the rivers, and in all the inhabited places of the country.

16 **I will seek that which was lost, and bring again that which was driven away**, and will bind up that which was broken, and will strengthen that which was sick: but I will destroy the fat and the strong; I will feed them with judgment.

20 Therefore thus saith the Lord God unto them; Behold, I, even I, will judge between the fat cattle and between the lean cattle.

21 Because ye have thrust with side and with shoulder, and pushed all the diseased with your horns, till ye have scattered them abroad;

22 Therefore will I save my flock, and they shall no more be a prey; and I will judge between cattle and cattle.

23 **And I will set up one shepherd over them, and he shall feed them, even my servant David; he shall feed them, and he shall be their shepherd**.

Verse 23 is actually referring to the Savior during His millennial reign. "David" is often used in the scriptures to refer to descendants of King David. This includes Jesus (see Matthew 1:1–16). He will reign personally on the earth during the Millennium as "Lord of lords and King of kings" (Revelation 17:14, 19:16) and is referred to here as "David." He will be our "Shepherd." Thus, one named David will indeed lead the Church, but it is the Savior during the thousand years of peace that will begin with the Second Coming (D&C 29:11.) This passage of scripture is not even a sign of the times.

Such misinterpreting of the scriptures can cause unjustified excitement and even worry. During my growing up years, when David O. McKay was the president of the Church, there was a persistent rumor to the effect that there was a prophecy that the Second Coming would take place during the time in the last days when a prophet named David was the president of the Church. Needless to say, it caused considerable excitement for some who believed it, especially as President McKay was getting very old. When he passed away and the rumor had not proven true, there was some disappointment among those who believed it, and even worse, there were some whose testimonies were shaken.

Later in my teaching career, I occasionally ran into another such rumor built up around Elder David B. Haight, when he was called to be an Apostle. It was whispered that, if he became the president of the Church, we would know that the Savior would come sometime during his administration.

We will now move on to several true signs of the times.

SIGN 2

THE DISCOVERY OF AMERICA AND THE ESTABLISHMENT OF THE UNITED STATES OF AMERICA

CATEGORY: FULFILLED

This is a very significant sign of the times. Before the Restoration could take place, this prophecy had to be fulfilled. The freedoms and environment in which the restoration of the Church could take place had to be established. Nephi prophesied the discovery of America by Christopher Columbus and the ensuing colonization by the pilgrims and the colonists as follows:

1 Nephi 13:12–15
12 And I looked and beheld a man [*Columbus*] among the Gentiles, who was separated from the seed of my brethren by the many waters; and I beheld the Spirit of God, that it came down and wrought upon the man; and he went forth upon the many waters, even unto the seed of my brethren [*the Lamanites*], who were in the promised land.

13 And it came to pass that I beheld the Spirit of God, that it wrought upon other Gentiles [*the Pilgrims*]; and they went forth out of captivity, upon the many waters.

14 And it came to pass that I beheld many multitudes of the Gentiles upon the land of promise; and I beheld the wrath of God, that it was upon the seed of my brethren; and they were scattered before the Gentiles and were smitten.

15 And I beheld the Spirit of the Lord, that it was upon the Gentiles [*the colonists*], and they did prosper and obtain the land for their inheritance; and I beheld that they were white, and exceedingly fair and beautiful, like unto my people before they were slain.

Nephi continued, prophesying the establishment of the United States of America (bold added for emphasis):

1 Nephi 13:16–19
16 And it came to pass that I, Nephi, beheld that the Gentiles who had gone forth out of captivity did humble themselves before the Lord; and the power of the Lord was with them.

17 And I beheld that their mother Gentiles [*Great Britain*] were gathered together upon the waters, and upon the land also, to battle against them [*the 13 Colonies*].

18 And I beheld that the power of God was with them, and also that the wrath of God was upon all those that were gathered together against them to battle.

19 And I, Nephi, beheld that the Gentiles that had gone out of captivity were delivered by the power of God out of the hands of all other nations.

1 Nephi 22:7
7 And it meaneth that the time cometh that after all the house of Israel have been scattered and confounded, that **the Lord God will raise up a mighty nation among the Gentiles** [*the United States of America*], yea, even upon the face of this land; and by them shall our seed be scattered.

The Savior also prophesied the establishment of the United States as recorded in Third Nephi (bold added for emphasis):

3 Nephi 21:4
4 For it is wisdom in the Father that they should be established in this land, and be

INSPIRATION OF CHRISTOPHER COLUMBUS

BY JOSE MARIA VELASCO

set up as a free people by the power of the Father, that these things might come forth from them unto a remnant of your seed, that the covenant of the Father may be fulfilled which he hath covenanted with his people, O house of Israel;

By the way, some may suggest that this prophecy is not very current and its fulfillment occurred so far in the past that it should not be considered as a sign of the last days. Actually, in the whole context of the history of the earth since the fall of Adam and Eve, the establishment of the United States of America is very recent. Consider that the earth has seven thousand years from the Fall of Adam and Eve to the end of the Millennium and the little season that follows (see D&C 77:6). Thus, the founding of the United States is a relatively recent event in the history of things and is appropriately considered a sign signaling that the Second Coming is getting relatively near.

Perhaps you are aware that many sailors and explorers before Columbus had seen or set foot on the north American continent. The Vikings spoke of it. Sailors took their ships past the mouth of the Columbia River on the western edge of the continent, seeing that vast waterway to the interior, but not exploring it. These, along with many others had seen and knew of this land but did not attempt or succeed in serious exploring and colonizing efforts. Knowing what we do about the hand of the Lord in preserving this land for His purposes in the last days, it becomes obvious that the prophecy of Lehi was literally fulfilled regarding it (bold added for emphasis):

2 Nephi 1:6–8
6 Wherefore, I, Lehi, prophesy according to the workings of the Spirit which is in me, that **there shall none come into this land save they shall be brought by the hand of the Lord**.

7 Wherefore, this land is consecrated unto him whom he shall bring. And if it so be that they shall serve him according to the commandments which he hath given, it shall be a land of liberty unto them; wherefore, they shall never be brought down into captivity; if so, it shall be because of iniquity; for if iniquity shall abound cursed shall be the land for their sakes, but unto the righteous it shall be blessed forever.

8 And behold, **it is wisdom that this land should be kept as yet from the knowledge of other nations**; for behold, many nations would overrun the land, that there would be no place for an inheritance.

SIGN 3

A PROPHET NAMED "JOSEPH" TO BE RAISED UP IN THE LAST DAYS

CATEGORY: FULFILLED

Joseph, who was sold into Egypt, prophesied that the Lord would raise up a "seer" out of his posterity who would restore the true gospel in the last days (see 2 Nephi 3:11–13). He further prophesied that that prophet would have his name (Joseph) and would also be named after his father, in other words would be Joseph Jr.

One of the interesting miracles that we see in conjunction with the naming of Joseph Smith Jr. is that he was not the first son born to Joseph Smith Sr., and his wife, Lucy Mack Smith. Usually, if a husband and wife determine to name a boy after the husband, they give that name to the first son born to them. This is logical, since they don't know whether or not they will have any more sons. In the case of Joseph and Lucy, they had an unnamed son born sometime between mid 1796 and early 1797. Another son was born in 1798. They ended up naming him Alvin. Yet another son was born in 1800. They named him Hyrum. Next, came a daughter, whom they named Sophronia. Finally, in 1805, the prophesied son was born to them. No doubt, inspiration prevailed upon their minds as they contemplated what to name this little fellow. Likewise, we imagine there was much excitement in heaven as this great and noble spirit son of God, foreordained to be the mighty prophet of the Restoration, was finally sent to earth. Father and Mother Smith decided to name him Joseph Smith Jr. As you know, the adversary mounted severe opposition almost immediately that continued throughout his life. However, Joseph in Egypt had also prophesied that "they that seek to destroy him shall be confounded" (2 Nephi 3:14.) In other words, he would be protected until he had completed his earthly mission.

SIGN 4

THE COMING FORTH OF THE BOOK OF MORMON

CATEGORY: FULFILLED

The coming forth of the Book of Mormon is a pivotal sign of the times in signaling that the dispensation of the fulness of times and the ensuing last days have arrived. Ezekiel referred to the Bible as "the stick of Judah" and to the Book of Mormon as "the stick of Joseph." In the last days, the Book of Mormon will join with the Bible as a testimony of Christ. This very significant sign of the times is prophesied in Ezekiel as follows (bold added for emphasis):

Ezekiel 37:15–19
15 The word of the Lord came again unto me, saying,

16 Moreover, thou son of man, take thee one stick [*symbolic of the Bible*], and write upon it, For Judah, and for the children of Israel his companions: then take another stick [*symbolic of the Book of Mormon*],

and write upon it, For Joseph, the stick of Ephraim, and *for* all the house of Israel his companions:

17 And join them one to another into one stick; and they shall become one in thine hand.

18 And when the children of thy people shall speak unto thee, saying, Wilt thou not shew us what thou meanest by these?

19 Say unto them, Thus saith the Lord God; Behold, I will take **the stick of Joseph**, which is in the hand of Ephraim, and the tribes of Israel his fellows, and will put them with him, even **with the stick of Judah**, and make them one stick, and they shall be **one in mine hand**.

We mentioned above that the coming forth of the Book of Mormon is a major sign that the last days have begun. This is clearly stated in the Book of Mormon, as follows (bold added for emphasis):

3 Nephi 21:1–2
1 And verily I say unto you, **I give unto you a sign**, that ye may know the time when these things [*the gathering and events in the last days as described in 3 Nephi, chapters 20–23*] shall be about to take place—that I shall gather in, from their long dispersion, my people, O house of Israel, and shall establish again among them my Zion;

2 And behold, **this is the** thing which I will give unto you for a **sign**—for verily I say unto you **that when these things which I declare unto you, and which I shall declare unto you hereafter of myself, and by the power of the Holy Ghost which shall be given unto you of the Father, shall be made known unto the Gentiles** [*in other words, when the Book of Mormon comes forth*] that they may know concerning this people who are a remnant of the house of

PORTRAIT OF
JOSEPH SMITH JR.

Jacob, and concerning this my people who shall be scattered by them;

The Savior continues, again explaining that when the record of His dealings with His people in the Americas (the Book of Mormon) comes forth to the remnant of the Lamanites, it is a sign that the last days have begun. In 3 Nephi 21:7, He instructs the people (bold added for emphasis):

> 7 **And when** these things come to pass that **thy seed shall begin to know these things—it shall be a sign unto them**, that they may know that the work of the Father hath already commenced unto the fulfilling of the covenant which he hath made unto the people who are of the house of Israel.

It has often been said that the Book of Mormon is the best "missionary" in the Church. Great numbers of people have been converted by reading it. President Benson continually encouraged members to "flood the earth" with the Book of Mormon. In the October 1988 general conference of the Church, he said:

> The Book of Mormon is the instrument that God designed to "sweep the earth as with a flood, to gather out [His] elect" (Moses 7:62). This sacred volume of scripture needs to become more central in our preaching, our teaching, and our missionary work.

During our second mission as Church Educational System missionaries, my wife and I had a young man in our classes who had been converted at age 14 by reading the Book of Mormon. He told us that he had answered a Mormon Ad and had ordered a free copy of the Book of Mormon. It changed his life completely. Through a continuing series of miracles in his behalf, he is now serving as a full-time missionary. It all began with the Book of Mormon.

From his early youth, Parley P. Pratt, one of the first Apostles of the Church in this dispensation,

had sought the true gospel. His seeking eventually put him in contact with the teachings of Alexander Campbell, of Virginia, and an associate, Sidney Rigdon, who was preaching on the American frontier near where Parley resided. He attended meetings where Sidney preached. This, in turn, led him to firmly believe in faith, repentance, baptism by immersion, and the gift of the Holy Ghost, but that the power was not on earth to administer these ordinances.

While living on the frontier farm with his young wife, who was named Thankful, he was prompted that they should leave their modest home and travel east to visit relatives and friends in their hometown in eastern New York. Arriving in Rochester, Parley felt strongly that he should interrupt his journey and travel south into the Palmyra area. He bid farewell to his wife, assuring her that he would catch up with her soon.

By now, Parley had become a lay preacher of sorts, and as he traveled south about 10 miles, he determined to set up an appointment to do some preaching that evening. In the course of traveling about the neighborhood giving out invitations, he encountered an old Baptist who talked to him at length about a strange book that had recently been published by a young man from Palmyra, purportedly translated from gold plates. Parley was prompted to take an interest in the book. The Baptist deacon promised him that he could take a look at the book the next day, if he would come by his house. In his own words, Parley P. Pratt tells what happened next:

> Next morning I called at his house, where, for the first time, my eyes beheld the "BOOK OF MORMON"—that book of books— that record which reveals the antiquities of the "New World" back to the remotest ages, and which unfolds the destiny of its people and the world for all time to come;— that Book which contains the fulness of the gospel of a crucified and risen Redeemer:—

that Book which reveals a lost remnant of Joseph, and which was the principal means, in the hands of God, of directing the entire course of my future life.

I opened it with eagerness, and read its title page. I then read the testimony of several witnesses in relation to the manner of its being found and translated. After this I commenced its contents by course. I read all day; eating was a burden, I had no desire for food; sleep was a burden when the night came, for I preferred reading to sleep.

As I read, the spirit of the Lord was upon me, and I knew and comprehended that the book was true, as plainly and manifestly as a man comprehends and knows that he exists. My joy was now full, as it were, and I rejoiced sufficiently to more than pay me for all the sorrows, sacrifices and toils of my life. I soon determined to see the young man who had been the instrument of its discovery and translation. (*Autobiography of Parley P. Pratt*, 1973, Deseret Book, 37)

Parley traveled to Palmyra, New York, and asked around for Joseph Smith. He was told that Joseph lived some two to three miles from there (in Manchester). As he approached the Smith family farm, he met a man who was herding some cows. He asked the stranger for the whereabouts of Joseph Smith and was told that he currently resided in Pennsylvania (Harmony, Pennsylvania), which was over 100 miles away. Parley asked the man if any of Joseph's family were around, and the man herding the cows informed him that he was Joseph's brother Hyrum. Parley told him of his interest in the Book of Mormon, whereupon Hyrum Smith invited him to come into his house where the two spent most of the night in conversation.

Among other things, Parley told Hyrum of his feeling that priesthood authority was lacking as were apostles and other priesthood authorities necessary to properly maintain the church as

Christ had organized it. He concluded that the whole world was without authorized baptism.

The result of this time spent with Hyrum Smith was that Parley P. Pratt was converted. As he departed the next morning to walk 30 miles to fulfill a preaching commitment he had made for that evening, Hyrum presented him with a copy of the Book of Mormon. As he stopped to rest occasionally on his journey, he commenced to read the book again, delighted to have his own copy of the Book of Mormon. He arrived in time to fill his speaking appointment. A large crowd attended the meeting. He filled another preaching appointment the next evening, finding much interest among the people in his message. He was urged by the crowd to stay and continue teaching them, but he was extremely anxious to return to Hyrum Smith's residence and request baptism.

After traveling the 30 miles back to Hyrum's home, Parley stayed overnight there. The next morning, they walked about 25 miles to the Peter Whitmer Sr. farm in Fayette, New York, arriving in the evening, where Parley said he was warmly welcomed by the little branch of the Church there. After resting the night, he was baptized the next day by Oliver Cowdery, in Seneca Lake. The Book of Mormon had a powerful convert!

SIGN 5
THE RESTORATION OF THE PRIESTHOOD AND THE PRIESTHOOD KEYS
CATEGORY: FULFILLED

This is a an important sign of the last days. Without the priesthood, which is the authority of God, delegated to man to act in His name (D&C 20:73; 138:30), the Church cannot exist. Without the restoration of priesthood keys, which are the power and authority to

100 SIGNS

THEREFORE, THE
KEYS OF THIS
DESPENSATION
ARE COMMITTED
INTO YOUR
HANDS.

D & C   110:16

control and direct the use of the priesthood by all priesthood holders, and to preside over all members, order would not exist and the Church would not remain unified and the same in inspired form and function throughout the world. Several years ago, I attended a sacrament meeting in Marseille, France. While I understood scarcely a word that was said, I did understand most everything that went on. I understood the sacrament. I felt the Spirit as talks were given and prayers were said. The Saints radiated the same love and goodness as at home. The sameness and order of the Church prevailed and I felt at home.

Not long ago, a recent convert in our ward expressed his appreciation for the order in the Church. He said that it is a major factor that attracted him to the Church in the first place. It helped lead him to the waters of baptism. Keys of the priesthood do indeed bring and maintain order in the Church.

The Bible informs us that in the last days, before the coming of the Lord, this priesthood and its attendant powers and keys will be once again available to man on earth. For example, in Malachi we read that Elijah is to be sent to earth before the coming of the Lord:

> Malachi 4:5–6
> 5 Behold, I will send you Elijah the prophet before the coming of the great and dreadful day of the Lord [*the Second Coming*]:
> 6 And he shall turn the heart of the fathers to the children, and the heart of the children to their fathers, lest I come and smite the earth with a curse.

We learn from Doctrine and Covenants 110:11–16 that Moses, Elias, and Elijah came to Joseph Smith and Oliver Cowdery in the Kirtland Temple and restored priesthood keys, including the keys of sealing (bold added for emphasis):

D&C 110:11–16

11 After this vision closed, the heavens were again opened unto us; and **Moses appeared** before us, and committed unto us the **keys of the gathering of Israel** from the four parts of the earth, and the leading of the ten tribes from the land of the north.

12 After this, **Elias appeared**, and committed the **dispensation of the gospel of Abraham**, saying that in us and our seed all generations after us should be blessed.

13 After this vision had closed, another great and glorious vision burst upon us; for **Elijah the prophet**, who was taken to heaven without tasting death, **stood before us, and said:**

14 Behold, **the time has fully come**, which was spoken of by the mouth of Malachi—testifying that he [*Elijah*] should be sent, before the great and dreadful day of the Lord come—

15 **To turn the hearts of the fathers to the children, and the children to the fathers**, lest the whole earth be smitten with a curse—

16 Therefore, **the keys of this dispensation are committed into your hands**; and **by this ye may know that the great and dreadful day of the Lord [*the Second Coming*] is near, even at the doors**.

As you can see at the end of verse 16, above, this restoration of priesthood keys is a powerful sign of the times, signifying to all who understand that the coming of the Lord is indeed drawing near.

Jeremiah makes reference to a "new covenant" that will be made in the last days (see heading to Jeremiah 31 in our LDS Bible). Covenants must be made through the power of the priesthood. Therefore, in order for this "new covenant" to be made, the priesthood must be restored (bold added for emphasis):

Jeremiah 31:31–33

31 Behold, the days come, saith the Lord, that **I will make a new covenant** with the house of Israel, and with the house of Judah:

32 Not according to the covenant that I made with their fathers in the day that I took them by the hand to bring them out of the land of Egypt; which my covenant they brake, although I was an husband unto them, saith the Lord:

33 But this shall be the covenant that I will make with the house of Israel; After those days, saith the Lord, **I will put my law in their inward parts, and write it in their hearts; and will be their God, and they shall be my people**.

The priesthood and the keys that go with it have been restored as prophesied in the last days. For example, the Aaronic Priesthood was restored to Joseph Smith and Oliver Cowdery as recorded in the Doctrine and Covenants (bold added for emphasis):

D&C 13:1

1 Upon you my fellow servants, in the name of Messiah **I confer the Priesthood of Aaron**, which holds the keys of the ministering of angels, and of the gospel of repentance, and of baptism by immersion for the remission of sins; and this shall never be taken again from the earth, until the sons of Levi do offer again an offering unto the Lord in righteousness.

Peter, James, and John restored the Melchizedek Priesthood to Joseph Smith and Oliver Cowdery in the spring of 1829. (See Bible Dictionary, "Melchizedek Priesthood.") Though no specific date is given, this momentous event is referred to in the Doctrine and Covenants as follows (bold added for emphasis):

D&C 27:12–13

12 And also with Peter, and James, and John, whom I have sent unto you, **by whom I have ordained you and confirmed you to be apostles**, and especial witnesses of my name, and bear the keys of your ministry and of the same things which I revealed unto them;

13 Unto whom I have committed the keys of my kingdom, and a dispensation of the gospel for the last times; and for the fulness of times, in the which I will gather together in one all things, both which are in heaven, and which are on earth;

Priesthood keys were thus a vital part of the "restoration of all things, which God hath spoken by the mouth of all his holy prophets since the world began." (Acts 3:21.)

Later in this book (sign 31), we will say more about the coming of Elijah to restore the keys of the sealing power.

SIGN 6
THE RESTORATION OF THE TRUE CHURCH OF JESUS CHRIST
CATEGORY: FULFILLED

We are promised in the Bible and elsewhere that when the last days arrive, the people of the earth will once again have the privilege of joining the true Church of Jesus Christ. Thus, the Great Apostasy or falling away from the true Church established by the Savior during His mortal ministry will be brought to a close. The Apostle Paul spoke of this apostasy, which would occur before the Savior's return, as follows (bold added for emphasis):

2 Thessalonians 2:1–3

1 Now we beseech you, brethren, by the coming of our Lord Jesus Christ, and by our gathering together unto him,

2 That ye be not soon shaken in mind, or be troubled, neither by spirit, nor by word, nor by letter as from us, as that **the day of Christ** [*the Second Coming*] is at hand.

3 Let no man deceive you by any means: for *that day shall not come,* **except there come a falling away first**, and that man of sin be revealed, the son of perdition;

The Apostle Peter prophesied the restoration of the true Church of Jesus Christ in the last days before the Second Coming (bold added for emphasis):

Acts 3:19–21

19 Repent ye therefore, and be converted, that your sins may be blotted out, when the times of refreshing shall come from the presence of the Lord;

20 And he shall send **Jesus Christ**, which before was preached unto you:

21 **Whom the heaven must receive until the times of restitution of all things**, which God hath spoken by the mouth of all his holy prophets since the world began.

Isaiah prophesied the Restoration and the ensuing gathering of Israel in the last days, before the coming of Christ (bold added for emphasis):

Isaiah 2:1–3

1 The word that Isaiah the son of Amoz saw concerning Judah and Jerusalem.

2 And it shall come to pass **in the last days**, that **the mountain of the Lord's house** [*the restored Church*] **shall be established** in the top of the mountains, and shall be exalted above the hills; and all nations shall flow unto it.

3 And many people shall go and say, Come ye, and let us go up to the mountain of the Lord, to the house of the God of Jacob; and he will teach us of his ways, and we will walk in his paths: for out of Zion shall go forth the law, and the word of the Lord from Jerusalem.

Moroni quoted another prophecy of Isaiah about the restoration of the true Church in the last days as he appeared to Joseph Smith and instructed him. (Joseph Smith—History 1:40.)

Isaiah 11:11–12

11 And it shall come to pass **in that day** [*the last days*], *that* **the Lord shall set his hand again the second time to recover the remnant of his people**, which shall be left, from Assyria, and from Egypt, and from Pathros, and from Cush, and from Elam, and from Shinar, and from Hamath, and from the islands of the sea.

12 And **he shall set up an ensign for the nations, and shall assemble the outcasts of Israel, and gather together the dispersed of Judah from the four corners of the earth**.

Daniel clearly prophesied the restoration of the gospel and the true Church, foretelling that it would eventually fill the whole earth and would continue growing right up to the Second Coming (bold added for emphasis):

Daniel 2:35, 44–45

35 Then was the iron, the clay, the brass, the silver, and the gold, broken to pieces together, and became like the chaff of the summer threshingfloors; and the wind carried them away, that no place was found for them: and **the stone** [*the restored Church in the last days*] that smote the image **became a great mountain, and filled the whole earth**.

44 And in the days of these kings shall the God of heaven set up a kingdom, which shall never be destroyed: and the kingdom shall not be left to other people, but it shall break in pieces and consume all these kingdoms, and **it shall stand for ever**.

45 Forasmuch as thou sawest that the stone was cut out of the mountain without hands, and that it brake in pieces the iron, the brass, the clay, the silver, and the gold; the great God hath made known to the king what shall come to pass hereafter: and the dream is certain, and the interpretation thereof sure.

The Apostle Paul alerted the Ephesian saints that in the dispensation of the fulness of times (the last major gospel dispensation before the Second Coming), the gospel would be restored completely.

Ephesians 1:10

10 **That in the dispensation of the fulness of times he might gather together in one all things in Christ**, both which are in heaven, and which are on earth; even in him:

We will include yet one more New Testament prophecy of the Restoration, one that is quite familiar to many members of the Church.

Revelation 14:6

6 And I saw another angel fly in the midst of heaven, **having the everlasting gospel to preach unto them that dwell on the earth**, and to every nation, and kindred, and tongue, and people,

This prophecy became significant to John Taylor. As a young man in England, he had a vision in which he saw "an angel in the heavens, holding a trumpet to his mouth, sounding a message to the nations" (B. H. Roberts, *The Life of John Taylor*, Salt Lake City, Bookcraft, 1963, 27–28). While he didn't understand the significance of this vision at the time, it later became a strong witness to him as he became acquainted with the restored gospel and joined the Church. He later became the third president of the Church.

Under the guidance of the Spirit, people throughout the world are being prepared to accept the true gospel. It has been restored. They are searching for it. They wonder if it is to be found anywhere on earth today. It is. It has been restored. It is a completed sign of the times and its blessings are being miraculously made available increasingly throughout the earth.

SIGN 7

ONCE RESTORED IN THE LAST DISPENSATION, THE TRUE CHURCH WILL NEVER AGAIN BE LOST THROUGH APOSTASY

CATEGORY: BEING FULFILLED

Perhaps you've noticed that every time the gospel was established or restored throughout history, it eventually was taken away because of apostasy. Thus, it is very significant and comforting to know that, according to prophecy, when the Church is restored in the last dispensation (our day), it will never be taken away again. It will never die out again.

Several years ago, while I was serving as a stake president, a once-faithful member of my stake got caught up with a group of apostates who had determined for themselves that the First Presidency and Quorum of the Twelve were leading the Church away from the pure gospel restored by Joseph Smith. Consequently, he moved his family to a remote location out of state where they could associate with this break-off group. Some months later, he happened to be back in town on business and I chanced to run into him downtown. He was pleasant and respectful and desired to chat. He soon led the discussion to his actions in affiliating with such a group, and he was curious as to what I thought about it. I asked him if he still believed in the scriptures, including the Bible. He answered emphatically yes! I asked him if he had read the clear prophecy in Daniel that the Church, once restored in the last dispensation, would never go astray. With a concerned look on his face, he said no. I invited him to read Daniel 2:44 and then get back to me when convenient. A short while later, he contacted me, stating with deep

LDS CONFERENCE CENTER

SALT LAKE CITY, UTAH

appreciation that he had never noticed this scripture before.

Daniel 2:44

44 And in the days of these kings [*the last dispensation*] shall the God of heaven set up a kingdom, **which shall never be destroyed: and the kingdom shall not be left to other people**, but it shall break in pieces and consume all these kingdoms, and it shall stand for ever.

The prophesy clearly states that, once the true church has been restored again in the last days, it will "never be destroyed." And then Daniel double emphasizes this fact by saying "the kingdom shall not be left to other people." This good man, who had been temporarily deceived, honestly accepted this prophecy of Daniel as the word of God, realizing now that the Church, once restored in the last dispensation, would never be turned over to others. He expressed gratitude to me for pointing it out in the scriptures and shortly thereafter moved his family back, resuming faithful activity in the Church.

SIGN 8

THE CHURCH WILL BE ESTABLISHED IN THE TOPS OF THE MOUNTAINS

CATEGORY: FULFILLED

Isaiah prophesied that in the last days, the "mountain of the Lord's house shall be established in the top of the mountains." As with so much of Isaiah, this prophecy can have many meanings in its fulfillment. It can refer to temples. It can refer to the Church. It can refer to the Conference Center at Church headquarters in Salt Lake City. It can refer to a future temple yet to be built in the mountains of Jerusalem (D&C 133:13). For our purposes

here, we will emphasize the aspect that the Church would be established in the tops of the mountains and that people throughout the world would come unto it.

Isaiah 2:2–3

2 And it shall come to pass **in the last days**, that the mountain of **the Lord's house shall be established in the top of the mountains**, and shall be exalted above the hills; and **all nations shall flow unto it.**

3 And **many people** shall go and **say**, Come ye, and **let us go up to the mountain of the Lord, to the house of the God of Jacob**; and he will teach us of his ways, and we will walk in his paths:

Surely this prophecy is being fulfilled as people throughout the world look to Salt Lake City, Utah, the headquarters of the true Church of Jesus Christ of Latter-day Saints, established as it were in the tops of the mountains, for guidance from the Lord's living prophets in the last days. This sign of the times is especially wonderfully fulfilled during each general conference, as members and interested people throughout the world "go up to the mountain of the Lord," in person, electronically, and in print to be taught in His ways.

SIGN 9

THE CHURCH WILL GROW TO FILL THE ENTIRE EARTH

CATEGORY: BEING FULFILLED

In Daniel, chapter 2, we read his exciting prophecy about the spread of the true Church and gospel throughout the whole earth. Daniel explains King Nebuchadnezzar's dream in which the Church was seen as a stone, cut "out of the mountain without hands," which rolled forth and filled the whole earth in the last days.

"Without hands" means that it is God's work, not man's.

Daniel 2:35, 44–45

35 Then was the iron, the clay, the brass, the silver, and the gold, broken to pieces together, and became like the chaff of the summer threshing floors; and the wind carried them away, that no place was found for them: and **the stone** that smote the image **became a great mountain, and filled the whole earth**.

44 And in the days of these kings **shall the God of heaven set up a kingdom, which shall never be destroyed**: and the kingdom shall not be left to other people, but it shall break in pieces and consume all these kingdoms, and **it shall stand for ever**.

45 Forasmuch as thou sawest that the **stone was cut out of the mountain without hands**, and that it brake in pieces the iron, the brass, the clay, the silver, and the gold; the great **God hath made known to the king what shall come to pass hereafter**: and the dream *is* certain, and the interpretation thereof sure.

There are many accounts that bear witness of the fact that this sign of the times is being fulfilled in marvelous ways. Things are happening behind the scenes to prepare for the spread of the gospel throughout the world, including penetrating into countries that now seem off-limits to the spread of the gospel.

For example, many years ago, one of my former seminary students told me what had happened to him and his companion as they attempted to teach the gospel in a foreign country whose government was unfriendly to the Church. They had run into so many legal restrictions and government regulations that their work was virtually stopped. In desperation, they decided to go to government headquarters and work their way office by office until they either got to someone who had authority to cut through the legal restrictions so they could do their work, or until they got evicted from the region. Needless to say, they had prayed much about the situation, and this was what they felt prompted to do.

As they entered the government headquarters building, they began to work their plan. As expected, they met bureaucrats in each office who referred them on to the next higher official's office. No one was willing to consider their request for a permit to preach the gospel. This continued for some time until they began to feel that they were wasting their time and the Lord's time. The bureaucracy seemed hopeless. They determined to keep trying for a few more offices since they were now into an area in the building where the offices were quite large and the furnishings rather expensive. Miraculously, no one stopped them. Rather, they simply kept getting referred to higher officials. Finally, they found themselves in an extravagantly furnished, spacious office area. The staff member who controlled access to this particular official rang his office and was instructed to usher the two young men in.

Upon entering, the missionaries nervously approached the official, who was sitting at his large desk, and stopped a few feet before reaching him. He looked up, put his pen down, stared at them for a few moments, and then smiled and said, "You're Americans, aren't you?" in excellent English.

They answered "Yes, sir." He then asked them to tell him where in the United States they were from. My former seminary student told me that, at this point, his main concern was how to explain to the man where Springville, Utah, is, as well as the location of his companion's rural Idaho town. Instead, they merely said that they were from the United States and lived east of California. The official smiled and said, "Yes, of course, but be more specific than that. Tell me exactly where you live." My young missionary said, "I live in Springville, Utah, which is about six miles south of Provo, which is about fifty miles south of Salt Lake City." The man quickly came around his desk and vigorously shook their hands saying, "You're Mormon missionaries, aren't you? I know exactly where Springville is. I like Mormons! I went to Brigham Young University in Provo. They treated me very well there. Sit down. What can I do for you?"

A very pleasant conversation followed. Then they explained their problem, and this high government official took immediate action that allowed them to continue the work of the Lord in that area.

Here is yet another example of how the Lord is preparing things for the preaching of the gospel in the entire world. Some years ago, the Friday devotional speaker at the institute of religion where I was teaching spoke of some LDS businessmen friends who had journeyed to communist China after the doors of that country had partially opened. They hoped to invest successfully in developing businesses there because trade relations with outside investors had opened up. While there, the men were hosted by a government-sponsored young factory worker who spoke excellent English. At the end of their excursion in China, which lasted several weeks, their young host shepherded them to the airport, where they awaited their flight home to Utah. A tender friendship had grown between them and the young Chinese interpreter, and as the time of their departure approached, the young man surprised them by presenting them with a wonderful gift.

In their businessmen minds, they quickly calculated that the gift would have cost their host at least one month's wages, and they had nothing to give him in return. Acquiring a gift for him had skipped their minds and they were

caught completely off guard. However, one of the businessmen had been reading in his leather-bound triple combination scriptures while awaiting the plane, and a quick-thinking colleague snatched the book from the hands of his friend and presented it to the young Chinese, explaining that this book was a gift from them to him, that it contained sacred writings that were most prized by these men, and that it would be an honor to them if he would accept it and read it.

The young man caressed the leather cover of the book and the gold-leafed pages, noting the fine quality of the very thin pages of the book. He then held the LDS scriptures close to his chest and expressed both gratitude and astonishment that they would give him such a precious treasure. The plane arrived and they parted with deep emotion.

Some months later, the LDS businessmen again flew to China, this time to go ahead with some business deals. Again, the communist government provided an interpreter and host, and, to their delight, it was the same young man. As they happily chatted and caught each other up on events which had occurred during their absence, the young man excitedly told them that he had been promoted to be foreman over 5,000 Chinese factory workers. He further reported that they all studied English together at the factory for one hour each day. He asked them, "And guess what we read as we study English?" The answer astonished the men and caused great joy in their hearts. "The Book of Mormon!"

The young foreman had made copies of pages from the Book of Mormon out of the triple combination the men had given him at the airport. He was using these scriptures to teach English to his workers at the factory. Just think of a future day when missionaries are allowed to preach in that region of the country. Some of the

SLAVES SHALL
RISE UP AGAINST
THEIR MASTERS,
WHO SHALL BE
MARSHALED AND
DISCIPLINED FOR WAR.

D & C 87:4

seeds that were planted will have taken root and already be awaiting further nourishment. Thus, in this, and no doubt in countless other ways, the way is being prepared for the going forth of the gospel to "all nations, kindreds, tongues and people" (D&C 42:58).

Here is one last example of this preparation for the gospel to spread throughout the earth in fulfillment of this great prophecy of Daniel. Some years ago, I was told by an LDS serviceman who served in the Gulf War that members of the Church were allowed to meet together in Church services by the Arab nations in which they were stationed. This was highly unusual, he told me, because no other Christian religions were allowed to do so on Arab soil. When asked the reason for this surprising permission, he simply said that high-ranking Arab government officials had such respect for the Church that they allowed it. One limitation was that members were not allowed to meet in groups of more than thirty-five. In the October 2001 general conference of the Church, President Gordon B. Hinckley emphasized the growth of the Church. He said, "We are now a global organization. We have members in more than 150 nations." We have missionaries in unprecedented numbers circling the globe. And with modern technology, the gospel message can be transmitted to members and nonmembers alike in the farthest flung reaches of the world. Indeed, the prophecy of Daniel is being fulfilled before our very eyes!

SIGN 10

THE CIVIL WAR WILL START IN SOUTH CAROLINA

CATEGORY: FULFILLED

One of the striking prophecies that is to be fulfilled in the last days, alerting people that the final scenes before the Second Coming are

getting close, is that the Civil War will start in South Carolina. It will be the beginning of "wars that will shortly come to pass, beginning at the rebellion of South Carolina." From that time, "war will be poured out upon all nations, beginning at this place [South Carolina]" (D&C 87:1–2). It has, of course, already taken place, and we are now watching war being "poured out upon all nations."

This "Civil War Prophecy" was given on Christmas Day, 1832, making it 28 years before the Civil War began by South Carolina as Fort Sumter was fired upon on April 12, 1861. Such a prophecy is strong proof that Joseph Smith was indeed a prophet of the living God and is an amazing witness that the gospel is true.

SIGN 11

SLAVES WILL RISE UP AGAINST THEIR MASTERS

CATEGORY: BEING FULFILLED

On December 25, 1832, the Prophet Joseph Smith gave a sweeping prophecy that is sometimes referred to as "a prophecy on wars." It is contained in the Doctrine and Covenants as section 87. Within this section, we see a specific prophecy that is also one of the signs of the times and that will continue to be fulfilled as the time of the Second Coming draws closer. It is found in verse 4 (bold added for emphasis):

> D&C 87:4
> 4 And it shall come to pass, after many days, **slaves shall rise up against their masters**, who shall be marshaled and disciplined for war.

As we consider this prophecy, we must be careful not to place it in too narrow of a context in our own minds. Some might have a tendency to restrict its fulfillment to the rising up of the slaves against their masters in the past history of the United States. This would be far too narrow in scope. In this prophecy, the word, "slaves," refers to oppressed people everywhere during the last stages of the world before the Savior's coming. This would include rebellion against oppressive regimes and cultures. It can include women fighting for equal rights, men fighting for equal opportunity, children leaving family and cultural tradition in order to gain higher education, factions within countries demanding fair representation in their governments, and so forth. A quote from the *Doctrine and Covenants Student Manual, Religion 325*, 1981, used by our Institutes of Religion, page 195, is helpful here:

D&C 87:4–5

Who Are the "Slaves" Who Shall Rise Up Against Their Masters?

This prophecy begins with reference to the Civil War, which was fought over the issue of slavery. Many have therefore assumed that the slaves mentioned in D&C 87:4 were the blacks who fled north and fought in the Union armies against their former masters. Although that action partially fulfilled the prophecy, Elder Joseph L. Wirthlin suggested a further fulfillment: "In many cases I am quite sure we all think this has to do particularly with the slaves in the Southern States, but I believe, brethren and sisters, that it was intended that this referred to slaves all over the world, and I think of those, particularly in the land of Russia and other countries wherein they have been taken over by that great nation and where the people are actually the slaves of those individuals who guide and direct the affairs of Russia and China, and where the rights and the privilege to worship God and to come to a knowledge that Jesus Christ is his Son is denied them." (in Conference Report, October 1958, 32)

And so it is not just by chance that there is so much political turmoil and "rising up" to shake off the shackles of oppression and unrighteous dominion all around us in our day. It is the ongoing fulfillment of this prophecy, one of many prophecies designed to bear witness that every word given by God through His prophets will be fulfilled. It is another reminder to the watchful and faithful that the coming of the Lord is near.

SIGN 12
A FULL END OF ALL NATIONS
CATEGORY: YET TO BE FULFILLED

At the end of Doctrine and Covenants 87:6, we find a prophecy about "the full end of all nations," meaning that as the Millennium begins and the Savior takes over to rule as "Lord of lords, and King of kings" (Revelation 17:14), all other governments will cease to be. We will enjoy a "theocracy" or "government by God" during the thousand years of peace. Many of the signs of the times in the last days will lead up to this prophesied end of all other governments and rulers. Let's read this verse (bold added for emphasis):

D&C 87:6
6 And thus, with the sword and by bloodshed the inhabitants of the earth shall mourn; and with famine, and plague, and earthquake, and the thunder of heaven, and the fierce and vivid lightning also, shall the inhabitants of the earth be made to feel the wrath, and indignation, and chastening hand of an Almighty God, until the consumption decreed hath made **a full end of all nations**;

In the last verse of section 87, the Savior concludes with vital and comforting counsel to those who seek to keep His commandments and desire to avoid the extreme turmoil and emotional trauma that is now accompanying these signs of the times leading up to the millennial reign of Christ. (Bold added for emphasis:)

<u>D&C 87:8</u>
8 Wherefore, **stand ye in holy places, and be not moved**, until the day of the Lord come [*the Second Coming*]; for behold, it cometh quickly, saith the Lord. Amen.

Through living the gospel, we are blessed with many "holy places," among which are righteous homes, temples, our church meetings, seminaries, institutes of religion, and gatherings and activities with family and friends who have similar goals and respect for the ways of God.

SIGN 13
SCATTERED ISRAEL WILL BE GATHERED
CATEGORY: BEING FULFILLED

Before the coming of the Lord, there will be a great gathering of Israel out of the entire world. For thousands of years, Israel has been being scattered. And who is Israel? Answer: The descendants of Abraham, Isaac, and Jacob, plus all those who have joined them in the covenants of the true gospel. Jacob had twelve sons (Genesis 29–30; 35:18). Jacob's name was changed to "Israel." Thus, the "Children of Israel" are the "Children of Jacob" and their descendants. They are the descendants of Abraham and Sarah. The Lord made a covenant with Abraham, which clearly indicated that his posterity would spread the gospel and the priesthood throughout the world. In the Pearl of Great Price we read the following (bold added for emphasis):

<u>Abraham 2:9–11</u>
9 And I will make of thee a great nation, and I will bless thee above measure, and make thy name great **among all nations**, and thou shalt be a blessing unto thy seed after

thee, that in their hands **they shall bear this ministry and Priesthood unto all nations**;

10 And I will bless them through thy name; for as many as receive this Gospel shall be called after thy name, and shall be accounted thy seed, and shall rise up and bless thee, as their father;

11 And I will bless them that bless thee, and curse them that curse thee; and in thee (that is, in thy Priesthood) and in thy seed (that is, thy Priesthood), for I give unto thee a promise that this right shall continue in thee, and **in thy seed** after thee (that is to say, the literal seed, or the seed of the body) **shall all the families of the earth be blessed**, even with the blessings of the Gospel, which are the blessings of salvation, even of life eternal.

As mentioned above, Israel has indeed been scattered all over the earth. In about 721 BC (see Bible Dictionary, Chronology, 721 BC) Assyria took ten of the tribes of Israel captive and led them away to the north. These have become known as the lost ten tribes. Their return is one of the signs of the times (see sign 23 in this book). The Jews were scattered several times throughout history, including the Babylonian captivity about 587 BC.

So, the direction for Israel has been outward throughout the centuries, into the entire world. When the gathering of Israel begins in earnest, we know that the last days have arrived. Nephi taught of the scattering and gathering of Israel as follows (bold added for emphasis):

<u>1 Nephi 10:12–14</u>
12 Yea, even my father spake much concerning the Gentiles, and also concerning the house of Israel, that they should be compared like unto an olive tree, whose branches should be broken off and should be **scattered upon all the face of the earth.**

13 Wherefore, he said it must needs be that we should be led with one accord into the land of promise, unto the fulfilling of the

word of the Lord, that **we should be scattered upon all the face of the earth.**

14 And **after the house of Israel should be scattered they should be gathered together again**; or, in fine, after the Gentiles had received the fulness of the Gospel, the natural branches of the olive tree, or the remnants of the house of Israel, should be grafted in, or come to the knowledge of the true Messiah, their Lord and their Redeemer.

Nephi again speaks of the gathering of Israel in the latter days as follows (bold added for emphasis):

<u>1 Nephi 19:16</u>
16 Yea, then will he remember the isles of the sea; yea, and **all the people who are of the house of Israel, will I gather in**, saith the Lord, according to the words of the prophet Zenos, from the four quarters of the earth.

Isaiah speaks of this last days gathering many times. In this next reference, it appears that Isaiah has seen many forms of our modern transportation system, which will be used by converts as they gather to be with the Saints, both in terms of gathering to Zion as well as in gathering to attend general conference, etc. We will add a few explanatory notes and use bold for emphasis.

<u>Isaiah 5:26–30</u>
26 And **he will lift up an ensign** [*flag, rallying point; the true gospel*] **to the nations from far**, and will hiss [*whistle; a signal to gather*] unto them from the end of the earth: and, behold, **they shall come with speed swiftly** [*modern transportation*]:

27 **None shall be weary nor stumble** among them; **none shall slumber nor sleep**; neither shall the girdle of their loins be loosed [*change clothes*], nor the latchet of their shoes be broken [*they will travel so fast

that they won't need to change clothes or even take their shoes off*]:

28 **Whose arrows are sharp, and all their bows bent** [*perhaps describing the body of a sleek airliner, like an arrow, and the swept back wings like a bow*], **their horses' hoofs shall be counted like flint** [*making sparks like the wheels on a train?*], and their wheels like a whirlwind [*airplanes, trains?*]:

29 **Their roaring shall be like a lion** [*the noise of airplanes, trains, etc.?*], they shall roar like young lions: yea, they shall roar, and **lay hold of the prey** [*take in their passengers?*], **and shall carry it away safe, and none shall deliver it** [*the converts, i.e., none will stop the gathering of Israel in the last days*].

30 **And in that day** [*the last days*] they shall roar against them like the roaring of the sea: and **if one look unto the land, light is darkened in the heavens thereof** [*conditions in the last days, war, smoke, pollutions, spiritual darkness, etc.?*]

And how is this final "gathering" to be accomplished? The answer is simple. The Lord will do it.

<u>D&C 39:11</u>
11 And if thou do this, I have prepared thee for a greater work. Thou shalt preach the fulness of my gospel, which **I have sent forth in these last days**, the covenant which I have sent forth **to recover my people, which are of the house of Israel.**

An article in the July 1998 *Ensign*, by Paul K. Browning, emphasized this aspect of the last days gathering. Quoting from the article, entitled "Gathering Scattered Israel: Then and Now," pages 54–61:

As members of The Church of Jesus Christ of Latter-day Saints, we are taught that these are the last days and that many of the signs having to do with the Savior's Second

100
SIGNS

Coming are taking place in our lifetime. One of the signs we discuss is found in the tenth article of faith: "We believe in the literal gathering of Israel and in the restoration of the ten tribes." Indeed, the doctrine of the gathering is an important part of our understanding about what is to happen before the Savior's return to earth.

As Joseph's seed brings others into the Church, these new members are then commissioned likewise to go and spread the gospel. In the aggregate, millions will be gathered to help them in their return to the Lord. But in individual specificity, the Lord told Jeremiah that sometimes the gathering entity will be small: "I will take you one of a city, and two of a family, and I will bring you to Zion" (Jeremiah 3:14). Thus, it is only through the work of thousands of missionaries and millions of Church members that those among the nations who want to return actually "return." In the beginning decades of the Church, converts were encouraged to relocate to places where the Church was headquartered, whether that was Kirtland, Nauvoo, or Salt Lake City. That particular era has passed. Today those who join the Church are encouraged to gather to its stakes—or to build new stakes. Jacob of the Book of Mormon foresaw this development: "They shall be gathered home to the lands of their inheritance, and shall be established in all their lands of promise" (2 Nephi 9:2).

President Harold B. Lee emphasized this understanding of what it means to gather when he said, "The place of gathering for the Mexican Saints is in Mexico; the place of gathering for the Guatemalan Saints is in Guatemala; the place of gathering for the Brazilian Saints is in Brazil; and so it goes throughout the length and breadth of the whole earth. ("Strengthen the Stakes of Zion," *Ensign*, July 1973, 5)

Jacob, Nephi's brother, makes it clear in the allegory of the tame and wild olive trees (see Jacob 5) that the blessings pertaining to the house of

Israel belong to all those who are obedient and all who choose to join the gathering.

One of the most important aspects of the gathering is whether or not you, personally, are being successfully gathered to Christ. We were discussing this topic in an institute of religion class when a young man raised his hand and asked permission to tell the class how he had been "gathered." What followed was a touching and beautiful account of how he had been "gathered" to the gospel and the Church from an abusive home and much of difficulty and despair.

Years ago, before going on a mission as a young elder, I worked a summer on the railroad to earn money for my mission. As it happened, there were many on that shift who were antagonistic toward the Church. One man in particular took delight in harassing me because I was an active Latter-day Saint. His wife was a faithful member and he constantly complained about the bishop and about the tithing and offerings she paid, claiming, among other things, that the bishop's new car came as a result of money she and other members paid to the Church. He had a cabin on a nearby reservoir and often said that he would never give up fishing and recreation there and replace it with attending boring meetings on Sunday. Furthermore, he told me several times that it would do him no good to have his cabin if he gave up his "two day" weekends. He was otherwise friendly to me and I took his jabs about the Church in stride and without much reaction.

When the time came, I departed for a two-and-a-half-year mission to Austria. Upon returning, I was again offered the job on the railroad and I readily took it to help with my tuition at the university. To my great surprise and joy, one day while we were waiting in the office for the next train to arrive, this man turned in his swivel chair and said, "Dave, you'll never guess what happened to me while you were gone!" I waited with great curiosity for him to continue. I had already noticed that he was wearing a thin blue shirt with a vague suggestion of temple garments underneath, but I had discounted that as a very remote possibility. He continued, saying that, during my absence, he had joined the Church, sold his cabin on the reservoir, and was very content and happy. He and his wife had been sealed in the temple and were active together in the Church. Another example of the "gathering" of individuals that leads to the large scale gathering of Israel in these last days.

In summary, it is clear that ancient prophets foresaw the day of a second gathering. It must have thrilled them to look down the corridors of time and see both the tens of millions of Israel's remnants and many others who would respond to the call to be gathered with covenant Israel.

SIGN 14

ALL WILL HEAR THE GOSPEL IN THEIR OWN TONGUE

CATEGORY: BEING FULFILLED

As we study this sign of the times, we sense that the dramatic development of technology and transportation since the restoration of the gospel is playing a key role in its fulfillment. The prophecy that all will hear the gospel in their own tongue is found in many places in the scriptures. For our purposes, we will use the following two verses (bold added for emphasis):

D&C 90:10–11
10 And then cometh the day when the arm of the Lord shall be revealed in power in convincing the nations, the heathen nations, the house of Joseph, of the gospel of their salvation.

11 For it shall come to pass in that day, that **every man shall hear the fulness of the gospel in his own tongue, and in his own language**, through those who are ordained unto this power, by the administration of the Comforter, shed forth upon them for the revelation of Jesus Christ.

Just imagine the scope of the work performed by the Church today in translating and providing the scriptures in all of the languages in which the gospel is being preached throughout the world. Think of the role of computer technology and broadcasting and communication technology, as well as advances in transportation and missionary work in bringing the gospel to all the world in such a way that each can be taught in his or her own language. While we still have much more to accomplish in fulfilling this sign of the times, the current progress in accomplishing it is both mind boggling and exciting.

While working as a curriculum writer for the Church, several of us were shown a number of devices that would facilitate bringing the gospel to individuals in their own languages. Among the several devices discussed were an inexpensive wristband containing all of the missionary discussions with a miniature speaker and solar powered. The presenters told us that this had been designed for countries with remote villages whose inhabitants spoke several different dialects. The thought was that missionaries could leave such bands with interested native dialect speakers, then come back a few days later and answer their questions and pursue further discussion with a translator present.

In another setting, several of us were shown a solar-powered device made from very inexpensive components mass-produced for solar powered yard lighting. The entire standard works plus many other audio talks from the Church could be installed on it. The idea was to thus make the Book of Mormon, especially, available to people in developing nations whose reading skills were below that needed to read the scriptures. The possibilities are endless.

And right now, with the rapid development of smart phones and other personal handheld devices, it is possible for people throughout the world to hear and see the scriptures and other media produced by the Church in their own language and at their own convenience. They have almost unlimited resources available to study the gospel right in the palm of their hand!

SIGN 15

RIGHTEOUSNESS AND TRUTH WILL "SWEEP THE EARTH AS WITH A FLOOD"

CATEGORY: BEING FULFILLED

This is a most encouraging sign of the times. In the Pearl of Great Price, we read (bold added for emphasis):

Moses 7:62
62 And righteousness will I send down out of heaven [*the restoration of the gospel through heavenly visions and manifestations*]; and truth will I send forth out of the earth [*the Book of Mormon*], to bear testimony of mine Only Begotten; his resurrection from the dead; yea, and also the resurrection of all men; and **righteousness and truth will I cause to sweep the earth as with a flood**, to gather out mine elect from the four quarters of the earth, unto a place which I shall prepare, an Holy City, that my people may gird up their loins [*may be prepared*], and be looking forth for the time of my coming; for there shall be my tabernacle, and it shall be called Zion, a New Jerusalem.

We are obviously living in the day and age when the fulfillment of this sign is underway. We have seen an amazing increase in the number of young elders and sisters "flood" the Church's MTCs

since the lowering of ages for worthy young men and women to serve missions. We are watching as temples begin to "dot the earth." The Church is in most nations. The Book of Mormon is "flooding the earth." Miracles are occurring daily as it is translated into more and more languages. At the time of this writing, the entire Book of Mormon has been translated into 95 languages, and portions of it have been translated into 24 more languages. The fulfillment of this sign will continue right into the Millennium.

And, as mentioned in the discussion of sign #14 in this chapter, the proliferation of smart phones and other personal electronic devices is literally flooding the earth with the capability of studying the scriptures, reading general conference talks, watching general conference sessions, accessing Church media productions, and a host of other good and worthy things designed to promote righteousness and truth throughout the earth.

It is interesting and encouraging to note that, even though wickedness will continue to increase right up to the Second Coming (D&C 84:97), righteousness will likewise increase, and ultimately triumph over all evil.

SIGN 16

THE CHURCH WILL BE BROUGHT OUT OF OBSCURITY

CATEGORY: BEING FULFILLED

Accompanying the prophecy in Daniel 2:35 that the Church in the last days will go forth to fill the whole earth is the statement by the Savior at the beginning of the Doctrine and Covenants that the Church is to be brought out of obscurity (in other words, will go from hardly being known to being widely known throughout the world). We will quote it here (bold added for emphasis):

D&C 1:30

30 And also those to whom these commandments were given, might have power to lay the foundation of this church, and to **bring it forth out of obscurity** and out of darkness, the only true and living church upon the face of the whole earth, with which I, the Lord, am well pleased, speaking unto the church collectively and not individually—

It is thrilling to watch "the only true and living church upon the face of the whole earth" literally coming forth out of obscurity in our day. It is gratifying to watch as the "Mormons" become known throughout the world because of numerous initiatives of the Church, including our humanitarian services. The Mormon Tabernacle Choir does untold good through music and the spoken word. Temple open houses promote the doctrine of eternal families around the globe. The words of the living prophets and apostles are transmitted throughout the world via the Internet. And on and on as the work of the Lord rolls forth prior to His Second Coming.

SIGN 17

THE NAME OF JOSEPH SMITH WILL BE SPOKEN OF FOR GOOD AND EVIL IN ALL NATIONS

CATEGORY: BEING FULFILLED

Joseph, who was sold into Egypt, prophesied that, in the last days, a "seer" would be raised up by the Lord to restore the gospel. He specifically prophesied that this prophet's name would be "Joseph" and that he would be named after his father (2 Nephi 3:4–15). Thus, Joseph in Egypt gave a significant sign of the times, namely, that in the last days, a choice seer would be raised up by the Lord to become the prophet of the Restoration for the last dispensation which would lead up to the Second Coming. Joseph

Smith became the fulfillment of this ancient prophecy.

What a surprise it must have been for young Joseph when Moroni told him that his "name should be had for good and evil among all nations, kindreds, and tongues, or that it should be both good and evil spoken of among all people" (Joseph Smith—History 1:33). For an obscure upstate New York backwoods farm boy of seventeen to be told that people throughout the world would know about him must have caused deep reflection and some concern on his part.

In our day, we are watching this prophecy being fulfilled in dramatic fashion, as the name of Joseph Smith continues to be both praised and vilified throughout the world in ever increasing frequency and scope. It is so spoken of on a large scale by mass media and on a very small scale in the smallest villages and individual homes and huts. He is praised and derided, honored and cursed, in almost every language and dialect on earth.

Knowing this prophecy by Moroni is helpful to those of us who honor and revere Joseph Smith when we hear negative things about him. In fact, it can be a testimony strengthener for us as we realize that each attempt to tear him down is yet another fulfillment of this prophecy.

I remember hearing a returned missionary speak in sacrament meeting and recount his anger when he and his companion were accosted by a drunk man cursing them and Joseph Smith on a dirt road in a small, high mountain village in South America after they had finished a spiritual discussion in a humble home there. His anger soon turned to awe and testimony as his senior companion reminded him that the drunken man was fulfilling Moroni's prophecy about Joseph Smith. It was even more significant since the man had obtained his alleged information about the Prophet from sources elsewhere in the village who were unfriendly to the Church.

SIGN 18

MOTHER EARTH WILL REJOICE TO FINALLY BE FREE OF WICKEDNESS

CATEGORY: YET TO BE FULFILLED

Apparently, this sign of the times will be fulfilled when the earth is cleansed of wickedness at the time of the Second Coming. Thus, it will be one of the last to be fulfilled. Enoch saw in vision that the earth does not like wickedness upon her. He heard the earth lamenting the evil and corruption upon her during the meridian of time when the Savior performed His mortal mission. He heard the earth ask when she would obtain rest from the wickedness and corruption of sin upon her. (Bold added for emphasis:)

Moses 7:47–49

47 And behold, Enoch saw the day of the coming of the Son of Man, even in the flesh; and his soul rejoiced, saying: The Righteous is lifted up, and the Lamb is slain from the foundation of the world; and through faith I am in the bosom of the Father, and behold, Zion is with me.

48 And it came to pass that **Enoch looked upon the earth; and he heard a voice from the bowels thereof, saying: Wo, wo is me, the mother of men; I am pained, I am weary, because of the wickedness of my children. When shall I rest, and be cleansed from the filthiness which is gone forth out of me? When will my Creator sanctify me, that I may rest, and righteousness for a season abide upon my face?**

49 And when **Enoch heard the earth mourn,** he wept, and cried unto the Lord, saying: O Lord, wilt thou not have compassion upon the earth? Wilt thou not bless the children of Noah?

Enoch's concern for the earth and her feelings was heightened as the vision continued. He sympathized with the earth and joined her by asking "When shall the earth rest?" He was shown that the earth would not yet rest from sin upon her during the Savior's mortal ministry. (Bold added for emphasis:)

Moses 7:54–58

54 And it came to pass that Enoch cried unto the Lord, saying: **When the Son of Man cometh in the flesh, shall the earth rest?** I pray thee, show me these things.

55 And the Lord said unto Enoch: Look, and he looked and beheld the Son of Man lifted up on the cross, after the manner of men;

56 And he heard a loud voice; and the heavens were veiled; and all the creations of God mourned; and the earth groaned; and the rocks were rent; and the saints arose, and were crowned at the right hand of the Son of Man, with crowns of glory;

57 And as many of the spirits as were in prison came forth, and stood on the right hand of God; and the remainder were reserved in chains of darkness until the judgment of the great day.

58 And again Enoch wept and cried unto the Lord, saying: **When shall the earth rest?**

The answer from the Savior was that the earth will finally have her desired rest and enjoy peace upon her after the wicked are destroyed at His coming and the thousand years of millennial peace begin. (Bold added for emphasis:)

Moses 7:60–61

60 And the Lord said unto Enoch: As I live, **even so will I come in the last days**, in the days of wickedness and vengeance, to fulfil the oath which I have made unto you concerning the children of Noah;

MOTHER EARTH BEING
CLEANSED OF WICKEDNESS

61 **And the day shall come that the earth shall rest**, but before that day the heavens shall be darkened, and a veil of darkness shall cover the earth; and the heavens shall shake, and also the earth; and great tribulations shall be among the children of men, but my people will I preserve;

While many consider the earth to be simply an inanimate planet that serves as host to many ecosystems and mankind, the scriptures give us to understand that it is indeed a living thing. This leads to more interesting questions, for which we have no answers. But at least we know that the earth is a living thing and will die and resurrect. (Bold added for emphasis:)

D&C 88:25–26
25 And again, verily I say unto you, the earth abideth the law of a celestial kingdom, for it filleth the measure of its creation, and transgresseth not the law—

26 Wherefore, it shall be sanctified; yea, notwithstanding **it shall die, it shall be quickened again**, and shall abide the power by which it is quickened, and the righteous shall inherit it.

In fact, we learn from the Doctrine and Covenants that the creations of God are capable of having happiness (bold added for emphasis):

D&C 77:2–3
2 Q. What are we to understand by the four beasts, spoken of in the same verse?

A. They are figurative expressions, used by the Revelator, John, in describing heaven, the paradise of God, **the happiness of** man, and of **beasts**, and of **creeping things**, and of the **fowls** of the air; that which is spiritual being in the likeness of that which is temporal; and that which is temporal in the likeness of that which is spiritual; the spirit of man in the likeness of his person, as also the spirit of the beast, and every other creature which God has created.

3 Q. Are the four beasts limited to individual beasts, or do they represent classes or orders?

A. They are limited to four individual beasts, which were shown to John, to represent **the glory of the classes** of beings in their destined order or sphere of creation, **in the enjoyment of their eternal felicity**.

We also learn that plants have souls (a spirit and physical body). In the Pearl of Great Price, we are taught (bold added for emphasis):

Moses 3:9
9 And out of the ground made I, the Lord God, to grow **every tree**, naturally, that is pleasant to the sight of man; and man could behold it. And it **became also a living soul**. For it was spiritual in the day that I created it; for it remaineth in the sphere in which I, God, created it, yea, even all things which I prepared for the use of man; and man saw that it was good for food. And I, the Lord God, planted the tree of life also in the midst of the garden, and also the tree of knowledge of good and evil.

And so, as we strive to take good care of the earth and be ecologically responsible and wise, we can have an added sense of kinship with the earth and God's creations upon her because of these brief revelations about her.

SIGN 19
THE LOST TEN TRIBES WILL RETURN
CATEGORY: YET TO BE FULFILLED

We are going to be rather conservative as we discuss this well-known sign of the times. You may wish to nudge it a bit toward the "being fulfilled" category because of the number of converts to the Church in foreign lands, as well as many domestically, whose patriarchal blessings indicate that they are from tribes of

100 SIGNS

AND THE DAY SHALL
COME THAT THE
EARTH SHALL REST,
BUT BEFORE THAT DAY
THE HEAVENS SHALL
BE DARKENED.

MOSES 7:61

Israel who are a part of the lost ten tribes. This is fine and is not a problem. However, while there is an obvious gathering of Israel taking place right now, including many from remnants of all of the tribes of Israel scattered throughout the world, the scriptures seem to indicate that a large group known as the lost ten tribes will return before the Second Coming. For this reason, we will consider this sign of the times to be primarily in the "yet to be fulfilled" category. The Doctrine and Covenants gives fascinating details about their return as follows:

D&C 133:26–33

26 And they who are in the north countries shall come in remembrance before the Lord; and their prophets shall hear his voice, and shall no longer stay themselves; and they shall smite the rocks, and the ice shall flow down at their presence.

27 And an highway shall be cast up in the midst of the great deep.

28 Their enemies shall become a prey unto them,

29 And in the barren deserts there shall come forth pools of living water; and the parched ground shall no longer be a thirsty land.

30 And they shall bring forth their rich treasures unto the children of Ephraim, my servants.

31 And the boundaries of the everlasting hills shall tremble at their presence.

32 And there shall they fall down and be crowned with glory, even in Zion, by the hands of the servants of the Lord, even the children of Ephraim.

33 And they shall be filled with songs of everlasting joy.

Apostle James E. Talmage, in his book, *Articles of Faith*, comments on the return of the lost ten tribes as follows:

Restoration of the Lost Tribes—From the scriptural passages already considered, it is

plain that, while many of those belonging to the Ten Tribes were diffused among the nations, a sufficient number to justify the retention of the original name were led away as a body and are now in existence in some place where the Lord has hidden them. To them the resurrected Christ went to minister after His visit to the Nephites, as before stated. Their return constitutes a very important part of the gathering, characteristic of the dispensation of the fulness of times.

To the scriptures already quoted as relating to their return, the following should be added. As a feature of the work of God in the day of restoration we are told: "And they who are in the north countries shall come in remembrance before the Lord; and their prophets shall hear his voice, and shall no longer stay themselves; and they shall smite the rocks, and the ice shall flow down at their presence. And an highway shall be cast up in the midst of the great deep. Their enemies shall become a prey unto them, And in the barren deserts there shall come forth pools of living water; and the parched ground shall no longer be a thirsty land. And they shall bring forth their rich treasures unto the children of Ephraim, my servants. And the boundaries of the everlasting hills shall tremble at their presence. And there shall they fall down and be crowned with glory, even in Zion, by the hands of the servants of the Lord, even the children of Ephraim. And they shall be filled with songs of everlasting joy. Behold, this is the blessing of the everlasting God upon the tribes of Israel, and the richer blessing upon the head of Ephraim and his fellows" (D&C 133:26–34).

From the express and repeated declaration, that in their exodus from the north the Ten Tribes are to be led to Zion, there to receive honor at the hands of those who are of Ephraim, who necessarily are to have previously gathered there, it is plain that Zion is to be first established. (James E. Talmage, *Articles of Faith* [Salt Lake City: Deseret Book, 1981], 308)

Did you notice in the last paragraph of Elder Talmage's writing, quoted above, that he said, concerning the tribe of Ephraim, that they "necessarily are to have previously gathered" to Zion, before others of the lost ten tribes are to be gathered in large numbers? Thus, it is interesting to note that even though Ephraim is one of the lost ten tribes, a large number of them have already been gathered and have prepared and are preparing for the return of the rest of the lost tribes.

Occasionally, members of the Church may hear debates as to whether or not the ten tribes are "lost" in the sense that they are scattered throughout the nations of the world and consequently do not know who they are, or whether they are lost as a large group and are hidden somewhere by the Lord. In other words, the debate centers around whether or not they are currently together as a group. There is wisdom in not trying to be a "purist" on this matter, saying, "Either they are scattered all over or they are together as a group." It could well be that many of them are scattered abroad in all nations in addition to there being a large group together, whose whereabouts are unknown and whose return will be rather spectacular.

It is significant to note that when Moses appeared in the Kirtland Temple, as recorded in Doctrine and Covenants 110:11, and conferred the keys of gathering upon Joseph Smith and Oliver Cowdery, there seemed to be a differentiation between the "gathering of Israel" and the "leading of the ten tribes from the land of the north." The verse reads as follows (bold added for emphasis):

> D&C 110:11
> 11 After this vision closed, the heavens were again opened unto us; and Moses appeared before us, and **committed unto us the keys** of the **gathering of Israel** from the four parts of the earth, **and** the **leading of the ten tribes from the land of the north**.

This seems to imply that they are two separate undertakings in the last days. From this verse we are also given to understand that our modern prophets hold not only the keys of the gathering of Israel, but also the keys of leading the ten tribes from the north, since Moses gave these keys to Joseph and Oliver, and since these keys have been handed down continuously to the present day.

It will be helpful here to briefly review who the tribes of Israel are and who the lost ten tribes of Israel are.

Abraham and Sarah had Isaac (Genesis 21:1–3). Isaac and Rebekah had Jacob (Genesis 25:20–26). Jacob and his four wives had twelve sons (Genesis 29–30). **Jacob's name was changed to "Israel" (Genesis 32:28). Thus, Jacob's twelve sons and the nations that came from them are called "the children of Israel."**

Abraham made covenants with God, which, when kept faithfully, would lead to exaltation. These covenants and promises were to be passed down to his posterity through Isaac and Jacob. In conjunction with this "Abrahamic Covenant," He and his posterity were given the responsibility to take the gospel and blessings of the priesthood to all the world. (Bold added for emphasis:)

> Abraham 2:8–11
> 8 My name is Jehovah, and I know the end from the beginning; therefore **my hand shall be over thee**.
>
> 9 And **I will make of thee a great nation**, and **I will bless thee above measure** [*exaltation*], and **make thy name great among all nations**, and thou shalt be a blessing unto **thy seed** after thee, that in their hands they **shall bear this ministry and Priesthood unto all nations**;

100 SIGNS

10 And I will bless them through thy name; **for as many as receive this Gospel shall be called after thy name, and shall be accounted thy seed**, and shall rise up and bless thee, as their father;

11 And I will bless them that bless thee, and curse them that curse thee; and in thee (that is, in thy priesthood) and in thy seed (that is, thy priesthood), for I give unto thee a promise that this right shall continue in thee, and in thy seed after thee (that is to say, the literal seed, or the seed of the body) shall all the families of the earth be blessed, even with the blessings of the Gospel, which are the blessings of salvation, even of life eternal [*exaltation*].

The Bible Dictionary in the back of the 1989 version of the LDS Bible explains how the twelve tribes eventually divided into two kingdoms, Judah and Israel, also referred to as "the southern kingdom" and "the northern kingdom" respectively. "Judah" consisted of the tribes of Judah and Benjamin, and "Israel" consisted of the other ten tribes. Eventually, gross wickedness among the ten tribes led to their capture by the Assyrians in about 722 BC. Thus, they became the "lost ten tribes." A little over 100 years later, Judah, or the southern kingdom, was carried away captive by the Babylonians. Lehi and his family escaped this captivity by departing from the Jerusalem area into the wilderness in 600 BC as commanded by the Lord (1 Nephi 2:1–4).

Bible Dictionary

Israel, Kingdom of. The division of the house of Israel into two kingdoms at approximately 925 BC had been prophesied by Ahijah (1 Kgs. 11:31–35). The immediate cause was a revolt of the people against the heavy taxes levied by Solomon and his son Rehoboam. **Ten tribes formed the northern kingdom**, with headquarters at Shechem in Samaria. They were known as Israel, or the northern kingdom, or Ephraim, since Ephraim was the dominant group among them. Their first king was Jeroboam, an Ephraimite; he was followed later by such kings as Omri and Ahab (who ruled with his Phoenician wife Jezebel). **The southern kingdom, consisting of the tribes of Judah and Benjamin, was headquartered at Jerusalem**.

The northern kingdom soon went into apostasy and adopted many practices of Baalism, notwithstanding the ministries of such great prophets as Elijah and Amos. After a history of over 200 years and a series of 19 kings, the kingdom **was captured by the Assyrians and the people carried away captive into Assyria. They have therefore become known as the "lost ten tribes."**

Since their captivity they have never yet returned to their homeland, but extensive promises and prophecies speak of the time when they of the "north countries" shall return when they are ready to obey the gospel. The gathering of the lost tribes is to be a more spectacular event than the children of Israel coming out of Egypt in Moses' day. Prophecies of their return are: Isa. 11:10–16; Jer. 3:18; 16:14–21; 1 Ne. 22:4–12; 2 Ne. 10:21–22; 3 Ne. 15:13–15; 16:1–5; D&C 133:26–35.

We will include another bit of information here, associated with lineage and the twelve tribes that is relevant to patriarchal blessings. Have you ever noticed that when it comes to declaration of lineage during patriarchal blessings, there are actually thirteen options as far as specific tribes of Israel are concerned? This is because the tribe of Joseph is divided between his sons, Manasseh and Ephraim. Thus, specific tribes that could be declared by the patriarch under inspiration, are:

1. Reuben	8. Asher
2. Simeon	9. Issachar
3. Levi	10. Zebulon
4. Judah	11. Ephraim
5. Dan	12. Manasseh

6. Naphtali   13. Benjamin

7. Gad

Joseph received the birthright portion of his father, Isaac's, possessions, which was a double portion. His double portion was divided up between his sons, Ephraim and Manasseh. You can see this as you look at a map of the Land of Canaan at the time the land was divided up among the tribes of the children of Israel under the direction of Joshua (Joshua, chapters 14 through 19). You won't find the tribe of Joseph on the map, but you will find the tribes or nations of Ephraim and Manasseh.

SIGN 20

THE TIMES OF THE GENTILES WILL BE FULFILLED

CATEGORY: BEING FULFILLED

Simply put, during the days of the Savior's mortal ministry, the gospel was taken by Him and His disciples formally only to the Jews. After His resurrection and ascension to heaven, He instructed His Apostles and disciples to take the gospel to the Gentiles also (Mark 16:15; Acts 10, heading). While there are many definitions of "Gentile," in this case, the word simply means "anyone who is not a Jew."

Thus, during the Savior's earthly ministry, the gospel was taken first to the Jews and then to the Gentiles. In the last days, before the Second Coming of Christ, the gospel will be taken first to the Gentiles, and then to the Jews. The phrase "times of the Gentiles" refers to the great last-days missionary effort in taking the gospel to the Gentiles. It appears a number of times in the scriptures in one form or another. We will consider two passages of scripture that contain this exact phrase. Speaking of the Jews, Luke

recorded this sign of the times as follows (bold added for emphasis):

Luke 21:24
24 And they shall fall by the edge of the sword, and shall be led away captive into all nations: and Jerusalem shall be trodden down of the Gentiles, **until the times of the Gentiles be fulfilled**.

In Doctrine and Covenants 45:25, this same prophecy is given, and the context is that of the last days. We will include some verses before and after for context and use bold for emphasis.

D&C 45:22–28
22 Ye say that ye know that **the end of the world cometh**; ye say also that ye know that the heavens and the earth shall pass away;

23 And in this ye say truly, for so it is; but these things which I have told you shall not pass away until all shall be fulfilled.

24 And this I have told you concerning **Jerusalem**; and when that day shall come, shall a **remnant** be **scattered among all nations**;

25 But **they shall be gathered again**; **but they shall remain until the times of the Gentiles be fulfilled.**

26 And in that day shall be heard of wars and rumors of wars, and the whole earth shall be in commotion, and men's hearts shall fail them, and they shall say that Christ delayeth his coming until the end of the earth.

27 And the love of men shall wax cold, and iniquity shall abound.

28 And when **the times of the Gentiles** is come in, **a light shall break forth among them that sit in darkness, and it shall be the fulness of my gospel;**

We are living in the day when this prophecy is being fulfilled. We are living in the "times of the Gentiles." The gospel is being taken to the "Gentiles" through the vast and far-reaching missionary effort of the Church and by the great upsurge in media efforts by the Church

100 SIGNS

that reach even into the most remote and far-flung corners of the globe. However, as you have probably observed, we are not yet taking the gospel to the Jews as a formal initiative. It is not yet time. While there are some wonderful individual members and converts to the Church who are of the tribe of Judah, the Lord has not yet given the signal to begin concerted efforts to preach the gospel to the Jews. In fact, as you are perhaps aware, at the time of the publishing of this book, members of the Church who visit the Holy Land are specifically instructed by the Church not to engage in conversations about the Church with citizens of Israel there, nor to answer any of their questions about the gospel. This is because of an agreement between the First Presidency and the government of Israel that was negotiated when the Church determined to build the BYU Jerusalem Center some years ago.

While I was serving as a stake president, one of our missionary couples called me one day from their mission field and with great concern asked me if it was true that they were not allowed to baptize a Jewish couple they had taught who were citizens of Israel. As it turned out, they had met and taught this wonderful couple, and they had expressed a desire to be baptized. When the zone leader of the mission came to interview the couple for baptism, he discovered that they were citizens of Israel and indicated to them and to my missionary couple that they could not be baptized at this time. It would violate the agreement between the Israeli Government and our First Presidency that we would neither proselytize nor baptize any citizens of Israel, until such time as the Israeli government requested and gave permission for us to do so.

The missionaries asked on the phone if such a policy were in place and if so, would I please call the Brethren and confirm that it was still in place. I told them that, as far as I knew, such a policy was still in place, but that I would call Church headquarters in Salt Lake City and confirm it. I did so and was told that it is still in force. I then called the missionaries and explained that it was still the case and that their investigators could rest assured that the time would come when they could join the Church, but that that time had not yet arrived. Also, I suggested that the missionary couple assure their investigators that the Lord would look at their hearts and would accept of their desire to be baptized, so that if they continued to live the principles of the gospel as best they could, and if conditions never changed such that they could receive baptism in this life, they would surely have that opportunity in the spirit world.

While we don't know for sure when the Jews will get the opportunity to receive the gospel on a large scale, many suppose that it will be at the time when the Savior appears to them on the Mount of Olives, just outside of Jerusalem at a time when there is much destruction in Jerusalem and that region of Israel (Zechariah 14:2–4). Sign 97 in this chapter discusses this appearance of the Master, which is one of the significant signs of the times.

SIGN 21

THERE WILL BE MUCH DESPAIR, DEPRESSION, EMOTIONAL INSTABILITY, AND GLOOM AND DOOM

CATEGORY: BEING FULFILLED

People seem to be flocking to therapists, counselors, psychologists, ministers, social workers, and others for help in unprecedented numbers. All around us, there is much depression, despair, hopelessness, and lack of motivation to do anything. In Luke 22:26, we find this sign of the times. As you read this verse, quoted next, you will see the phrase "men's hearts failing them," which refers to giving up hope, having no more courage, having no faith, and so forth. We will read this verse in context with verses 25 and 27 in order to get the last days setting of this prophecy (bold added for emphasis).

Luke 21:25–27
25 And **there shall be signs** in the sun, and in the moon, and in the stars; and upon the earth distress of nations, with perplexity; the sea and the waves roaring;

26 **Men's hearts failing them** for fear, and for looking after those things which are coming on the earth: for the powers of heaven shall be shaken.

27 And **then shall they see the Son of man coming** in a cloud with power and great glory.

This same sign of the times is given also in the Doctrine and Covenants as well as in the Pearl of Great Price. They read as follows (bold added for emphasis):

D&C 45:26
26 And in that day shall be heard of wars and rumors of wars, and the whole earth shall be in commotion, and **men's hearts shall fail them**, and they shall say that Christ delayeth his coming until the end of the earth.

D&C 88:91
91 And all things shall be in commotion; and **surely, men's hearts shall fail them**; for fear shall come upon all people.

Moses 7:65–66
65 And it came to pass that Enoch saw the day of the coming of the Son of Man, in the last days, to dwell on the earth in righteousness for the space of a thousand years;

66 But **before that day** he saw great tribulations among the wicked; and he also saw the sea, that it was troubled, and **men's hearts failing them**, looking forth with fear for

the judgments of the Almighty God, which should come upon the wicked.

Fortunately for the Saints in the last days, there is peace and stability in living the gospel, including following the living prophets. We have constant guidance from the Lord through them and through the gift of the Holy Ghost. We, of all people on earth, have the best chance of following the Savior's counsel about the signs of the times recorded in Matthew 24:6, as well as in Joseph Smith—Matthew 1:23, wherein He said "see that ye be not troubled." There is peace in righteous doing. We have no need to get caught up in the depression and despair that has become such a common and pervasive problem of our times. In fact, if we were to get caught up in it, we would not being doing a very good job of following our latter-day prophets. President Monson gave wonderful counsel on this topic in the April 2009 general conference. He said:

It would be easy to become discouraged and cynical about the future—or even fearful of what might come—if we allowed ourselves to dwell only on that which is wrong in the world and in our lives. Today, however, I'd like us to turn our thoughts and our attitudes away from the troubles around us and to focus instead on our blessings as members of the Church. . . .

How might we have joy in our lives, despite all that we may face? Again from the scriptures: "Wherefore, be of good cheer, and do not fear, for I the Lord am with you, and will stand by you."

The history of the Church in this, the dispensation of the fulness of times, is replete with the experiences of those who have struggled and yet who have remained steadfast and of good cheer as they have made the gospel of Jesus Christ the center of their lives. This attitude is what will pull us through whatever comes our way. It will not remove our troubles from us but rather will enable us to face our challenges, to meet them head on, and to emerge victorious.

This is clear counsel. Following it will not only bless our own lives with a greater ability to avoid being caught up in negatives but will also help us be a positive influence for those around us.

SIGN 22

IN SPITE OF GROSS WICKEDNESS AND SPIRITUAL DARKNESS UPON THE EARTH, THE LORD'S COVENANT PEOPLE WILL BE PRESERVED

CATEGORY: BEING FULFILLED

This is a very significant prophetic promise. It brings reassurance and calm. Because of it, we can be completely confident that the Church will continue to grow and prosper in the last days, despite the efforts of Satan and his followers to stop it or at least slow it down. (Bold added for emphasis:)

Moses 7:61
61 And the day shall come that the earth shall rest, but before that day the heavens shall be darkened, and a veil of darkness shall cover the earth; and the heavens shall shake, and also the earth; and great tribulations shall be among the children of men, **but my people will I preserve**;

Knowing this allows us as individuals and as a church to confront setbacks, trials, and tribulations with full faith that the blessings of heaven will see us through and that our personal destinies and those of the Church will gloriously triumph ultimately. Knowing this can make the difference between discouragement and despair and bright confidence and fortitude as we go through life.

Throughout the early history of the Church in this dispensation, its enemies repeatedly sought to snuff out the infant Church. But despite their efforts, the Church was protected. It grew despite setbacks, and the enemies failed. Mobs tried to destroy Joseph Smith and get the gold plates before the Church was even organized. But he was protected, even though it required extreme exertion on his part, and the enemies failed. Efforts to thwart and destroy the young Church in New York caused the exodus of the saints to Ohio, where the Church continued to grow.

When apostasy in Kirtland made it look to some as if the Restoration were doomed, the righteous and faithful were protected in sufficient numbers that they could gather to Missouri where the Church continued to grow. The enemies of the prophesied restoration of the gospel continued to fail.

When Joseph Smith and others were jailed for the winter in Liberty Jail in Missouri, many thought the Church was doomed to die out. Later, they looked with glee at the scene of misery and destitution that engulfed the half-frozen and starving Saints as they trudged across the frozen snow and ice to Illinois. While Joseph and the others were languishing in the miserable dungeon that ironically was named "Liberty Jail," a powerful revelation, constituting sections 121–123 of the Doctrine and Covenants, was given in which the Lord again detailed that the enemies of the Church would continue to fail. (Bold added for emphasis:)

D&C 121:11–23
11 And they who do charge thee with transgression, their hope shall be blasted, and their prospects shall melt away as the hoar frost melteth before the burning rays of the rising sun;

12 And also that God hath set his hand and seal to change the times and seasons, and to blind their minds, that they may not understand his marvelous workings; that he may prove them also and take them in their own craftiness;

13 Also because their hearts are corrupted, and the things which they are willing to bring upon others, and love to have others suffer, may come upon themselves to the very uttermost;

14 That they may be disappointed also, and their hopes may be cut off;

15 And not many years hence, that they and their posterity shall be swept from under heaven, saith God, that not one of them is left to stand by the wall.

16 **Cursed are all those that shall lift up the heel against mine anointed**, saith the Lord, and cry they have sinned when they have not sinned before me, saith the Lord, but have done that which was meet in mine eyes, and which I commanded them.

17 But those who cry transgression do it because they are the servants of sin, and are the children of disobedience themselves.

18 And those who swear falsely against my servants, that they might bring them into bondage and death—

19 Wo unto them; because they have offended my little ones they shall be severed from the ordinances of mine house.

20 Their basket shall not be full, their houses and their barns shall perish, and they themselves shall be despised by those that flattered them.

21 They shall not have right to the priesthood, nor their posterity after them from generation to generation.

22 It had been better for them that a millstone had been hanged about their necks, and they drowned in the depth of the sea.

23 Wo unto all those that discomfort my people, and drive, and murder, and testify against them, saith the Lord of Hosts; **a** generation of vipers shall not escape the damnation of hell.

The revelation went on to confirm the bright future for the Lord's covenant people. The Church is to be preserved, and it extends ultimately to each faithful member.

D&C 121:26–29

26 God shall give unto you knowledge by his Holy Spirit, yea, by the unspeakable gift of the Holy Ghost, that has not been revealed since the world was until now;

27 Which our forefathers have awaited with anxious expectation to be revealed in the last times, which their minds were pointed to by the angels, as held in reserve for the fulness of their glory;

28 A time to come in the which nothing shall be withheld, whether there be one God or many gods, they shall be manifest.

29 All thrones and dominions, principalities and powers, shall be revealed and set forth upon all who have endured valiantly for the gospel of Jesus Christ.

The Church grew and thrived in Nauvoo. Converts from far and wide gathered there.

100 SIGNS

SIGN 23

THERE WILL BE EXTRAORDINARILY WIDESPREAD SELFISHNESS AND LACK OF CARING FOR OTHERS

CATEGORY: BEING FULFILLED

The Apostle Paul wrote to Timothy prophesying of evils and conditions that will be widespread in the last days. (See heading to 2 Timothy, chapter 3, in the LDS edition of the Bible.) The conditions warned about extreme selfishness as given in the following verse (bold added for emphasis):

2 Timothy 3:2
2 For men shall be **lovers of their own selves**, covetous, boasters, proud, blasphemers, disobedient to parents, **unthankful**, unholy,

We see this selfishness and lack of caring for the welfare of others all around us. It is, in fact, a rather prominent sign of the times. It is the opposite of the charity and caring taught by the gospel of Jesus Christ. Here again, we are fortunate in our wards and branches to dwell as it were in a society of Saints, where love, thoughtfulness, service to one another, and deep kindness are a part of our daily living. Indeed, the gospel environment protects us to a great degree from the Satan-sponsored emotional and spiritual ravages of the last days.

This selfishness and lack of caring for others, which is such a widespread and extraordinarily prominent sign of the times in the last days, has been around to some degree ever since the beginning. We see it in the life and attitude of Cain after he slew Abel, his righteous brother. When Cain was called to accountability by the Lord, he hardly even mentioned Abel. He was only concerned with his own plight. Notice how this is evident in his response. Watch for his use of "me," "I," "my," and "mine" (bold added for emphasis):

Moses 5:35–39
35 And the Lord said: What hast thou done? The voice of thy brother's blood cries unto me from the ground.

36 And now thou shalt be cursed from the earth which hath opened her mouth to receive thy brother's blood from thy hand.

37 When thou tillest the ground it shall not henceforth yield unto thee her strength. A fugitive and a vagabond shalt thou be in the earth.

38 And Cain said unto the Lord: Satan tempted **me** because of my brother's flocks. And **I** was wroth also; for his offering thou

didst accept and not **mine**; **my** punishment is greater than **I** can bear.

39 Behold thou hast driven **me** out this day from the face of the Lord, and from thy face shall **I** be hid; and **I** shall be a fugitive and a vagabond in the earth; and it shall come to pass, that he that findeth **me** will slay **me**, because of **mine** iniquities, for these things are not hid from the Lord.

SIGN 24
COUPLES WILL AVOID MARRIAGE AND OPENLY LIVE TOGETHER
CATEGORY: BEING FULFILLED

Many years ago when I was serving as a young missionary in Austria, it was common for us to use 1 Timothy 4:3 to show that churches that taught celibacy were a fulfillment of one of the signs of the times (bold added for emphasis):

1 Timothy 4:1–3
1 Now the Spirit speaketh expressly, that in the latter times [*the last days*] some shall depart from the faith, giving heed to seducing spirits, and doctrines of devils;

2 Speaking lies in hypocrisy; having their conscience seared with a hot iron;

3 **Forbidding to marry**, and commanding to abstain from meats, which God hath created to be received with thanksgiving of them which believe and know the truth.

Obviously, that interpretation of Paul's prophecy about this sign of the times was too narrow. We are seeing a devastating trend toward "forbidding to marry" in the widespread practice of living together, having children, and so forth, without the covenants and commitments of formal marriage. As the Church holds firm to the God-given laws concerning the sacred nature of marriage and the necessity of formalizing it by covenants, more and more pressure is placed on the Church to change its stand. We are most fortunate as a people and as members of the Church to have living prophets, seers, and revelators, who are "steadfast and immovable" (Mosiah 5:15) in teaching us the word and will of God on this and other vital issues for the survival of a healthy society.

SIGN 25

THE MARK OF THE BEAST IN THEIR FOREHEADS

CATEGORY: BEING FULFILLED

As mentioned in chapter 3 of this book, there is much misunderstanding about "the mark of the beast" as found in Revelation, chapter 13. You may wish to read this part of chapter 3 again as you study this sign of the time.

The Apostle John was given a marvelous vision in which he saw much about the last days. It is recorded as the book of Revelation in the Bible. Among many other things, he saw frightening beasts representing Satan's stranglehold on many in our day. He saw the "mark of the beast" on their foreheads, symbolizing their loyalty to him and his evil ways. If you look at the heading for Revelation 13 in your LDS Bible, you will see that the "fierce-looking beasts" referred to in this chapter of the Bible "represent degenerate earthly kingdoms controlled by Satan" in the last days. Let's read Revelation 13:13–16, the actual verses that are the basis of most discussions about the "mark of the beast." I will add some verses before for context and add some explanatory notes as we read. Then, I will discuss the prophecy. I will use bold to point out the "mark of the beast" parts of the reference.

Revelation 13:13–16

13 And he doeth great wonders [*Satan and his evil angels can be spectacular in their tempting*], so that he maketh fire come down from heaven on the earth in the sight of men [*a counterfeit of Elijah's miracle, 1 Kings 18:38*],

14 And deceiveth them [*the wicked and foolish and many of those who are ignorant of the laws of God*] that dwell on the earth by the means of those miracles which he had power to do in the sight of the beast; saying to them that dwell on the earth, that they should make an image to [*i.e., worship*] the beast, which had the wound by a sword, and did live. [*Revelation 13:3. In other words, Satan will do all he can to get all people to follow him, to "worship" him by living wickedly in the last days.*]

15 And he had power to give life [*make wickedness attractive*] unto the image of the beast [*symbolic of various forms of wickedness which the wicked made in verse 14 by following Satan's instructions*], that the image of the beast should both speak, and cause that as many as would not worship the image of the beast should be killed [*people's "idols" can take over their lives and cause them to die spiritually, and physically in wars, plagues, etc. Also, the wicked can cause great trouble, temporarily, for the righteous*].

16 And he causeth all [*all who follow Satan; the righteous are not part of this group because they have the seal of God in their foreheads as mentioned in Revelation 7:3*], both small and great, rich and poor, free and bond, to **receive a mark** in their right hand, or **in their foreheads** [*symbolically indicating that they are loyal to Satan and the wickedness he sponsors*]:

In the culture of the Bible, "forehead" was symbolic of "loyalty." Thus we see faithful Jews wearing phylacteries even today (see Bible Dictionary, under "Phylacteries") tied to their foreheads, symbolizing loyalty and obedience to their God. Notice also in Revelation 14:1 that there are a 144,000 righteous who have the

100 SIGNS

"Father's name written in their foreheads," which symbolizes loyalty and obedience to the Father. (Bold added for emphasis:)

> Revelation 13:17
> 17 And that no man might buy or sell, save he that had **the mark**, or the name **of the beast**, or the number of his name. [*Satan exercises great control over economies where the majority are wicked or allow wickedness; the righteous today would do well to follow the counsel of the prophets regarding self-sufficiency and staying out of unnecessary debt, etc.*]

Verses 16 and 17 are examples of the importance of carefully considering context when interpreting verses of scripture. If one were to read only these verses, the conclusion could be that, in the last days, "all" (verse 16) people will eventually come under the power of Satan and wicked people under his control, and thus have the "mark of the beast" upon them. This would be very depressing and could cause people to give up hope. However, if we examine other verses in Revelation, we see the truth. For example, read Revelation 14:1, where we see 144,000 with the Father's name in their foreheads, rather than the mark of the beast in their foreheads. Furthermore, in Revelation 20:4, we see righteous people who do not have the mark of the beast "which had not worshipped the beast, neither his image, neither had received his mark upon their foreheads, or in their hands." Thus we see that "all" (Revelation 13:16) do not come under Satan's control, rather "all" the foolish or wicked do, who "wondered after the beast" (verse 3).

Verse 17 implies much financial bondage in the last days associated with the "mark of the beast." If we follow the council of the Brethren, we will not come under this bondage. For example, Elder L. Tom Perry counseled:

Live strictly within your income and save something for a rainy day. Incorporate in your lives the discipline of budgeting that which the Lord has blessed you with . . . avoid excessive debt. Necessary debt should be incurred only after careful, thoughtful prayer and after obtaining the best possible advice. We need the discipline to stay well within our ability to pay. Wisely we have been counseled to avoid debt as we would avoid the plague. . . . It is so easy to allow consumer debt to get out of hand. If you do not have the discipline to control the use of credit cards, it is better not to have them. A well-managed family does not pay interest—it earns it. The definition I received from a wise boss at one time in my early business career was 'Thems that understands interest receives it, thems that don't pays it.' . . . Acquire and store a reserve of food and supplies that will sustain life. Obtain clothing and build a savings account on a sensible, well-planned basis that can serve well in times of emergency. As long as I can remember, we have been taught to prepare for the future and to obtain a year's supply of necessities. I would guess that the years of plenty have almost universally caused us to set aside this counsel. I believe the time to disregard this counsel is over. With events in the world today, it must be considered with all seriousness. (L. Tom Perry, *Ensign*, November 1995, 36)

In summary, Satan and the degenerate earthly kingdoms controlled by him in the last days, symbolized by beasts in Revelation, chapter 13, will wield devastating power over nations and people who symbolically have the "mark of the beast in their foreheads," or in other words, who are loyal to him and his wicked ways. On the other hand, those who are loyal to God and His righteous ways will symbolically have the "Father's name written in their foreheads" (Revelation 14:1) or will have "been born of

God" and will have "received his image in [their] countenances" (Alma 5:14).

SIGN 26
GREAT TRIBULATION AMONG THE WICKED
CATEGORY: BEING FULFILLED

It seems to be a common tendency to think that the wicked are free to live their lives as they want to. Being "free" from the restraints of religion and the laws of society appears quite attractive to many. The collective result of gross wickedness among large numbers of people is great misery and suffering among the wicked themselves. As their main goal becomes the plundering and destruction of others, their own circumstances, including living conditions and fear of discovery, become abject and stark. We often see this among terrorist groups. They live lives of squalor and uncertainty and cause their own families and people to suffer greatly. Often education is undervalued and suppressed, and brutality, tyranny, and isolation are the order of the day. Enoch saw this in great magnitude as a sign of the times in the last days (bold added for emphasis):

> Moses 7:65–66
> 65 And it came to pass that Enoch saw the day of the coming of the Son of Man, in the last days, to dwell on the earth in righteousness for the space of a thousand years;
>
> 66 But **before that day he saw great tribulations among the wicked**; and he also saw the sea, that it was troubled, and men's hearts failing them, looking forth with fear for the judgments of the Almighty God, which should come upon the wicked.

Alma taught his son, Corianton, that "wickedness never was happiness" (Alma 41:10). Indeed, we are witnessing this on an unprecedented scale as we see personal wickedness and lack of moral courage and integrity undermine the stability of individuals, families, nations, companies, sports franchises, communities, and society in general. Wickedness is indeed bringing tribulation to those who choose to ignore conscience and go against the laws of God.

The Doctrine and Covenants provides a scathing pronouncement as to the results of wickedness (bold added for emphasis).

> D&C 121:13–14
> 13 Also because their hearts are corrupted, and the things which they are willing to bring upon others, and love to have others suffer, **may come upon themselves to the very uttermost**;
>
> 14 That they may be disappointed also, and their hopes may be cut off;

SIGN 27
EVER LEARNING, AND NEVER COMING TO THE KNOWLEDGE OF THE TRUTH
CATEGORY: BEING FULFILLED

The Apostle Paul included this sign of the times in the last days as one of many such signs he pointed out to Timothy (bold added for emphasis):

> 2 Timothy 3:1–7
> 1 This know also, that in the last days perilous times shall come.
>
> 2 For men shall be lovers of their own selves, covetous, boasters, proud, blasphemers, disobedient to parents, unthankful, unholy,
>
> 3 Without natural affection, trucebreakers, false accusers, incontinent, fierce, despisers of those that are good,
>
> 4 Traitors, heady, highminded, lovers of pleasures more than lovers of God;

100
SIGNS

5 Having a form of godliness, but denying the power thereof: from such turn away.

6 For of this sort are they which creep into houses, and lead captive silly women laden with sins, led away with divers lusts,

7 Ever learning, and never able to come to the knowledge of the truth.

It is interesting that the Lord would include verse 7, above, as a sign of the times specifically denoting the last days. Since the dawn of history, people have sought knowledge and individuals have given much effort to pursue studies in science, philosophy, religion, history, and so forth, without successfully coming to a knowledge of truth. So, why would this be a sign of the times in the last days?

One possibility might be that with the amazing increase in scientific discoveries and capabilities for research and discovery, especially since the restoration of the gospel through Joseph Smith, the vast majority of the earth's population should be pointed in the direction of believing in God as the Creator of all things. But this does not seem to be the case. The overwhelming majority of the earth's population still doesn't know the simple truths readily available in the restored gospel of Jesus Christ. We have rockets with mind-boggling scientific instruments and cameras and other devices probing deep into the reaches of interstellar space, sending back marvelous evidence of the Creator's work, and yet many still reject the idea that there is a God. Medical science makes astounding strides daily in understanding the God-created miracle of the human body, and yet many intentionally avoid giving any credibility or even consideration to the "truth" that we are created in the image of God (Genesis 1:27).

It seems that while advances in science and technology continue to increase exponentially, there is less and less mention of God in our media. While in previous generations there was often concern and debate about public events, concerts, sporting events, and so forth being held on the Sabbath, now it is no longer even a topic of public discussion or concern, or even awareness, for the vast majority. In times past, what God says in the Bible was influential in determining local and national laws and policies. Now, most lawmakers don't seem to even think of it or are reluctant to say anything about the Lord's laws and commandments for fear of incurring public scorn and wrath.

There are probably many other ways in which this sign of the times is being fulfilled in our day, perhaps including the taking of God out of public schools; taking prayer out of local government; and removing Christmas scenes, the Ten Commandments, Christian statues and art, and so forth from public venues. The net result for the majority is that God is further and further from their minds. Situational ethics prevail, and absolute truths are no longer considered reasonable or applicable. The net result for society is that the other signs of the last days mentioned by Paul in verses 2–6 have become the norm. Thus, more and more, people throughout the world are "ever learning, and never able to come to a knowledge of the truth."

One additional possibility that we should consider as one of the ways in which this sign of the times is being fulfilled in these last days comes from the Prophet Joseph Smith (bold added for emphasis):

D&C 123:12

12 For there are many yet on the earth among all sects, parties, and denominations, who are blinded by the subtle craftiness of men, whereby they lie in wait to deceive, and **who are only kept from the truth because they know not where to find it—**

As you know, one of the great aspects of the work of the Lord in the last days is that of missionary work. The gospel must be preached to every "nation, and kindred, and tongue, and people" (Revelation 14:6). As the great latter-day work of gathering Israel continues to go forth, more and more sincere individuals will no longer be "kept from the truth because they know not where to find it" and will be enabled to learn and now, finally, "come to the knowledge of the truth."

SIGN 28
WIDESPREAD SUPPRESSION OF PERSONAL CONSCIENCE
CATEGORY: BEING FULFILLED

Have you noticed how open and blatant wickedness no longer seems to bring with it humiliation and shame? Public figures get caught in compromising situations, affairs, corruption, and so forth, but keep right on going, seeking votes, re-election, or whatever. Many seem to relish the attention and additional popularity such behavior unfortunately brings in our day. Paul described this to Timothy as a sign of the times in the last days (bold added for emphasis):

> 1 Timothy 4:1–2
> 1 Now the Spirit speaketh expressly, that in the latter times [*last days*] some shall depart from the faith, giving heed to seducing spirits, and doctrines of devils;
> 2 Speaking lies in hypocrisy; **having their conscience seared with a hot iron**;

In other words, such individuals have repeatedly ignored and pushed back against their conscience to the point that it has been pretty much withdrawn according to the laws of agency. One of the sad things about this whole situation is that many of the public seem to relish what they are seeing in the lives of these leaders and celebrities. Rather than being offended and repulsed by such lifestyles and rejecting public figures so involved, such exposure of high profile behavior seems to validate and reflect approval on their own personal choices and corruption. Therefore, they embrace these public figures all the more. Thus, they, themselves, seem likewise to fulfill this prophecy personally. Their own consciences appear to have been repressed to the point that they have nearly ceased to function, having likewise been figuratively "seared with a hot iron."

SIGN 29
THE JEWS WILL RETURN TO JERUSALEM
CATEGORY: FULFILLED AND BEING FULFILLED

For all practical purposes, this major sign of the times has been fulfilled. Sponsored by Great Britain in the United Nations, the Jews became a nation in 1948. Thus, the Jews have now returned to the Holy Land and have their own nation and their own government. In the April 1960 general conference of the Church, Elder George Q. Morris of the Council of the Twelve, said that the Jews have returned (bold added for emphasis):

> A third item is God's promise that he would gather Jews to Jerusalem, and I think perhaps we may well now not continue the saying the Jews are going to gather in Jerusalem. **I think now we may well say they have gathered**. (In Conference Report, April 1960, 100–1)

Thus, we do not need to wait for this sign of the times to be fulfilled. They are back. However, since the Jews continue to return, virtually daily, some may wish to include the category "being fulfilled" also as we consider this prophecy.

Joseph Smith prophesied the return of the Jews as he spoke to members of the Church in April 1843 (bold added for emphasis):

> **Judah must return, Jerusalem must be rebuilt**, and the temple, and water come out from under the temple, and the waters of the Dead Sea be healed. It will take some time to rebuild the walls of the city and the temple, &c.; and **all this must be done before the Son of Man will make His appearance**. There will be wars and rumors of wars, signs in the heavens above and on the earth beneath, the sun turned into darkness and the moon to blood, earthquakes in divers places, the seas heaving beyond their bounds; then will appear one grand sign of the Son of Man in heaven. But what will the world do? They will say it is a planet, a comet, &c. But the Son of Man will come as the sign of the coming of the Son of Man, which will be as the light of the morning cometh out of the east. (Joseph Smith, *History of The Church of Jesus Christ of Latter-day Saints,* introduction and notes by B. H. Roberts, 7 vols. [Salt Lake City: The Church of Jesus Christ of Latter-day Saints, 1932–51], 5:337)

In the Doctrine and Covenants, the Jews are instructed to flee to Jerusalem in the last days. This verse reads as follows:

> D&C 133:13
> 13 And let them who be of Judah flee unto Jerusalem, unto the mountains of the Lord's house.

In yet another passage from the Doctrine and Covenants, we read the following (bold added for emphasis):

> D&C 45:24–25
> 24 And this I have told you concerning Jerusalem; and when that day shall come, shall a remnant be scattered among all nations;

> 25 But **they shall be gathered again**; but they shall remain until the times of the Gentiles be fulfilled.

And so it is that the return of the Jews is a major sign of the times. As we watch this and so many other prophecies being fulfilled, our testimonies should grow and be strengthened. Surely, the Lord is most kind and generous to give us so much obvious evidence that the gospel is true.

SIGN 30
THE JEWS ACCEPT THE TRUE GOSPEL
CATEGORY: YET TO BE FULFILLED

Although there are some faithful, individual Jewish members of the Church already, the fulfillment of this prophecy will not come until large numbers of Jews accept Jesus Christ as the Promised Messiah and join the true Church through baptism and confirmation. Nephi speaks of the time when the Jews will finally believe in Christ:

> 2 Nephi 30:7
> 7 And it shall come to pass that the Jews which are scattered also shall begin to believe in Christ; and they shall begin to gather in upon the face of the land; and as many as shall believe in Christ shall also become a delightsome people.

Zechariah spoke of the "grace" or opportunity to believe in Christ that would be extended to the Jews in the last days when the Savior preserves them from destruction and appears to them. We understand that this will lead to the conversion of large numbers of our Jewish brothers and sisters. Zechariah tells us (bold added for emphasis):

Zechariah 12:7–10

7 **The Lord also shall save the tents of Judah** first, that the glory of the house of David and the glory of the inhabitants of Jerusalem do not magnify themselves against Judah.

8 **In that day shall the Lord defend the inhabitants of Jerusalem**; and he that is feeble among them at that day shall be as David; and the house of David shall be as God, as the angel of the Lord before them.

9 And it shall come to pass in that day, that **I will seek to destroy all the nations that come against Jerusalem**.

10 And I **will pour upon the** house of David, and upon the **inhabitants of Jerusalem, the spirit of grace** and of supplications: and they shall look upon me whom they have pierced, and they shall mourn for him, as one mourneth for his only son, and shall be in bitterness for him, as one that is in bitterness for his firstborn.

Zechariah 13:6

6 And *one* shall say unto him, **What *are* these wounds in thine hands**? Then he shall answer, Those with which I was wounded *in* the house of my friends.

The Doctrine and Covenants sheds further light upon this scene as follows (bold added for emphasis):

D&C 45:51–53

51 And then shall the Jews look upon me and say: What are these wounds in thine hands and in thy feet?

52 **Then shall they know that I am the Lord**; for I will say unto them: These wounds are the wounds with which I was wounded in the house of my friends. I am he who was lifted up. I am Jesus that was crucified. I am the Son of God.

53 And then shall they weep because of their iniquities; then shall they lament because they persecuted their king.

On September 10, 1859, Charles W. Penrose also spoke of this great conversion of the Jews in an article in the *Millennial Star* (bold added for emphasis):

His [Christ's] next appearance will be among the distressed and nearly vanquished sons of Judah. At the crisis of their fate, when the hostile troops of several nations are ravaging the city and all the horrors of war are overwhelming the people of Jerusalem, he will set his feet upon the Mount of Olives, which will cleave and part asunder at his touch. Attended by a host from heaven, he will overthrow and destroy the combined armies of the Gentiles, and appear to the worshipping Jews as the mighty Deliverer and Conqueror so long expected by their race; and while love, gratitude, awe, and admiration swell their bosoms, the Deliverer will show them the tokens of his crucifixion and disclose himself as Jesus of Nazareth, whom they had reviled and whom their fathers put to death. **Then will unbelief depart from their souls, and the blindness in part which has happened unto Israel be removed.** ("The Second Advent," Charles W. Penrose, *Millennial Star*, vol. 21, Sept. 10, 1859, 582–83)

SIGN 31

THE PROPHET ELIJAH WILL COME TO RESTORE THE KEYS OF SEALING

CATEGORY: FULFILLED

This sign of the times was fulfilled on Sunday, April 3, 1836, in the Kirtland Temple in Ohio when the Prophet Elijah appeared to the Prophet Joseph Smith and Oliver Cowdery and gave them the keys of sealing families together forever. This monumental event is recorded in the Doctrine and Covenants as follows (bold added for emphasis):

KIRTLAND TEMPLE

BY SCOTT JARVIE

D&C 110:13–16

13 After this vision had closed, another great and glorious vision burst upon us; for **Elijah** the prophet, who was taken to heaven without tasting death, **stood before us**, and said:

14 Behold, the time has fully come, which was spoken of by the mouth of Malachi—testifying that he [*Elijah*] should be sent, before the great and dreadful day of the Lord come—

15 To turn the hearts of the fathers to the children, and the children to the fathers, lest the whole earth be smitten with a curse—

16 Therefore, **the keys of this dispensation are committed into your hands; and by this ye may know that the great and dreadful day of the Lord is near, even at the doors.**

It is very interesting to note that many faithful Jews still celebrate the Passover every year. And as part of their Passover celebration, they have a place setting at the table for Elijah. During the services, they ceremoniously open the door to invite Elijah to come in and take his place of honor at their table, if it so happens that he comes that year. It is a tender and reverent token of their faith that the prophecy about the return of Elijah will be fulfilled. The prophecy is found in Malachi as follows (bold added for emphasis):

Malachi 4:5–6

5 Behold, **I will send you Elijah the prophet before the coming of the great and dreadful day of the Lord**:

6 And he shall turn the heart of the fathers to the children, and the heart of the children to their fathers, lest I come and smite the earth with a curse.

It is also significant to note that the coming of the Prophet Elijah to Joseph Smith and Oliver Cowdery took place on Easter Sunday. Yes, Sunday, April 3, 1836 (see heading to Doctrine and Covenants, section 110), was Easter Sunday,

which means that Jews throughout the world were celebrating Passover when he came.

Thus, the keys of sealing have been restored, as prophesied, and the work of sealing the living and dead as family units is going forth upon the earth.

The great strides seen recently in the family history program of the Church are mind-boggling to say the least. The Spirit of Elijah is resting mightily upon the work of researching our ancestors and providing the ordinances for their salvation. The ready access on personal computers and other personal electronic devices for researching our own family lines, for indexing, and a host of other activities for helping to save our dead ancestors has brought excitement and testimony in unprecedented degree.

Elder David A. Bednar gave a stirring and much-referred-to sermon in the October 2011 general conference of the Church in which he invited all members, especially the youth, to become involved in family history. We will include some brief excerpts from his talk here. He first gave a brief review of who Elijah was and defined the Spirit of Elijah. He then directed his attention to the young people of the Church and said:

It is no coincidence that FamilySearch and other tools have come forth at a time when young people are so familiar with a wide range of information and communication technologies. Your fingers have been trained to text and tweet to accelerate and advance the work of the Lord—not just to communicate quickly with your friends. The skills and aptitude evident among many young people today are a preparation to contribute to the work of salvation.

Next, Elder Bednar invited the youth of the Church to study about Elijah and experience for themselves the Spirit of Elijah, which is a special manifestation of the Spirit that inspires and impels family history work. Among other things, he said, again addressing the youth:

> I encourage you to study, to search out your ancestors, and to prepare yourselves to perform proxy baptisms in the house of the Lord for your kindred dead (see D&C 124:28–36)

He also encouraged young people in the Church to use their skills to help other members of the Church in their family history work. He then continued. Note the prophecies and promises contained in the next excerpt.

> As you respond in faith to this invitation, your hearts shall turn to the fathers. The promises made to Abraham, Isaac, and Jacob will be implanted in your hearts. Your patriarchal blessing, with its declaration of lineage, will link you to these fathers and be more meaningful to you. Your love and gratitude for your ancestors will increase. Your testimony of and conversion to the Savior will become deep and abiding. And I promise you will be protected against the intensifying influence of the adversary. As you participate in and love this holy work, you will be safeguarded in your youth and throughout your lives.

Our family can bear personal witness to the effects of the Spirit of Elijah on research efforts. A good example is found on my wife's side of the family. For decades, efforts to connect up the genealogy going back on her father's side in Germany were fruitless. Time and money was spent to no avail. The ancestors who lived in the United States had been researched successfully, but when it came to connecting across the ocean to Germany, it was repeatedly a dead end.

Then, one of our daughters was called to the Germany Hamburg Mission. When she was set apart for her mission, she was told that she would be instrumental in bridging the missing information to connect her grandfather's line to his ancestors in Germany. Throughout her mission, she awaited the fulfillment of that promise, but it did not come. Finally, on the evening before her departure for home, at a farewell get-together held in one of the wards in her mission, a long-time member struck up a conversation with her. In the course of that chat, she discovered that he was a professional genealogist and he was certain that he could find the missing records. He had access to archives in the relevant area of Germany.

Long story short, he agreed to check on it, and in the process was put in touch by an archivist with a relative of my wife's father who was compiling his family history, but had been unsuccessful in finding the missing ancestor who emigrated to America several generations ago. Excitedly, information was exchanged, and in the end, we visited with the man from Germany. He told us he had come to Salt Lake some years ago, hoping to find the missing families for his research in the Church's family history library. But, unbeknown to him, the man's name, who emigrated from Germany, had been changed at Ellis Island when he and his family arrived in America, because the agent there did not know how to spell the German name.

We received the family history book containing our family history with joy, and the resulting ordinance work has been accomplished for over one thousand individuals.

SIGN 32
THE SAINTS WILL BE FEW IN NUMBER, BUT THE POWER OF GOD WILL BE WITH THEM
CATEGORY: BEING FULFILLED

This is a very comforting prophecy and sign of the times for members of the Church living in the last days. We will quote this prophecy, given in the Book of Mormon (bold added for emphasis):

1 Nephi 14:12–14

12 And it came to pass that I beheld the church of the Lamb of God, and its **numbers were few**, because of the wickedness and abominations of the whore who sat upon many waters; nevertheless, I beheld that the church of the Lamb, who were the saints of God, were also upon all the face of the earth; and their dominions upon the face of the earth were small, because of the wickedness of the great whore whom I saw.

13 And it came to pass that I beheld that the great mother of abominations did gather together multitudes upon the face of all the earth, among all the nations of the Gentiles, to fight against the Lamb of God.

14 And it came to pass that I, Nephi, beheld **the power of the Lamb of God**, that it **descended upon the saints of the church of the Lamb**, and upon the covenant people of the Lord, who were scattered upon all the face of the earth; **and they were armed with righteousness and with the power of God in great glory**.

This pleasant and encouraging prophecy is being fulfilled in quiet and sacred ways among the members of the Church throughout the earth. Covenant-keeping individuals and families feel this power and assurance from God. Branches, wards, and stakes feel the outpouring of the Spirit as they gather in worship, and in their daily lives as they serve one another and nonmember friends, neighbors, and relatives. The whole Church at general conference time feels "the power of the Lamb of God" as we are instructed by the Lord's prophets, seers, and revelators, and the Holy Ghost bears witness and teaches us in our hearts and minds.

SIGN 33

CHRIST WILL COME TO HIS TEMPLE

CATEGORY: FULFILLED AND BEING FULFILLED

One of the signs of the times is that, in the last days before the Second Coming, there will be an appearance of the Lord in His temple. In Malachi 3:1, we are told specifically that the Lord will come to His temple before the Second Coming. The verse reads as follows (bold added for emphasis):

Malachi 3:1

1 Behold, I will send my messenger, and he shall prepare the way before me: and **the Lord**, whom ye seek, **shall suddenly come to his temple**, even the messenger of the covenant, whom ye delight in: behold, he shall come, saith the Lord of hosts.

In order for this to take place, there would have to be a temple built. The early Saints built the first temple of this dispensation in Kirtland, Ohio, and the Savior came to it as described in the Doctrine and Covenants (bold added for emphasis):

D&C 110:1–10

1 The veil was taken from our minds, and the eyes of our understanding were opened.

2 **We saw the Lord standing upon the breastwork of the pulpit**, before us; and under his feet was a paved work of pure gold, in color like amber.

3 His eyes were as a flame of fire; the hair of his head was white like the pure snow; his countenance shone above the brightness of the sun; and his voice was as the sound of the rushing of great waters, even the voice of Jehovah, saying:

4 I am the first and the last; I am he who liveth, I am he who was slain; I am your advocate with the Father.

WE SAW THE LORD STANDING UPON THE BREASTWORK OF THE PULPIT, BEFORE US.

D & C 110:2

5 Behold, your sins are forgiven you; you are clean before me; therefore, lift up your heads and rejoice.

6 Let the hearts of your brethren rejoice, and let the hearts of all my people rejoice, who have, with their might, built this house to my name.

7 For behold, **I have accepted this house**, and my name shall be here; and I will manifest myself to my people in mercy in this house.

8 Yea, I will appear unto my servants, and speak unto them with mine own voice, if my people will keep my commandments, and do not pollute this holy house.

9 Yea the hearts of thousands and tens of thousands shall greatly rejoice in consequence of the blessings which shall be poured out, and the endowment with which my servants have been endowed in this house.

10 And **the fame of this house shall spread to foreign lands**; and this is the beginning of the blessing which shall be poured out upon the heads of my people. Even so. Amen.

Obviously, the Savior has also come to other temples built unto Him by the Saints in these latter days. Therefore, this prophecy continues to be fulfilled in marvelous ways. But it appears that the basic fulfillment of this particular prophecy occurred in the Kirtland Temple.

SIGN 34

GENEALOGICAL RESEARCH AND INTEREST IN FAMILY HISTORY WILL SPREAD AS NEVER BEFORE

CATEGORY: BEING FULFILLED

This is a most fascinating prophecy to watch as it is being fulfilled. This sign of the times is to be a great surge of interest in seeking information about one's ancestors. It includes the sealing of ancestors together as families, after the keys to

do so are restored by Elijah, as discussed with sign number 21 in this book. In Malachi, we read the following (bold added for emphasis):

> Malachi 4:5–6
> 5 Behold, I will send you Elijah the prophet before the coming of the great and dreadful day of the Lord:
>
> 6 And **he shall turn the heart of the fathers to the children, and the heart of the children to their fathers**, lest I come and smite the earth with a curse.

This prophecy is being fulfilled marvelously and obviously! In 1997, it was reported in *American Demographics* that 64 million Americans had written their own family history or had drawn up a family tree. Additionally, it was stated that some 100 million were at that time involved in searching for their roots. In fact, the only hobbies that were more popular than learning about family history were stamp collecting, gardening, and coin collecting. (See *Utah County Journal*, Vol. 28, Issue 3, Sunday, January 12, 1997.) Now, some 16 years since that article was written, many sources report that family history is the number one hobby in the country.

As you have no doubt observed, this interest in learning about one's ancestors continues to grow. Well over half of the patrons who come to the Church's Family History facility in Salt Lake City are not members of the Church. Yet, the "Spirit of Elijah" is upon them, and they are drawn into this marvelous work.

President Boyd K. Packer spoke of the influence of family history work on the living as well as upon the dead:

> Family history work has the power to do something *for* the dead. It has an equal power to do something *to* the living. Family history work of Church members has a refining, spiritualizing, tempering influence on those

DANGERS UPON
THE WATERS

who are engaged in it. They understand that they are tying their family together, their living family here with those who have gone before.

Family history work in one sense would justify itself even if one were not successful in clearing names for temple work. The process of searching, the means of going after those names, would be worth all the effort you could invest. The reason: You cannot find names without knowing that they represent people. You begin to find out things about people. When we research our own lines we become interested in more than just names or the number of names going through the temple. Our interest turns our hearts to our fathers—we seek to find them and to know them and to serve them. ("Your Family History: Getting Started," *Ensign*, August 2003,12–17)

Thus it is that the ongoing fulfillment of this great prophecy, which is a prominent sign of the times, bears specific witness that the gospel is true and that the Savior will come as promised.

SIGN 35

DANGERS UPON THE WATERS

CATEGORY: BEING FULFILLED

This particular sign of the times is much misunderstood and is often the focus of misinformation and incorrect advice. It comes from the Doctrine and Covenants, section 61. The problem is that some verses of this revelation are very specific to the time it was given (1831) as well as to "these waters" (verse 5, which would be the rivers upon which the Saints were traveling in those days, including the Missouri River). Other parts of the revelation can be considered a "sign of the times," such as verses 4, 14, and 15. We will quote some of the relevant verses from this section, adding commentary as we go and bolding for emphasis.

D&C 61:4–6

4 Nevertheless, I suffered it that ye might bear record; behold, there are **many dangers upon the waters, and more especially hereafter** [*in the future*];

5 For I, the Lord, have decreed in mine anger many destructions upon the waters; yea, and **especially upon these waters**. [*The rivers and waters the Saints were using to travel to and from Missouri, etc.*]

6 Nevertheless, all flesh is in mine hand, and he that is faithful among you shall not perish by the waters.

D&C 61:13–19

13 And now, behold, for your good I gave unto you a commandment concerning these things; and I, the Lord, will reason with you as with men in days of old.

14 Behold, I, the Lord, in the beginning blessed the waters [*see Genesis 1:20–22*]; but **in the last days, by the mouth of my servant John, I cursed the waters**. [*See Revelation 16:3–4.*]

15 Wherefore, **the days will come that no flesh shall be safe upon the waters**. [*Future prophecy, a sign of the times. Perhaps including pollution, toxic waste, oil spills, Giardia, etc.*]

16 And it shall be said in days to come that none is able to go up to the land of Zion upon the waters, but he that is upright in heart. [*Specific reference to travel to Missouri in that day.*]

17 And, as I, the Lord, in the beginning cursed the land [*Genesis 3:17*], even so in the last days have I blessed it [*D&C 104:14–18*], in its time, for the use of my saints, that they may partake the fatness thereof. [*A prophecy that the productivity of the land will greatly increase in the last days. No doubt we are seeing agricultural science contribute significantly to the fulfillment of this prophecy.*]

18 And now I give unto you a commandment that what I say unto one I say unto all, that you shall **forewarn your brethren concerning these waters**, that they come not in journeying upon them, lest their faith

fail and they are caught in snares; [*A specific reference to traveling on those rivers in flood season back then.*]

19 I, the Lord, have decreed, and **the destroyer rideth upon the face thereof**, and I revoke not the decree. [*Satan will wield power and cause troubles with water in the last days.*]

D&C 61:22

22 And **it mattereth not unto me**, after a little, if it so be that they fill their mission, **whether they go by water or by land**; let this be as it is made known unto them according to their judgments hereafter. [*In other words, use common sense. It is appropriate for Latter-day Saints to travel in watercraft, as long as they use common sense.*]

In conclusion, it is obvious that one of the signs of the times is that there will be extra dangers upon the waters. This can include more frequent, more violent storms, oil spills, toxins being poured into rivers and streams, acid rain, warships, torpedoes, the spread of destructive algae, etc. We will deal more with some of this in the next sign we consider. However, there is much misinformation and even LDS "mythology" that has grown up around the issue of "dangers upon the water." For instance, missionaries are not allowed to go swimming during their missions. Some members attribute this to the notion that some evil force awaits to pull them under and drown them. Yet, in some missions, including Elder John H. Groberg's mission when he was a young missionary to the South Pacific, travel by boat, ship, canoe, or whatever is almost a daily necessity. Perhaps one of the real reasons that missionaries are not allowed to go swimming is that the scenery at the beach or in the swimming pool is too immodest. In other words, very little fabric is used for a large number of swimming suits, which can make it difficult, if not impossible, for missionaries to avoid lustful

thoughts. Lustful thinking drives the Spirit away (See D&C 42:23).

SIGN 36
WIDESPREAD DESPISING OF GOOD PEOPLE (THE CRAB PRINCIPLE)
CATEGORY: BEING FULFILLED

Yet another prophesied aspect of the gross wickedness and spiritual darkness that will cover the earth in the last days is the widespread intentional tearing down of the reputations and personal lives of good people. Many years ago, I was taught to beware of the so-called "crab principle." To illustrate this destructive behavior, the teacher described to us a large bowl in which a few crabs had been placed. One crab alone in the bowl could, after some effort, stretch out sufficiently to hook a claw over the edge of the bowl and pull itself up and over, thus escaping. However, with more crabs in the bowl, when one was about to escape, the others would invariably pull the successful escape artist back down, thus rendering success impossible. This same principle seems to be operative to such an extent in our day that it was prophesied as one of the signs of the times. Muckrakers destroy good people's reputations and honest efforts to serve by finding embarrassing tidbits and blowing them out of proportion in the public eye. It is called "character assassination" and is often used in politics. The Apostle Paul prophesied this as a sign of the times in the last days (bold added for emphasis):

2 Timothy 3:1–3

1 This know also, that in the last days perilous times shall come.

2 For men shall be lovers of their own selves, covetous, boasters, proud, blasphemers, disobedient to parents, unthankful, unholy,

3 Without natural affection, trucebreakers, false accusers, incontinent, fierce, **despisers of those that are good**,

Knowing that this is a sign of the times can help us avoid such behavior. We can forgive and let others grow and progress, leaving their past behind. When we see this negative behavior prominent in the media, we can be aware of its destructive effect upon society and can use it to strengthen our testimonies, realizing that it is yet another fulfillment of prophecy.

SIGN 37

MUCH ECOLOGICAL DAMAGE WILL OCCUR IN THE LAST DAYS

CATEGORY: BEING FULFILLED

The book of Revelation especially points out this sign of the times, particularly in chapter 8. We will include some verses from chapter 8 here and bold some words and phrases so that you can see this prophecy of ecological damage at-a-glance.

Revelation 8:7–12

7 The first angel sounded, and there followed hail and fire mingled with blood, and they were cast upon the earth: and the third part of **trees** was burnt up, and all green grass was burnt up.

8 And the second angel sounded, and as it were a great mountain burning with fire was cast into the sea: and the third part of the **sea** became blood;

9 And the third part of the creatures which were in the **sea,** and had life, died; and the third part of the ships were destroyed.

10 And the third angel sounded, and there fell a great star from heaven, burning as it were a lamp, and it fell upon the third part of the **rivers**, and upon the **fountains of waters**;

11 And the name of the star is called Wormwood: and the third part of the **waters** became wormwood; and many men died of the **water**s, because they were **made bitter.**

12 And the fourth angel sounded, and the third part of the **sun** was smitten, and the third part of the **moon**, and the third part of the **stars**; so as the third part of them was darkened, and the day shone not for a third part of it, and the night likewise.

There are obviously many ways in which the damage to the environment indicated in the foregoing verses could be inflicted. In conclusion, it would appear from these and other verses in scripture that there will be prominent ecological damage and disturbance in the last days leading up to the coming of the Lord.

SIGN 38

VARIOUS FORMS OF "INDULGENCES" WILL BE IN USE

CATEGORY: BEING FULFILLED

This may sound a bit strange, since we generally think of indulgences as being the cause of Martin Luther's coming out in opposition to the dominant church in his life. Basically, indulgences were "payments in advance" for sins that were going to be committed. It was a source of much revenue for his church, and he was repulsed by the hypocrisy of it. So what form do indulgences take in our day, the last days? Mormon prophesied it as follows (bold added for emphasis):

Mormon 8:32

32 Yea, it shall come in a day [*the last days*] when **there shall be churches built up that shall say: Come unto me, and for your money you shall be forgiven of your sins**.

At first glance, this looks like the same practice that repulsed Martin Luther. But, when we look at it in context of our modern times, we see several "versions" of indulgences actively being offered and practiced in our day. For example, one verse informs us that congregants would hire teachers for their congregations who would teach the things they wanted to hear (bold added for emphasis):

> 2 Timothy 4:3
> 3 For the time will come when they will not endure sound doctrine; but after their own lusts shall **they heap to themselves teachers, having itching ears**;

In other words, people would hire teachers for their congregations who would have "itching ears," meaning that they would listen carefully to detect what would be pleasing to those paying their salaries and then teach accordingly. The Apostle Paul warned Timothy to be on the alert for this in his day. We see it in our day. Joseph Smith was told that, in his day, "they teach for doctrines the commandments of men, having a form of godliness, but they deny the power thereof" (Joseph Smith—History 1:19). The "commandments of men," in this context, would be the things members of a congregation want to hear that would seemingly give official religious sanction to their behaviors that violate the commandments of God.

It is indeed a common practice now among various organized churches to hire ministers who preach what the people want to hear. If they do not comply, they are fired and others hired in their place. Thus, we see many churches whose ministers teach that premarital sex is permissible, that practicing homosexual behavior is approved of God, that activities that violate the Sabbath are just fine, and the list goes on and on. It all boils down to paying for teachings in church that, in their minds, essentially make sins no longer sins, and thus, in effect, forgive sins for money.

SIGN 39
THE SUN WILL BE DARKENED AND THE MOON WILL BECOME AS BLOOD
CATEGORY: ?

For many years, as I spoke on the signs of the times at Know Your Religion lectures, Education Week, forums and in classes, I suggested to my students that we would be wise not to define nor to categorize this particular sign of the times. My reason for such thinking was that I had never heard a prophet even explain this prophecy, let alone say whether or not it had happened or was yet to be fulfilled. Then, in October general conference of 2001, in the Saturday morning session, President Gordon B. Hinckley said something that changed my mind on this prophecy. He taught (bold added for emphasis):

> The era in which we live is the fulness of times spoken of in the scriptures, when God has brought together all of the elements of previous dispensations. From the day that He and His Beloved Son manifested themselves to the boy Joseph, there has been a tremendous cascade of enlightenment poured out upon the world. The hearts of men have turned to their fathers in fulfillment of the words of Malachi. **The vision of Joel has been fulfilled wherein he declared**:

> Joel 2:28–32
> 28 And it shall come to pass afterward, that I will pour out my spirit upon all flesh; and your sons and your daughters shall prophesy, your old men shall dream dreams, your young men shall see visions:
> 29 And also upon the servants and upon the handmaids in those days will I pour out my spirit.

MOON TURNING TO BLOOD

30 And I will shew wonders in the heavens and in the earth, blood, and fire, and pillars of smoke.

31 **The sun shall be turned into darkness, and the moon into blood, before the great and the terrible day of the Lord come.**

32 And it shall come to pass, *that* whosoever shall call on the name of the Lord shall be delivered: for in mount Zion and in Jerusalem shall be deliverance, as the Lord hath said, and in the remnant whom the Lord shall call. ("Living in the Fulness of Times," *Ensign*, November 2001, 4)

As soon as our living prophet said that these words of Joel have been fulfilled, I accepted it on faith and continue to do so. However, I can also accept that faithful Saints can legitimately wonder whether or not President Hinckley was referring to some but not all of the verses in that scripture block. Until a prophet explains further, we will have to wait for additional understanding and clarification.

Other prominent references point to the sun being darkened and the moon being turned to blood. For instance (bold added for emphasis):

Matthew 24:29
29 Immediately after the tribulation of those days shall the **sun** be **darkened**, and the **moon shall not give her light**, and the stars shall fall from heaven, and the powers of the heavens shall be shaken:

Revelation 6:12
12 And I beheld when he had opened the sixth seal, and, lo, there was a great earthquake; and **the sun became black as sackcloth** of hair, and **the moon became as blood**;

As mentioned above, we will have to wait for a prophet to reveal the exact meaning of these words to us. In the meantime, many people have felt that this prophecy has to do with air pollution in the last days. However, there have no doubt been events in centuries past, such as earthquakes, volcanoes, and the like that would have caused great air pollution and thus darkened the sun and made the moon to appear as blood. And so, air pollution is probably not a good possibility for the fulfillment of this prophecy as a sign of the times.

Perhaps we need to rethink, after President Hinckley's words on this subject, and begin to wonder if the meaning could be more symbolic than literal. For example, in our gospel vocabulary, we often use the sun to symbolize celestial glory, heaven, light from above, and so forth. The moon often symbolizes terrestrial glory, which implies good and honorable people (see D&C 76:75) who keep the law of chastity, have moral integrity, etc. One possibility, though certainly not authoritative, could be that the sun's being darkened and the moon's becoming as blood would symbolize gross spiritual darkness in the final days preceding the Second Coming. It may symbolize that the vast majority of the inhabitants of the earth will cease to live according to either celestial or terrestrial law. It could mean that throughout the world there will be an overflowing flood of indulging in filth and spiritual pollution, adultery, fornication, homosexuality, pornography, dishonesty, crudeness, selfishness, and so on. And it could possibly be that President Hinckley's statement about Joel's prophecy includes the meaning that the wickedness on earth has now reached the point of fulfilling that prophecy, in addition to the fact that the Lord's Spirit is being poured out upon "all flesh." Whatever the case, for the purposes of this book, we will leave a question mark on this sign of the times, and we will look forward to additional authoritative instruction on the matter.

SIGN 40

THE CHURCH WILL BECOME WELL KNOWN THROUGHOUT THE EARTH

CATEGORY: BEING FULFILLED

This specific prophecy ties in closely with the prophecy that the Church will grow to fill the whole earth (Daniel 2:35). One of the things necessary for Daniel's prophecy to come to pass is having the Church itself and its members become better and better known. This prepares the way for the actual organization of the Church to become established throughout the world, bringing with it the true doctrines and priesthood ordinances that open the doors to salvation and exaltation. In the preface to the Doctrine and Covenants (section 1), the Lord revealed (bold added for emphasis):

> D&C 1:30
> 30 And also those to whom these commandments were given, might have power to lay the foundation of this church, and to **bring it forth out of obscurity** and out of darkness, the only true and living church upon the face of the whole earth, with which I, the Lord, am well pleased, speaking unto the church collectively and not individually—

"Obscurity" means "hardly known," "barely recognized," "of little or no consequence," and so forth. In our day, we thrill to see recognition of the Church increasing dramatically in many ways, including through the Tabernacle Choir, the "Mormon Helping Hands" yellow shirts seen on members helping with disaster cleanup, the Church's humanitarian aid, the broadcasting of general conference throughout the world, the great increase in missionaries, political candidates and public servants who are known as members of the Church, and myriad other ways, large and small, through with the

Church is becoming well-known. Mormon Ads and other uses of the media reach out to the world with greatly increasing positive impact. Individuals and families who faithfully live the gospel are quietly bringing the Church "out of obscurity" in their neighborhoods, communities, workplaces, schools, and wherever they go.

The fulfillment of this prophecy is a prerequisite series of concurrent events accompanying the spreading of the gospel to fill the whole earth, and we are privileged to watch and participate as it continues to gain momentum.

SIGN 41

DISEASES, PLAGUES, AND PESTILENCES WILL SWEEP THE EARTH IN SPITE OF MEDICAL ADVANCES AND TECHNOLOGY

CATEGORY: BEING FULFILLED

Advances in medical science are, for the most part, wonderful and serve as a great blessing from God to His children here on earth. Many of us owe our lives or the quality of life we enjoy to medical advances that have been achieved in our day. We owe a great debt of gratitude to the tireless efforts and great skill of medical practitioners who have dedicated their lives to curing disease and taking care of their patients.

However, in spite of all the advances in medical science, this sign of the times prophesies that great plagues, diseases, and pestilences will sweep the earth. God will not be mocked. The Prophet Joseph Smith spoke of the wicked throughout the world and warned what would happen if they reject the gospel and fight against truth (bold added for emphasis):

> D&C 109:30
> 30 And that all their works may be brought to naught, and **be swept away by the hail,**

THEY THAT **BELIEVE**
NOT IN **HIM** SHALL
BE DESTROYED, BOTH
BY **FIRE**, AND BY
TEMPEST, AND BY
EARTHQUAKES,
AND BY
BLOODSHEDS, AND
BY **PESTILENCE**,
AND BY **FAMINE**.

2 NEPHI 6:15

and by the judgments which thou wilt send upon them in thine anger, that there may be an end to lyings and slanders against thy people.

Jacob spoke of this sign of the times, referring to Isaiah's prophecy (bold added for emphasis):

2 Nephi 6:14–15
14 And behold, according to the words of the prophet, the Messiah will set himself again the second time to recover them (the restoration in the latter days); wherefore, he will manifest himself unto them in power and great glory, unto the destruction of their enemies, when that day cometh when they shall believe in him; and none will he destroy that believe in him.

15 And they that believe not in him shall be destroyed, both by fire, and by tempest, and by earthquakes, and by bloodsheds, and by pestilence, and by famine. And they shall know that the Lord is God, the Holy One of Israel.

In the Doctrine and Covenants, the Lord tells us (bold added for emphasis):

D&C 84:97
97 And plagues shall go forth, and they shall not be taken from the earth until I have completed my work, which shall be cut short in righteousness—

D&C 87:6
6 And thus, with the sword and by blood-shed the inhabitants of the earth shall mourn; and with famine, and plague, and earthquake, and the thunder of heaven, and the fierce and vivid lightning also, shall the inhabitants of the earth be made to feel the wrath, and indignation, and chastening hand of an Almighty God, until the consumption decreed hath made a full end of all nations;

In the Pearl of Great Price, the Savior repeats this prophecy of the last days (bold added for emphasis):

Joseph Smith—Matthew 1:29
29 Behold I speak for mine elect's sake; for nation shall rise against nation, and kingdom against kingdom; there shall be famines, and pestilences, and earthquakes, in divers places.

In conclusion, it is clear from these scriptural passages and others that God will not be mocked by people who seemingly get away with blatant sin because of medical advances. Rather, He will send plagues, pestilences, diseases, and so forth, to sweep the earth in an effort to get people to use their agency to repent and return to Him. We will finish our consideration of this sign of the times with a verse from the Doctrine and Covenants (bold added for emphasis):

D&C 45:31
31 And there shall be men standing in that generation, that shall not pass until they shall see an overflowing scourge; for a desolating sickness shall cover the land.

By the way, the phrase "desolating sickness" in verse 31, above, doesn't necessarily have to be limited to just one form of disease or plague. In fact, it may also include spiritual darkness, which is the worst form of disease.

SIGN 42
KNOWLEDGE, SCIENCE, AND TECHNOLOGY WILL INCREASE DRAMATICALLY
CATEGORY: BEING FULFILLED

This is a fascinating sign of the last days. We indeed live in a day of unprecedented advances in all forms of knowledge and technology. President Hinckley spoke of this during the

Saturday morning session of the October 2001 general conference of the Church:

> There has been more of scientific discovery during these years than during all of the previous history of mankind. Transportation, communication, medicine, public hygiene, the unlocking of the atom, the miracle of the computer, with all of its ramifications, have blossomed forth, particularly in our own era. During my own lifetime, I have witnessed miracle after wondrous miracle come to pass. ("Living in the Fulness of Times," *Ensign*, November 2001, 4)

We find this prophecy of a latter-day increase in knowledge in the book of Daniel (bold added for emphasis):

> Daniel 12:4
> 4 But thou, O Daniel, shut up the words, and seal the book, *even* to **the time of the end**: many shall run to and fro, and **knowledge shall be increased.**

It even sounds like the phrase "many shall run to and fro" could refer to modern transportation and the resulting hustle and bustle of society in the last days.

It is interesting to pay attention to the timing when so many of these advances have come onto the scene. If you were to take a large chalkboard and begin to plot inventions from about 4,000 BC and continue to the present day, putting one dot on the board for each invention that advanced the status of mankind, you would find very few dots until about the time of the restoration of the gospel through Joseph Smith. Then, the frequency of advances in all sorts of endeavor would begin to increase dramatically. Just a few examples follow:

1840s — The discovery of germs by Dr. Semmelweis, Vienna, Austria

1846 — The first large-scale demonstration of general anesthesia, Massachusetts General Hospital, Boston

1868 — The typewriter

1869 — The telegraph

1876 — The telephone

1877 — The phonograph

1877 — Arc welding

1879 — The lightbulb

1880s — The Kodak camera

1880 — The pneumatic tire

1884 — The fountain pen

1888 — The ballpoint pen

1890s — The automobile

1890s — Silent movies

1890s — Marconi's radio crystal

1891 — Forerunner of the zipper

1893 — Half-tone printing

1898 — Photographic paper

1899 — Magnetic tape recorder

1903 — Wright Brother's airplane

1907 — Radio tube

1915 — Tungsten filament for light bulbs, etc.

1920 — Talking movies

1934 — Television

1937 — Jet engine

1939 — Computer

1947 — Transistor

And if we were to attempt to continue the list up to the current day, it would be a virtually impossible task. In Doctrine and Covenants 88:73, the Lord said, "I will hasten my work in its time," and indeed He has inspired the means and technology to hasten the spread of the gospel throughout the world. If you look at the brief and limited list of inventions given above, you will note that many of the inventions have to do with communication and transportation. Certainly, this is part of the grand plan of the Lord to enable the true gospel to be preached to the entire world before the end comes (Matthew 24:14).

In the April 2013 general conference of the Church, Elder Richard G. Scott reminded us how valuable the technological advances of our day can be to us, when properly used and controlled. He said:

> You live in a world where technological advances occur at an astounding pace. It is difficult for many of my generation to keep up with the possibilities. Depending on how technology is used, these advances can be a blessing or a deterrent. Technology, when understood and used for righteous purposes, need not be a threat but rather an enhancement to spiritual communication.
>
> For example, many of us have a personal electronic device that fits into our pocket. We are seldom without its company; we may refer to it many times a day. Unfortunately, these devices can be a source of filth and wasted time. But, used with discipline, this technology can be a tool of protection from the worst of society.
>
> Who could have imagined not very many years ago that the full standard works and years of general conference messages would fit into your pocket? Just having them in your pocket will not protect you, but studying, pondering, and listening to

them during quiet moments of each day will enhance communication through the Spirit.

> Be wise in how you embrace technology. Mark important scriptures on your device and refer back to them frequently. If you young people would review a verse of scripture as often as some of you send text messages, you could soon have hundreds of passages of scripture memorized. Those passages would prove to be a powerful source of inspiration and guidance by the Holy Ghost in times of need.

SIGN 43

"THE WEAK THINGS OF THE EARTH SHALL BREAK DOWN THE MIGHTY AND STRONG ONES"

CATEGORY: BEING FULFILLED

This prophecy, found in the Doctrine and Covenants, is often used in reference to our humble missionaries, young and old, who serve throughout the world. Through diligent effort and the hand of the Almighty, they succeed in moving the work of the Lord forward against all odds. "Mighty and strong" forces rally against them; nevertheless, they are broken down and moved out of the way, allowing the Church with the saving doctrines and ordinances of the restored gospel to continue spreading. "Mighty and strong," highly educated individuals have their hearts melted by the simple and humble testimony born by a missionary. Government hazing and obstruction of missionary work is mandated to cease by sympathetic officials in power. The Lord said (bold added for emphasis):

D&C 1:12, 17–19
12 Prepare ye, prepare ye for that which is to come, for the Lord is nigh;

17 Wherefore, I the Lord, knowing the calamity which should come upon the

inhabitants of the earth, called upon my servant Joseph Smith, Jun., and spake unto him from heaven, and gave him commandments;

18 And also gave commandments to others, that they should proclaim these things unto the world; and all this that it might be fulfilled, which was written by the prophets—

19 **The weak things of the world shall come forth and break down the mighty and strong ones**, that man should not counsel his fellow man, neither trust in the arm of flesh—

Years ago, the wife of a former mission president in a Latin American mission spoke for Friday devotional at the institute of religion where I was teaching. She spoke of how the missionary work in a large city was being virtually brought to a halt by government bureaucrats and petty officials. The "mighty and strong" were standing in the way of the work of the Lord. The mission president had notified the missionaries in that city that he was pulling them out and sending them to another area that would be more fruitful. With three days to go before their transfer, the elders were tracting, but with little heart in it, just to try to feel that they were being faithful missionaries. Surprisingly, they were invited in by a man in a large home with servants. He was cordial and showed genuine interest in their message.

The missionaries avoided the normal commitment questions usually included in the discussion because they knew they would not be around to follow through. When they determined to excuse themselves and leave, the man asked them when they could come back and tell him more. They explained that they were being transferred and would not be able to make a return appointment. He insisted on being told the reason, so they briefly explained why they were being taken out

of the city. Upon hearing of the problem, he informed them that they would have no more such difficulties. He was the highest ranking official in that city and would issue and enforce orders that there was to be no more obstruction of their missionary efforts there. They excitedly called their mission president. They were allowed to remain and a great deal of success followed.

SIGN 44

THE RIGHTEOUS WISE WILL HAVE EXTRA OIL FOR THEIR LAMPS

CATEGORY: BEING FULFILLED AND YET TO BE FULFILLED

This is a rather encouraging sign of the times for thoroughly committed, faithful members of the Church (the "wise virgins") who are striving to have a supply of extra oil for their lamps, as explained in the Parable of the Ten Virgins, found in Matthew. The extra oil fortifies them so they can truly "endure to the end." The foolish virgins are likewise members of the Church, but are less committed, sometimes less active, on again, off again members. They believe the Church is true, believe in the Second Coming, and so forth, but, for now, are not willing to make full commitment to the gospel top priority in their lifestyles. Obviously, this sign of the times is now underway. It is being fulfilled in the lives of active, faithful members of the Church. But, its ultimate fulfillment is yet in the future and will be finally fulfilled at the time of the actual coming of Christ, when the righteous Saints, who have extra oil for their lamps are "caught up to meet him" (D&C 88:96.) Let's look at the Parable of the Ten Virgins (bold added for emphasis):

THE WEAK THINGS
OF THE WORLD
SHALL COME FORTH
AND BREAK
DOWN THE MIGHTY
AND STRONG ONES.

D & C   1:19

Matthew 25:1–13

1 Then shall the kingdom of heaven be likened unto ten virgins [*members of the Church, see McConkie,* Doctrinal New Testament Commentary, *Vol. 1, 684–685*], which took their lamps, and went forth to meet the bridegroom [*the Savior, when He arrives for the Second Coming*].

2 And five of them were wise, and five were foolish.

3 They that were foolish took their lamps, and **took no oil with them**:

4 But **the wise took oil in their vessels with their lamps**.

5 While the bridegroom tarried, they all slumbered and slept.

6 And at midnight there was a cry made, Behold, the bridegroom cometh; go ye out to meet him.

7 Then all those virgins arose, and trimmed their lamps.

8 And the foolish said unto the wise, Give us of your oil; for our lamps are gone out.

9 But the wise answered, saying, Not so; lest there be not enough for us and you: but go ye rather to them that sell, and buy for yourselves.

10 And while they went to buy, the bridegroom came; and they that were ready went in with him to the marriage: and the door was shut.

11 Afterward came also the other virgins, saying, Lord, Lord, open to us.

12 But he answered and said, Verily I say unto you, I know you not [*JST:"Ye know me not"*].

13 Watch therefore, for ye know neither the day nor the hour wherein the Son of man cometh.

As you can see from reading the parable, all ten virgins had oil in their lamps. But the five wise took extra olive oil in flasks with which to refill their lamps when the initial supply in the lamp itself ran out. All ten were expecting the Second

Coming. But it took longer to come than they expected. The five foolish did not have the extra reserves of spiritual strength and faithful deeds to endure to the end and thus be found worthy to meet the Bridegroom in person.

So the question becomes, how do we get extra reserves of oil for our lamps—in other words, for our lives? The opportunities are all around us. Faithfully attending church, accepting and fulfilling callings, personal scripture study, prayer, paying tithes and offerings, temple attendance, honesty and integrity in our personal and public lives, etc. We obtain wonderful quantities of oil for our lamps as we attend general conference, either in person or via the media, and then read and reread these powerful messages of the Lord's servants. Through reading and studying the Church magazines and the *Church News*, we find abundant supplies of additional oil that help keep us on the "strait and narrow path" (1 Nephi 8:20) by enlarging our souls and creating in us light and wells of strength to withstand the increasing pressures and distractions of the prophesied last days wickedness that surrounds us. Being nice to those around us is also an exceptionally good source of extra oil for our lamps.

SIGN 45

WARS AND RUMORS OF WARS WILL BECOME NORMAL LIFE

CATEGORY: BEING FULFILLED

This prophecy seems to indicate that wars and rumors of impending wars will become so commonplace that people will hardly pay any attention to them in the news. They will go about their daily lives and only particularly notice especially spectacular war news or those incidents that directly affect them. This is a much-prophesied sign of the times. We will give just a few of the many scripture references for this sign (bold added for emphasis).

Matthew 24:6
6 And ye shall hear of **wars and rumours of wars**: see that ye be not troubled: for all *these things* must come to pass, but the end is not yet.

Joseph Smith—Matthew 23
23 Behold, I speak these things unto you for the elect's sake; and you also shall hear of **wars, and rumors of wars**; see that ye be not troubled, for all I have told you must come to pass; but the end is not yet.

D&C 45:26
26 And in that day shall be heard of **wars and rumors of wars**, and the whole earth shall be in commotion, and men's hearts shall fail them, and they shall say that Christ delayeth his coming until the end of the earth.

Several years ago, I read in the newspaper that there were fifty-three declared wars going on at that time in various places throughout the world, plus many undeclared wars. I don't know how many there are today, but I suspect that there are many more than that. Perhaps one of our challenges as children of God living in such conditions in the last days is to avoid becoming callous to human suffering around us.

SIGN 46

THE LAST DAYS' SCOURGES OF THE LORD WILL INCREASE RIGHT UP TO THE SECOND COMING

CATEGORY: BEING FULFILLED

Some people have wondered whether or not there would be a period of peace upon the earth that would prepare the way and lead up to the Second Coming. According to the Doctrine and Covenants, such will not be the case. Rather, plagues, scourges, and calamities will be poured out with increasing intensity and frequency right up until the Savior comes. This is an ongoing sign of the times that is taking place all around us. It is an obvious witness that the scriptures are true, that there is a God, and that His word is being fulfilled. We see it consistently and relentlessly on the news. The Lord said (bold added for emphasis):

D&C 84:96–97
96 For I, the Almighty, have laid my hands upon the nations, **to scourge them for their wickedness**.

97 And plagues shall go forth, and **they shall not be taken from the earth until I have completed my work**, which shall be cut short in righteousness—

The Lord warned in the Doctrine and Covenants, section 88, verses 88–92, that, as people in the last days continue to ignore the gentle voice of warning of the missionaries, leaders, and members of the Church, He will, in effect, "turn up the volume" with scourges to get their attention. He said (bold added for emphasis):

D&C 88:89–91
89 For **after your testimony** cometh the testimony of earthquakes, that shall cause groanings in the midst of her, and men shall fall upon the ground and shall not be able to stand.

90 And also cometh the testimony of the voice of thunderings, and the voice of lightnings, and the voice of tempests, and the voice of the waves of the sea heaving themselves beyond their bounds.

91 And all things shall be in commotion; and surely, men's hearts shall fail them; for fear shall come upon all people.

NATURAL DISASTERS
WILL ABOUND

SIGN 47

FAMINES, EARTHQUAKES, TORNADOES, AND NATURAL DISASTERS WILL ABOUND

CATEGORY: BEING FULFILLED

This sign of the times is being fulfilled around the globe in obvious and observable ways. It too is mentioned in several scriptural references. We will use a reference from the Doctrine and Covenants for our example (bold added for emphasis):

D&C 45:33

33 And there shall be **earthquakes** also in divers places, and **many desolations**; yet men will harden their hearts against me, and they will take up the sword, one against another, and they will kill one another.

It is interesting to note that the Lord explains His reasoning behind sending these increased natural disasters upon the earth. In fact, He explains that these things follow on the heels of gentler approaches to bring His wayward children back to the blessings of the gospel. And when the inhabitants of the earth ignore these gentler approaches, the calm and fervent testimonies of members and missionaries sent throughout the earth to proclaim the message of peace and salvation through the gospel of Jesus Christ, then He uses more difficult-to-ignore ways to get their attention, that they might repent and come unto the Father through Christ (bold added for emphasis):

D&C 88:88–91

88 And **after your testimony** cometh wrath and indignation upon the people.

89 For **after your testimony** cometh the **testimony of earthquakes**, that shall cause groanings in the midst of her, and men shall fall upon the ground and shall not be able to stand.

90 And also cometh the **testimony of the voice of thunderings**, and the voice of **lightnings**, and the voice of **tempests**, and the voice of the **waves of the sea heaving themselves beyond their bounds.**

91 And **all things shall be in commotion**; and surely, men's hearts shall fail them; for fear shall come upon all people.

Occasionally, people are heard to suggest that there is actually not an increase in these natural disasters. Rather, it is just that we have more sensitive and better scientific instruments with which to measure and record these events. Some years ago, an acquaintance of mine wrote to a local meteorologist and asked him if this might be the case. His reply was definite. He said that there is definitely an increase both in frequency and intensity of these natural disasters. Something is going on. Since that time, there have been numerous articles in newspapers and magazines supporting the fact that nature seems to be more and more in commotion. This sign of the times is being fulfilled.

SIGN 48

ADDITIONAL SCRIPTURES WILL BE PUBLISHED

CATEGORY: FULFILLED AND YET TO BE FULFILLED

For all practical purposes, this prophecy has already been fulfilled. However, the day will come when the sealed portion of the Book of Mormon plates will be published. Also, under the direction of the First Presidency, additional scriptures could yet be published.

Isaiah foretold the coming forth of the Book of Mormon in the last days (bold added for emphasis):

2 Nephi 27:1 and 6

1 But, behold, **in the last days**, or in the days of the Gentiles—yea, behold all the nations of the Gentiles and also the Jews, both those who shall come upon this land and those who shall be upon other lands, yea, even upon all the lands of the earth, behold, they will be drunken with iniquity and all manner of abominations—

6 And **it shall come to pass that the Lord God shall bring forth unto you the words of a book** [*the Book of Mormon*], and they shall be the words of them which have slumbered.

Ezekiel likewise prophesied the coming forth of the Book of Mormon (bold added for emphasis):

Ezekiel 37:15–20

15 The word of the Lord came again unto me, saying,

16 Moreover, thou son of man, take thee one stick [*the Bible*], and write upon it, For Judah, and for the children of Israel his companions: then take **another stick** [*the Book of Mormon*], and write upon it, For Joseph, the stick of Ephraim, and for all the house of Israel his companions:

17 And join them one to another into one stick; and they shall become one in thine hand.

18 And when the children of thy people shall speak unto thee, saying, Wilt thou not shew us what thou meanest by these?

19 Say unto them, Thus saith the Lord God; Behold, I will take the stick of Joseph, which is in the hand of Ephraim, and the tribes of Israel his fellows, and will put them with him, even with the stick of Judah, and make them one stick, and they shall be one in mine hand.

20 And the sticks whereon thou writest shall be in thine hand before their eyes.

Verses 17 and 20, above, are being literally fulfilled as members of the Church throughout the world carry their LDS scriptures in their hand. Another fulfillment is found in the Topical Guide, Bible Dictionary, Index, and Guide to the Scriptures found in the back of our triple combination and quad. Yet additional fulfillment is found in a multitude of lesson manuals, Preach My Gospel, Strength of Youth, True to the Faith, Church magazines, and so forth where scripture references from the Bible and Book of Mormon, as well as other latter-day scriptures are bound together under one cover.

On April 23, 1834, the Lord revealed to Joseph Smith that additional scriptures, beyond the Bible and Book of Mormon, which were already in existence then, would be published to prepare His people for His coming. He said (bold added for emphasis):

D&C 104:58–59

58 And for this purpose I have commanded you to organize yourselves, even to **print my words, the fulness of my scriptures**, the revelations which I have given unto you, and which I shall, hereafter, from time to time give unto you—

59 **For the purpose of building up my church and kingdom on the earth, and to prepare my people for the time when I shall dwell with them, which is nigh at hand.**

This revelation resulted eventually in the publishing of the Doctrine and Covenants and the Pearl of Great Price.

SIGN 49
STRIKES, OVERTHROWING OF GOVERNMENTS, GANG WARFARE, VIOLENCE, AND DISRESPECT FOR AUTHORITY WILL INCREASE
CATEGORY: BEING FULFILLED

Elder Bruce R. McConkie summarized this sign of the last days as follows:

Strikes, anarchy, violence, to increase.— Not only do disasters and perils abound because of the unsettled conditions of the elements, but that same spirit of unrest is found among men themselves. The Lord's decree for this age is: "The whole earth shall be in commotion" (D&C 45:26). Signs of this commotion are seen daily in the untempered strikes and labor troubles that rock the economic world; in the violence, compulsion, and destruction of property that attend these strikes; in the unholy plots against our freedoms and free institutions; in the anarchy, rebellion, and crime that flow from great political movements which seek to destroy the agency of man and overthrow the governments of the world by force and violence. Communism and every other brutal and evil association or form of government are signs of the times. (*Mormon Doctrine*, 726)

Isaiah spoke of the disrespect for authority, for parents, and the resulting anarchy (lack of effective leadership in communities, nations, etc.), which would lead to the downfall of Jerusalem in ancient times. Satan will cause the same attitudes and trends to abound in the days directly preceding the Second Coming. Isaiah warned (bold added for emphasis):

Isaiah 3:5
5 And the **people shall be oppressed, every one by another**, and **every one by his neighbour**: the **child shall behave himself proudly against the ancient**, and **the base against the honourable**.

The Apostle Paul warned of these same conditions and prophesied that they would exist on a broad scale in the last days (bold added for emphasis):

2 Timothy 3:1–4
1 This know also, that **in the last days perilous times shall come**.

2 For men shall be lovers of their own selves, covetous, boasters, proud, blasphemers, **disobedient to parents**, unthankful, unholy,

3 Without natural affection, **trucebreakers**, false accusers, incontinent, fierce, **despisers of those that are good**,

4 **Traitors**, heady, highminded, lovers of pleasures more than lovers of God;

In the book of Helaman in the Book of Mormon, we find a very straightforward description of how governments, which were set up based on correct principles, can become corrupt, which leads to destructive strikes, anarchy, disrespect for good and honorable people and principles, and ultimately the destruction of society. Simply put, the steps are as follows:

1. The original government is established, based on the commandments of God.

2. Moral, righteous citizens endorse and support the government.

3. Over time, citizens become wicked and can't stand righteous laws.

4. The laws of the land are changed to support corrupt lifestyles of citizens.

5. People begin to use corrupt laws to support personal wickedness. They no longer ask, "What does the Bible say?" Rather, they ask, "Is it legal?"

6. Thus, corrupt laws corrupt people, and corrupt people continually pass additional corrupt laws until society becomes morally bankrupt.

7. People are no longer governed in their own hearts by the word of God and personal righteousness. Therefore, anarchy, violence, etc., lead to the destruction of society.

100 SIGNS

THIS KNOW ALSO, THAT

IN THE LAST DAYS PERILOUS TIMES SHALL COME.

2 TIMOTHY 3:1

This cycle of apostasy and corruption of governments originally established upon righteous principles is described in Helaman (bold added for emphasis):

> Helaman 4:21–23
>
> 21 Yea, they began to remember the prophecies of Alma, and also the words of Mosiah; and they saw that **they had been a stiff-necked people**, and that **they had set at naught the commandments of God**;
>
> 22 And that **they had altered and trampled under their feet the laws of Mosiah**, or that which the Lord commanded him to give unto the people; and they saw that **their laws had become corrupted**, and that **they had become a wicked people**, insomuch that they were wicked even like unto the Lamanites.
>
> 23 And **because of their iniquity** the church had begun to dwindle; and they began to disbelieve in the spirit of prophecy and in the spirit of revelation; and **the judgments of God did stare them in the face**.

As we watch this sign of the times being fulfilled, we would do well to follow the counsel of the Brethren who repeatedly have requested that we become involved in our own community and government entities in order to exert influence to stem the tide of corruption that is leading to the fulfillment of this prophecy.

SIGN 50

THERE WILL BE WIDESPREAD DISRESPECT FOR THAT WHICH IS SACRED AND HOLY

CATEGORY: BEING FULFILLED

Paul referred to this as "blasphemy," which means speaking and behaving disrespectfully regarding that which is sacred. He prophesied (bold added for emphasis):

> 2 Timothy 3:1–2
>
> 1 This know also, that in the last days perilous times shall come.
>
> 2 For men shall be lovers of their own selves, covetous, boasters, proud, **blasphemers**, disobedient to parents, unthankful, unholy,

No doubt you've seen much of the fulfillment of this sign of the times. Media is full of this kind of sacrilegious material. There seems to be competition among show hosts, commentators, celebrities, and others to see who can be more blatantly crude and immodest than the others. Open blasphemy and disrespect in media, entertainment, music, etc., for once-accepted Christian values and morals has become pretty much acceptable to the public. Previously held standards are completely ignored and trampled in the mire. Advertising targets younger and younger children.

SIGN 51

SEXUAL IMMORALITY, HOMOSEXUALITY, AND PORNOGRAPHY WILL ABOUND

CATEGORY: BEING FULFILLED

100 SIGNS

Many would wish that we could categorize this sign of the times as "fulfilled." However, since it will continue to get worse until the Savior comes, we must leave it as "being fulfilled." There are many warnings in the scriptures that this will be the case in the last days. It seems that the prophecy implies that sexual immorality will become so widespread and common in the last days that it will be considered to be the norm, and that anyone who does not get involved with these pernicious evils will be considered to be strange or abnormal.

The Apostle Paul speaks of this widespread evil that is to occur in the last days in his letter to

Timothy. We will use verses 1 and 6 (bold added for emphasis).

2 Timothy 3:1 and 6

1 This know also, that **in the last days perilous times shall come**.

6 For of this sort are they which creep into houses, and lead captive silly women laden with sins, **led away with divers lusts**,

In verse 6, above, Paul speaks of "divers lusts" (meaning various manifestations of lust) in prophesying about the last days. It is important for us to understand what he meant by this term. By the time he wrote this letter to Timothy, he had already defined a number of such lusts, including a variety of types of sexual immorality in more detail in his letter to the Romans. As we quote these verses from Romans, we will include some definitions of terms used by Paul in brackets, taken from *Strong's Exhaustive Concordance of the Bible*. Paul warned the Roman Saints as follows (bold added for emphasis):

Romans 1:24–31

24 Wherefore God also gave them up to uncleanness through the **lusts of their own hearts**, to **dishonour their own bodies between themselves** [*masturbation*]:

25 Who changed the truth of God into a lie, and worshipped and served the creature more than the Creator, who is blessed for ever. Amen.

26 For this cause God gave them up unto **vile affections**: for even **their women did change the natural use into that which is against nature** [*lesbianism*]:

27 And likewise also the **men, leaving the natural use of the woman, burned in their lust one toward another; men with men working that which is unseemly** [*homosexuality*], and receiving in themselves that recompence of their error which was meet.

28 And even as they did not like to retain God in *their* knowledge, God gave them over to a reprobate mind, to do those things which are not convenient [*things which are not proper*];

29 Being filled with all unrighteousness, **fornication**, wickedness, covetousness, maliciousness; full of envy, murder, debate, deceit, malignity; whisperers,

30 Backbiters, haters of God, despiteful, proud, boasters, inventors of evil things, disobedient to parents,

31 Without understanding, covenant breakers, **without natural affection**, implacable, unmerciful:

In "The Family: A Proclamation to the World," September 23, 1995, the First Presidency and Quorum of the Twelve Apostles included breaking of the law of chastity in the evils that would bring upon the world the calamities of the last days spoken of in scripture (bold added for emphasis):

We warn that **individuals who violate covenants of chastity**, who abuse spouse or offspring, or who fail to fulfill family responsibilities **will one day stand accountable before God**. Further, **we warn that the disintegration of the family will bring upon individuals, communities, and nations the calamities foretold by ancient and modern prophets.**

In spite of the warnings of our modern prophets, we watch as our society and the world in general become increasingly entangled in the evil web of pornography, sexual immorality, homosexuality, and a host of other evils associated with uncontrolled carnality, lust, and greed. We are no doubt seeing part of the fulfillment of a prophecy found in the Book of Mormon. Nephi says that in the last days, people will be "drunken with iniquity," in other words, out of control with wickedness. Surely, the huge emphasis on sexual immorality in our day is part of this sign of the times. Nephi tells us (bold added for emphasis):

<u>2 Nephi 27:1–2</u>

1 But, behold, **in the last days**, or in the days of the Gentiles—yea, behold all the nations of the Gentiles and also the Jews, both those who shall come upon this land and those who shall be upon other lands, yea, even **upon all the lands of the earth**, behold, **they will be drunken with iniquity and all manner of abominations—**

2 And when that day shall come they shall be visited [*punished*] of the Lord of Hosts, with thunder and with earthquake, and with a great noise, and with storm, and with tempest, and with the flame of devouring fire.

We read in the Doctrine and Covenants that sexual immorality, unrepented of, leads to the loss of the Spirit. When people lose the help of the Spirit, they become easy targets for the devil and his evil hosts. They lose their ability to reason clearly and to even see the dangers of sin.

<u>D&C 42:23</u>

23 And he that looketh upon a woman **to lust** after her shall deny the faith, and **shall not have the Spirit**; and if he repents not he shall be cast out.

One of the ways Satan is weakening people's resistance to the wiles of sexual immorality in our day is through the use of "politically correct" vocabulary to describe it. Such politically correct terminology is designed to take away any implication of wrongdoing or sin associated with immoral behavior. In the April 1996 general conference of the Church, Elder Neal A. Maxwell of the Quorum of the Twelve counseled members about such "politically correct" terminology when he said the following (bold added for emphasis):

The more what is **politically correct** seeks to replace what God has declared correct, the more ineffective approaches to human problems there will be, all reminding us of C. S. Lewis's metaphor about those who run around with fire extinguishers in times of flood. For instance, there are increasing numbers of victims of violence and crime, yet special attention is paid to the rights of criminals. Accompanying an ever-increasing addiction to pornography are loud alarms against censorship. Rising illegitimacy destroys families and threatens the funding capacities of governments; nevertheless, **chastity and fidelity are mocked**. These and other consequences produce a harsh cacophony. When Nero fiddled as Rome burned, at least he made a little music! **I have no hesitancy, brothers and sisters, in stating that unless checked, permissiveness, by the end of its journey, will cause humanity to stare in mute disbelief at its awful consequences**.

Ironically, as some people become harder, they use softer words to describe dark deeds. This, too, is part of being sedated by secularism! Needless abortion, for instance, is a **"reproductive health procedure,"** which is an even more "spongy expression" than **"termination of pregnancy"** (George McKenna, "On Abortion: A Lincolnian Position," *Atlantic Monthly*, Sept. 1995, 52, 54). "Illegitimacy" gives way to the wholly sanitized words **"nonmarital birth"** or **"alternative parenting"** (Ben J. Wattenberg, *Values Matter Most* [1995], 173). Church members will live in this wheat-and-tares situation until the Millennium. (Neal A. Maxwell, "Becometh As a Child," *Ensign*, May 1996, 68)

Several years ago, I began collecting "politically correct" terms used by the media and often required by government entities to describe what the word of the Lord calls sin and wickedness. A partial list follows:

Pro-choice: Implies agency is preserved in choosing abortion on demand, thus making an evil choice appear okay. Those who oppose this evil appear somehow anti-choice and thus, anti-God.

Free love: Again, this is an evil play on words, which tries to eliminate the concept of consequences.

Consenting adults: Implies an "okayness" if adults do it, even though it is a sin next to murder in seriousness (Alma 39:5).

Significant others: A sneaky description of one with whom adultery or fornication is committed.

Alternate lifestyles: Makes homosexuality, bisexuality, etc., look like harmless uses of agency.

Sexual preference: Treats homosexual behavior, etc., as a simple matter of personal preference, not sin.

Safe sex: As if illicit sex had no spiritual or emotional penalties at all.

Sexually active: Rather than calling them adulterers and fornicators, etc., thus attempting to remove any hint of wrongdoing or breaking God's commandments.

SIGN 52

MUCH BLOODSHED WILL PRECEDE THE SECOND COMING

CATEGORY: BEING FULFILLED

One of the signs of the times associated with the gross wickedness and spiritual darkness that will increase throughout the earth in the last days is that of widespread bloodshed. On April 2, 1843, the Prophet Joseph Smith prophesied the following (bold added for emphasis):

D&C 130:12
12 I prophesy, in the name of the Lord God, that the commencement of the difficulties which will cause **much bloodshed previous**

to the coming of the Son of Man will be in South Carolina.

We are seeing the fulfilling of this sign on a daily basis. The news is predominantly that of misery and bloodshed, with wars, killings, suicide bombings, mass graves discovered, murders, school shootings, ethnic cleansing with its associated mass murders, gang murders, use of chemical weapons for mass killings, domestic violence, and the reports go on and on.

By the way, it would be easy to get caught up in gloom and doom with all this going on in the world. But if we strive to do good, live the gospel, faithfully attend church, and fulfill our callings in the Church, we have peace, including peace of conscience. We surround ourselves with the fruits of the gospel in our lives. We associate with like-minded members of the Church and others of solid values and high standards, effectively creating for ourselves a buffer zone between us and the chaotic wicked world. We join with the Nephites spoken of in the Book of Mormon account of the "war years," recorded in Alma 43–62. They lived in an era of violence and warfare, strife and turmoil, yet we read (bold added for emphasis):

Alma 50:23
23 But behold **there never was a happier time among the people of Nephi**, since the days of Nephi, than in the days of Moroni, yea, even at this time, in the twenty and first year of the reign of the judges.

While these negative signs of the times can strengthen our testimonies because they too are observable witnesses that the words of God are being fulfilled, we need to be careful to avoid focusing and dwelling on them. Such behavior would certainly lead to discouragement and failure to "enjoy the journey," as President Thomas S. Monson has often counseled. It could lead us to get caught up in an alarmist mentality, which is certainly not the way our modern prophets and Apostles approach our day. The key is to use the fulfillment of negative signs to verify the truth of the gospel, but to focus on the positive signs of the times and enjoy watching their fulfillment. Such positive signs—the increasing numbers of missionaries, the rapid building of temples, the restoration of the gospel, the coming forth of the Book of Mormon, the restoration of the priesthood and keys of sealing, the rapidly accelerating gathering of Israel, and the translation of the scriptures and general conferences into a large number of languages—all combine to bring light, enjoyment, confidence, and a sense of purpose and optimism into our lives in these marvelous last days.

SIGN 53

THE DISINTEGRATION OF THE FAMILY WILL BRING PROPHESIED CALAMITIES IN THE LAST DAYS

CATEGORY: BEING FULFILLED

In our day, the First Presidency and Council of the Twelve Apostles gave this prophecy and warning on September 23, 1995. It is being fulfilled before our eyes. It is found in the second-to-last paragraph of "The Family: A Proclamation to the World." We will quote it here (bold added for emphasis).

> We warn that individuals who violate covenants of chastity, who abuse spouse or offspring, or who fail to fulfill family responsibilities will one day stand accountable before God. Further, **we warn that the disintegration of the family will bring upon individuals, communities, and nations the calamities foretold by ancient and modern prophets**.

You are no doubt aware of the constant efforts of local, state, national, and world governmental bodies to rework the definition of "family" to better fit the downward trends of modern society. The God-given definition of marriage between a man and a woman (Genesis 2:24) is under constant assault by Satan and his followers.

Most of the woes and ills of society can be traced to the lack of strong families where husband and wives lead in kindness and righteousness and teach their children the laws and ways of God that build strong communities and nations.

The Lord is constantly giving help, advice, and counsel through His chosen servants to enable us to build strong families. Perhaps you've noticed that the Lord is continuing to very clearly define "marriage" as between a man and a woman, and is providing much help for building strong families, including counsel and support for faithful Saints who find themselves in single-parenting situations.

On the other hand, because of the false ways and philosophies of the world, families continue to disintegrate all around us. Children are left without moral roots and guidance. Lawlessness, dishonesty, anarchy, corruption in business and government, selfishness, rampant self-indulgence, and sexual immorality are bringing unprecedented widespread personal and national calamities as prophesied.

SIGN 54

THE SPIRIT WILL STOP WORKING WITH THE WICKED

CATEGORY: BEING FULFILLED

When the Spirit stops working with the wicked, they lose their ability to think rationally or even begin to understand the need for personal righteousness. Righteous people are seen as their

100 SIGNS

I, THE LORD, AM ANGRY WITH THE WICKED; I AM HOLDING MY SPIRIT FROM THE INHABITANTS OF THE EARTH.

D & C 63:32

enemies and a threat to personal freedom and independence—a threat to the exercising of their agency. Without the Spirit, one's conscience has less and less influence, and evil deeds and cruelty become routine. In the Doctrine and Covenants, the Lord tells us that, already in 1831, He was holding His Spirit back because of widespread wickedness (bold added for emphasis):

D&C 63:32
32 I, the Lord, am angry with the wicked; **I am holding my Spirit from the inhabitants of the earth.**

As we read this verse, however, we must be careful to keep it in the larger context of all the scriptures. If we keep it in that larger context, we will see that His Spirit is indeed working with many people everywhere whose deeds and lifestyles have not put them beyond reach of its influence. (Bold added for emphasis:)

D&C 95:4
4 For the preparation wherewith I design to prepare mine apostles to prune my vineyard for the last time, that I may bring to pass my strange [*wonderful*] act, **that I may pour out my Spirit upon all flesh—**

Likewise, we read in the book of Joel that the Lord will pour out His Spirit upon all flesh prior to the Second Coming of Christ (bold added for emphasis):

Joel 2:28–29
28 And it shall come to pass afterward, that **I will pour out my spirit upon all flesh**; and your sons and your daughters shall prophesy, your old men shall dream dreams, your young men shall see visions:

29 And also upon the servants and upon the handmaids **in those days will I pour out my spirit.**

So, what is the main message of this sign of the times? Answer: That in the last days, because of

gross wickedness, great numbers of people will cease to feel the natural righteous emotions, feelings, common sense, wisdom, appreciation of beauty, nature, environment, worth of humans, and so forth, which are instilled and nourished by the Spirit. In place of these enlightened and enlightening attributes, they will be filled with the evil attributes and insensitivities listed by Paul in his warnings against wickedness found in several of his writings. We will consider two such references from his epistles here:

2 Timothy 3:1–7
1 This know also, that **in the last days perilous times shall come**.

2 For men shall be lovers of their own selves, covetous, boasters, proud, blasphemers, disobedient to parents, unthankful, unholy,

3 Without natural affection, trucebreakers, false accusers, incontinent, fierce, despisers of those that are good,

4 Traitors, heady, highminded, lovers of pleasures more than lovers of God;

5 Having a form of godliness, but denying the power thereof: from such turn away.

6 For of this sort are they which creep into houses, and lead captive silly women laden with sins, led away with divers lusts,

7 Ever learning, and never able to come to the knowledge of the truth.

Paul gives a similar but expanded list in his letter to the Roman members of the Church. We will include explanatory notes in brackets and bold for emphasis:

Romans 1:29–32
29 Being **filled with all unrighteousness** [*with all kinds of sins*], fornication [*sexual immorality*], wickedness [*depravity; see Strong's #4189*], covetousness, maliciousness [*meanness*]; full of envy, murder, debate [*strife, arguing*], deceit [*dishonesty*],

malignity [*plotting evil against others*]; whisperers [*gossipers*],

30 Backbiters [*slanderers; people who ruin other peoples' reputations*], haters of God, despiteful [*violent, overbearing*], proud, boasters, inventors of evil things [*thinking up more ways to be wicked*], disobedient to parents,

31 Without understanding [*foolish, stupid; see Strong's #0801*], covenantbreakers, without natural affection [*heartless*], implacable [*refuse to make covenants; see Strong's #0786*], unmerciful:

32 Who knowing the judgment of God [*they are sinning against knowledge*], that they which commit such things are worthy of death [*They know God's commandments and that people who commit such sins will die spiritually and will eventually be cut off from God*], not only do the same [*they not only commit such sins*], but have pleasure in them that do them [*they approve of and encourage others to commit such sins*]. [*In other words, members of the Church who have been taught the gospel and understand it, and still commit such sins, are very accountable. The effects on their spirituality are tragic. A major problem is that they not only commit such sins themselves, but they also encourage others to do the same.*]

JST—Romans 1:32
32 And some who, knowing the judgment of God, that they which commit such things are worthy of death, are inexcusable, not only do the same, but have pleasure in them that do them.

Perhaps you have had the disheartening experience of having a friend or loved one go inactive or leave the Church entirely and, consequently, have had firsthand experience with what happens when the Spirit stops working with someone due to lifestyle changes. When the individual was active in the gospel, you could have pleasant and productive discussions about shared values and the marvelous principles, doctrines, and applications of the plan of salvation. But now, after the person has been away from the Church for many years, you happen to run into him and, in the course of the conversation, it becomes apparent that in the intervening years, the standards of the gospel have not been a part of his life. To your dismay, it soon becomes evident that what is precious to you in the gospel has become a distant, hazy memory for him. Common talking points don't work anymore between you and your one-time good friend or relative.

I have had this happen on more than one occasion, and it has been startling and disappointing. It has driven home the value of remaining active in the Church and striving to keep the commandments in my life.

SIGN 55

PEACE WILL BE TAKEN FROM THE EARTH

CATEGORY: BEING FULFILLED

Again, as with the previous sign of the times, we must be careful to keep this sign in context. Obviously, peace is being taken from the earth. This sign is being fulfilled. There are wars and rumors of war. Violent civil wars rage on every hand. Gangs destroy the tranquility in once peaceful neighborhoods. Families are disintegrating. Violence and abuse are daily life for many. Movies make millions by making violence exciting. Even much of today's music is about violence and is violent itself. Mass media makes violence available everywhere. In the Doctrine and Covenants, the Lord tells us (bold added for emphasis):

D&C 1:35
35 For I am no respecter of persons, and will that all men shall know that the day speedily cometh; the hour is not yet, but is nigh at hand, when **peace shall be taken from the**

earth, and the devil shall have power over his own dominion.

As you can see in verse 35, above, when the Lord gave this revelation to Joseph Smith in 1831, He said, "The hour is not yet, but is nigh at hand," when this sign would begin to be fulfilled. Surely, it is underway now. But we must remember also that when we try our best to do right, there is peace in our hearts. When there is peace in our hearts, there is peace on earth for us. Also, there is wonderful peace in living among the Saints and in reading our scriptures and in creating righteous homes. In fact, the Lord provides great comfort in the following verse (bold added for emphasis):

D&C 1:36
36 And also **the Lord shall have power over his saints**, and shall reign in their midst, and shall come down in judgment upon Idumea, or the world.

Furthermore, the Lord reminds us of the peace and safety to be had in the congregations of the members of the Church (bold added for emphasis):

D&C 115:6
6 And that the **gathering together** upon the land of Zion, and **upon her stakes**, may be **for a defense, and for a refuge from the storm**, and from wrath when it shall be poured out without mixture upon the whole earth.

When we read the above-quoted scriptures, we come to the conclusion that, in the final days prior to the Second Coming, peace will largely be taken from the earth and its inhabitants. However, when we listen carefully to President Gordon B. Hinckley's counsel about being happy, as in the following quote, we soon realize that we live in a marvelous age, and that there can be much peace and beauty in our lives and in the world around us, when seen through the gift of the Holy Ghost.

> I do not know what we did in the preexistence to merit the wonderful blessings we enjoy. We have come to earth in this great season in the long history of mankind. It is a marvelous age, the best of all. As we reflect on the plodding course of mankind, from the time of our first parents, we cannot help feeling grateful. ("Living in the Fulness of Times," *Ensign*, November 2001, 4)

Likewise, when we listen to President Thomas S. Monson's repeated messages about "enjoying the journey," we realize that much depends on our attitude and faithfully living the gospel, when it comes to whether or not we, personally, have mostly peace in our lives. In the October 2008 general conference of the Church, he taught (bold added for emphasis):

> Let us relish life as we live it, **find joy in the journey**, and share our love with friends and family. One day each of us will run out of tomorrows.

SIGN 56

JERUSALEM WILL BE A "CUP OF TREMBLING" TO THOSE WHO ATTEMPT TO FIGHT AGAINST IT

CATEGORY: FULFILLED AND BEING FULFILLED

This sign of the times we can quite readily consider to be fulfilled. Israel has become a formidable military power, striking quickly and decisively against any who provoke its wrath. On the other hand, this prophecy continues being fulfilled on an almost daily basis. Therefore, we can go with either category on this one.

We should observe one caution when it comes to this prophecy. Many are inclined to say that all nations will be against Israel in the last days. A more careful reading of several of the prophecies about nations who fight against Israel in the final scenes before the Second Coming can lead us to understand that all nations will be involved with Jerusalem, "engaged at Jerusalem" (see heading to Zechariah, chapter 12, in LDS Bible). Thus, the prophecy that Jerusalem will be a "cup of trembling" applies to all nations who choose to fight against Israel. Let's look at some examples. First, a verse in Zechariah (bold added for emphasis):

Zechariah 12:2
2 Behold, **I will make Jerusalem a cup of trembling unto all the people round about, when they shall be in the siege both against Judah *and* against Jerusalem**.

The wording in Zechariah 12:3 and 9 leads us to understand that verse 2 (above) applies to nations who choose to fight against Israel. Verses 3 and 9 read as follows (bold added for emphasis):

Zechariah 12:3 and 9
3 And in that day will I make Jerusalem a burdensome stone for all people: all **that** burden themselves with it shall be cut in pieces, though all the people of the earth be gathered together against it.

9 And it shall come to pass in that day, *that* I will seek to destroy all the nations **that** come against Jerusalem.

The world has seen and continues to see dramatic evidence of the fulfillment of this prophecy. From a rational standpoint, it would be absurd to think that such a tiny nation as Israel, a scant 40 miles wide and 140 miles long (this varies from time to time, depending on political negotiations and agreements) could be the center of attention of the entire world and could wield military power that would intimidate much larger forces. As foretold by the Savior, in the following scripture reference, Israel has been trodden down by every

nation who desired to do so for about 2,000 years (bold added for emphasis):

Luke 21:24
24 And they shall fall by the edge of the sword, and shall be led away captive into all nations: and **Jerusalem shall be trodden down of the Gentiles, until the times of the Gentiles be fulfilled.**

Israel today has indeed become a terror to any nation who attacks it. It is indeed the fulfillment of prophecy. For instance, in June 1967, during what is known as the "Six-Day War," Israeli soldiers defeated a much larger enemy force and, among other things, retook Jerusalem.

Another example of the fulfillment of this prophecy may be found in the "Raid on Entebbe." Early in July 1976, my wife and I were in downtown Jerusalem climbing aboard a tour bus. We had noticed enthusiastic celebrating among people on the street, and asked our bus driver what was going on. He asked, "Haven't you heard?" We, of course, hadn't.

He went on to tell us of the rescue of Jewish hostages being held prisoners at the airport in Entebbe, Uganda, a rescue that had been completed that morning. According to him, a plane full of Jewish passengers had been commandeered by anti-Jewish terrorists who had taken them to Entebbe in Uganda, a country in eastern Africa. Having accomplished their deed, the terrorists mocked the nation of Israel and her citizens and made much political fodder out of the whole situation. Ultimately, the Jewish military determined to rescue the hostages.

They took three planes and flew the approximately 2,400 miles to Entebbe at night, flying so low as to be under radar range. They landed at the airport in Entebbe and took the hostages back after a brief firefight in which all but three or four hostages were saved. They quickly took off again and returned the beleaguered hostages to safety in Jerusalem. Such is the military status of Israel today. A prophecy fulfilled.

Israel continues to be mentioned virtually every day in the media. Again, just recently, when faced with a significant military threat, the response of its leaders was to say not to worry too much about them because they can take care of themselves. Israel's prominence on the stage of world politics continues to provide dramatic confirmation of the significance of the prophecies of God and the fact that He exists and all His words will be fulfilled (D&C 1:38).

SIGN 57

MANY WILL CLAIM THAT MIRACLES HAVE CEASED

CATEGORY: BEING FULFILLED

This sign of the times is just the opposite of the next sign listed in this chapter. Mormon warned that in the last days, many would claim that God no longer speaks to mankind and that miracles have ceased.

> 3 Nephi 29:6–7
> 6 Yea, **wo unto him that shall deny the revelations of the Lord, and that shall say the Lord no longer worketh by revelation, or by prophecy, or by gifts, or by tongues, or by healings, or by the power of the Holy Ghost!**
>
> 7 Yea, and **wo unto him that shall say at that day, to get gain, that there can be no miracle wrought by Jesus Christ**; for he that doeth this shall become like unto the son of perdition, for whom there was no mercy, according to the word of Christ!

Later, Mormon again foretold that the day would come, after the coming forth of the Book of Mormon and the restoration of the true church,

when many would claim miracles no longer take place.

> Mormon 8:26
> 26 And no one need say they shall not come, for they surely shall, for the Lord hath spoken it; for out of the earth shall they come, by the hand of the Lord, and none can stay it; and **it shall come in a day when it shall be said that miracles are done away**; and it shall come even as if one should speak from the dead.

In most of our discussions of the fulfillment of this prophecy, we tend to focus our attention on the teachings of other religions who claim that revelation has ceased and the scriptures are complete. Not long ago, I was having difficulty staying awake while driving so I tuned in to a Christian radio talk show. I have found that such stations often help keep me alert, either because of excellent discussions of Christian values, or because of false teachings that raise my ire and keep my mind busy countering their viewpoints. In this case, the host and guests adamantly taught that the cannon of scripture is complete, and thus there is no more revelation, including answers to prayer and manifestations from God through personal miracles. I was appalled! Many advocates of this point of view called in, offering strong opinions that this is indeed the case, stating that revelation, personal and otherwise, ceased with the Bible. They categorically said that no personal manifestations from God, including miracles, healings and intervention, protection, and so forth have taken place since the completion of the Bible. They went out of their way to deride and ridicule others who do not share this point of view. What a sad and damaging false belief and doctrine!

As stated above, most of our discussions on this topic focus on the beliefs and teachings of some

Christian religions. However, the fulfillment of prophecies that contain this sign of the times no doubt has a much broader application. We live in a day when skeptics of religion go to great lengths to discredit any belief in God. They replace the concept of divine intervention with a belief in pure coincidence. They teach that there is no life after death, no ultimate accountability. They teach that there is no such thing as absolute truth, replacing it with situational ethics. Such false teachings wreak havoc with society, commitment to family, moral integrity, and peace in general. Without a belief in God, in miracles, in accountability, and the stability that such beliefs foster, mankind is left to be "tossed to and fro, and carried about with every wind of doctrine, by the sleight of men, and cunning craftiness, whereby they lie in wait to deceive" (Ephesians 4:17).

Thus, in our day, the lack of belief in God results in widespread discounting or outright denying of miracles and other manifestations of the existence of God. It is a prominent sign of the times.

SIGN 58

MIRACLES WILL ABOUND

CATEGORY: BEING FULFILLED

This is a wonderful sign of the times, especially considering the predominantly wicked world of the last days that is the basis for many of the negative signs of the times. We see medical miracles, scientific marvels, divine intervention in rescuing people from natural disasters, personal and public miracles, technological miracles and discoveries, and a host of other miracles, public and private, which testify of a loving Heavenly Father and a loving Savior. Have you noticed that even though Satan and his evil followers are constantly destroying that which is good,

stirring things up and raging in the hearts of men and women in this final dispensation before the Second Coming, the power of God and His righteousness always have power to ultimately prevail? Thus, the power of God is concurrently being poured out upon all flesh as prophesied concerning these, the last days. Speaking of the last days prior to the Second Coming, Joel prophesied (bold added for emphasis):

> Joel 2:28
> 28 And it shall come to pass afterward [*meaning "in the last days," see heading to Joel 2 in your LDS Bible*], that **I will pour out my spirit upon all flesh**; and your sons and your daughters shall prophesy, your old men shall dream dreams, your young men shall see visions:

So many manifestations of this pleasant and encouraging sign of the times are all around us. We see a great number of miracles of healing. We note the relative speed at which our missionaries learn foreign languages, and often hear of the outright gift of tongues on special occasions. Miracles of conversion abound on a daily basis. The often simple and quiet miracle of receiving answers to prayers consistently bears witness of the tender care of a loving God.

The softening of hearts in those who formerly opposed participation in the gospel by family members is repeated in countless settings throughout the world. My wife and I saw this many times on our most recent mission as we served as CES missionaries teaching institute classes. For example, we had one student who joined the Church in his early teens. He was in an abusive home, and his mother and stepfather were very much against his joining the Church. He persisted and was finally baptized. The antagonism of his parents toward the Church and his faithful activity in it continued to fester. The members of his ward and his bishop were

I WILL POUR OUT MY SPIRIT UPON ALL FLESH; AND YOUR SONS AND YOUR DAUGHTERS SHALL PROPHESY.

JOEL 2:28

very supportive of him. One family especially picked him up each day and took him to early morning seminary as well as inviting them into their home often. He saw how a righteous home and family functioned and his testimony deepened.

With the help and encouragement of the bishop, he received his patriarchal blessing. When the envelope containing it arrived in the mail, his mother's anger against the Church boiled over. The envelope from the Church was another manifestation of his commitment to Mormonism and was the last straw. She quickly packed his things, purchased a one-way ticket to the city in another state where his biological father resided, and waited for him to come home from school. When he did, she met him at the door, told him he was no longer welcome there, handed him the envelope from the patriarch, the bus ticket, and his bags, and shut the door.

When he arrived to stay with his father, he was strictly forbidden to have any association with the Church in that city. For two long years, the only contact with the Church was reading and rereading his patriarchal blessing. He told us that one of the things he missed most was the sweet taste of the sacrament bread in his mouth. After the two years, his father's heart began to soften and he allowed his son to resume associating with the Church. Things progressed and he ended up attending a small university in the east and we met him as he attended institute classes that we were teaching.

Much to our delight, a year after our return home, we received word that he had received a mission call. Shortly before he flew out to an MTC in preparation for his foreign language mission, he called us and told us what had just taken place. He had determined to visit his sister and mother before he left. Much to his relief, hearts had been softened and he was welcomed with open arms.

His family attended church meetings with him and celebrated his mission call with a gathering in his honor. What a wonderful miracle! He now emails weekly to his mother and other relatives, along with a large number of admiring friends. He is a powerful servant of the Lord already, and his mission has just begun!

We witnessed other miracles of change of heart with many of our other students along with several nonmembers who were brought to class and to church by them. We witnessed similar miracles in the lives of students and other members who were striving to return to activity in the Church. Scenes like this are being repeated in settings throughout the world.

One example of the miracle of reactivation and recommitment took place several years ago when I was teaching in one of the Church's large institutes of religion in Utah. It was the beginning of the semester, about the second week of classes, when a student came into one of my classes a bit late. I interrupted my lesson to smile at him and welcome him to class, but he did not respond, and with a serious and somewhat sour face, he slumped into a desk on the front row. During the rest of the lesson, he glared at me and seemed not to respond to anything that was being taught and discussed. I planned on catching him at the end of class, but he slipped quickly out and I missed him. I thought to myself that he was one student I would not see in class again. I was wrong.

He came faithfully for the next two weeks, continuing at first to glare more than not but eventually started to have an inquisitive expression on his face. He sat between my teaching station and the classroom door and each day, he managed to slip quickly away at the end of class before I could catch him. Other students with questions and comments often precluded my getting over to him in time. Finally, at the end of the second week of class, he lingered afterward and asked if I had time to visit with him in my office. I did.

He expressed appreciation for the class and the Spirit that was felt strongly there and in the whole institute building. He told me that he was a returned missionary and lived in the far eastern part of the United States. After his mission, he had lapsed into inactivity and was enveloped in an attitude of skepticism and darkness, as far as the Church and life in general were concerned. During the next two years, he continued his downward slide, feeling at times that he had finally liberated himself from the fetters of the Church. He was pursuing a university education, and when occasionally asked by friends if he had ever considered going out to Utah to pursue his degree, he emphatically told them no, thinking to himself that surrounding himself again with members of the Church and their influence was the last thing he would ever consider doing.

Strangely, he ended up in Utah to pursue his degree at the university where I was teaching institute. He had no good explanation as to why he came west. He said it just happened. Some unexpected things fell into place and he simply came. He attended a semester and kept noticing a big building near campus with large numbers of students entering and leaving during breaks between classes. He was curious but did not take the time to check the building out. The signage on the building was not noticeable from his normal pedestrian routes.

Finally, at the beginning of his next semester, his curiosity got the best of him and he decided to investigate the building during a class break. He continued, telling me what happened next. He approached the south double doors to the building. As he opened the outside door, he was overwhelmed by a very strong and pleasant spirit. He told me that at that point, he said to

himself, "Whoa, this can't be for real. What is this?" He turned around and went back outside, deciding to try it again just to see if his mind was playing tricks on him or if there really was something to it.

He entered again and felt the same thing. With a grin on his face, he told me that he thought to himself that if the feeling was this strong between the double doors, what would it be like entering the foyer of the building? He entered, and as he was looking around, one of our young adult student council members was prompted to notice him, and she immediately walked over to him and welcomed him. She was cute. They chatted. He asked what building this was. She answered that it was the institute of religion. His resistance began to falter. She showed him around and gave him a class schedule. He decided to try attending a class and perhaps reconsider his inactive stance toward the Church.

He came to my class, still struggling with indecision, but liking the pleasant feeling and light that was gently flowing into his soul. It took him two more weeks to make up his mind to turn his life around. That was when he asked to see me after class. The miracle had begun and he returned to activity, relishing the cleansing power of the Atonement, experiencing a change of heart, and welcoming a new life of joy and optimism in the Church.

It is a day of miracles indeed! Perhaps one of the greatest miracles of all is that of a change of heart, a "new heart." In conjunction with the gathering of Israel in the last days, Ezekiel prophesied that those of Israel who would allow themselves to be gathered would have their old, stony heart replaced with a new heart (bold added for emphasis):

100
SIGNS

Ezekiel 36:24–28

24 For I will take you from among the heathen, and gather you out of all countries, and will bring you into your own land.

25 Then will I sprinkle clean water upon you, and ye shall be clean: from all your filthiness, and from all your idols, will I cleanse you.

26 **A new heart also will I give you**, and a new spirit will I put within you: and I will take away the stony heart out of your flesh, and I will give you an heart of flesh.

27 And I will put my spirit within you, and cause you to walk in my statutes, and ye shall keep my judgments, and do them.

28 And ye shall dwell in the land that I gave to your fathers; and ye shall be my people, and I will be your God.

Mormon, referring to the last days, spoke of "a God of miracles" (bold added for emphasis):

Mormon 9:11–19

11 But behold, **I will show unto you a God of miracles**, even the God of Abraham, and the God of Isaac, and the God of Jacob; and it is that same God who created the heavens and the earth, and all things that in them are.

12 Behold, he created Adam, and by Adam came the fall of man. And because of the fall of man came Jesus Christ, even the Father and the Son; and because of Jesus Christ came the redemption of man.

13 And because of the redemption of man, which came by Jesus Christ, they are brought back into the presence of the Lord; yea, this is wherein all men are redeemed, because the death of Christ bringeth to pass the resurrection, which bringeth to pass a redemption from an endless sleep, from which sleep all men shall be awakened by the power of God when the trump shall sound; and they shall come forth, both small and great, and all shall stand before his bar, being redeemed and loosed from this eternal band of death, which death is a temporal death.

14 And then cometh the judgment of the Holy One upon them; and then cometh the

time that he that is filthy shall be filthy still; and he that is righteous shall be righteous still; he that is happy shall be happy still; and he that is unhappy shall be unhappy still.

15 And now, **O all ye that have imagined up unto yourselves a god who can do no miracles**, I would ask of you, have all these things passed, of which I have spoken? **Has the end come yet? Behold I say unto you, Nay; and God has not ceased to be a God of miracles**.

16 Behold, **are not the things that God hath wrought marvelous in our eyes?** Yea, and who can comprehend the marvelous works of God?

17 Who shall say that it was not a miracle that by his word the heaven and the earth should be; and by the power of his word man was created of the dust of the earth; and **by the power of his word have miracles been wrought?**

18 And who shall say that Jesus Christ did not do many mighty miracles? And there were many mighty miracles wrought by the hands of the apostles.

19 And **if there were miracles wrought then, why has God ceased to be a God of miracles and yet be an unchangeable Being?** And behold, I say unto you he changeth not; if so he would cease to be God; and **he ceaseth not to be God, and is a God of miracles**.

When we couple the words of Mormon with the prophecy that miracles will abound in the last days, we have a wonderful continuing and increasing witness that God lives and His tender mercies, including the miracles of technology, medicine, transportation, and communication, will continue to increase in frequency and number as the Second Coming draws nigh.

SIGN 59

SECRET COMBINATIONS AND WORKS OF DARKNESS WILL PERMEATE SOCIETIES

CATEGORY: BEING FULFILLED

One of the signs of the signs of the times is that secret combinations and secret works of darkness, which devastated the Nephites, will permeate various nations and societies in the last days. Examples of secret combinations and the evil purposes of their adherents, found in the Book of Mormon, include (bold added for emphasis):

Helaman 2:8

8 And when the servant of Helaman had known all the heart of Kishkumen, and how **that it was his object to murder, and also that it was the object of all those who belonged to his band to murder, and to rob, and to gain power**, (and this was their secret plan, and their combination) the servant of Helaman said unto Kishkumen: Let us go forth unto the judgment–seat.

Helaman 6:21–23, 26

21 But behold, Satan did stir up the hearts of the more part of the Nephites, insomuch that they did unite with those bands of robbers, and **did enter into their covenants and their oaths**, that they would protect and preserve one another in whatsoever difficult circumstances they should be placed, **that they should not suffer for their murders, and their plunderings, and their stealings**.

22 And it came to pass that **they did have their signs, yea, their secret signs, and their secret words**; and this that they might distinguish a brother who had entered into the covenant, that whatsoever wickedness his brother should do he should not be injured by his brother, nor by those who did belong to his band, who had taken this covenant.

23 **And thus they might murder, and plunder, and steal, and commit whoredoms and all manner of wickedness**, contrary to the laws of their country and also the laws of their God.

26 Now behold, those secret oaths and covenants did not come forth unto Gadianton from the records which were delivered unto Helaman; but behold, **they were put into the heart of Gadianton by that same being who did entice our first parents to partake of the forbidden fruit**—

In the Book of Mormon, we read of what happened when the majority of the Nephites began supporting wicked leaders, many of whom were involved in these secret combinations. No doubt, we are seeing similar workings among many governments in the world today, as prophesied (bold added for emphasis):

Helaman 6:38–39

38 And it came to pass on the other hand, that **the Nephites did build them up and support them, beginning at the more wicked part of them, until they had overspread all the land of the Nephites**, and had seduced the more part of the righteous until they had come down to believe in their works and partake of their spoils, and to join with them in their secret murders and combinations.

39 And **thus they did obtain the sole management of the government, insomuch that they did trample under their feet and smite and rend and turn their backs upon the poor and the meek, and the humble followers of God**.

In a powerful testimony, President Ezra Taft Benson warned of secret combinations and works of evil in our day. He also testified that the power of God will strengthen the righteous and that they will ultimately come off triumphant. In the October 1988 general conference of the Church, he said (bold added for emphasis):

100 SIGNS

I testify that wickedness is rapidly expanding in every segment of our society. (See D&C 1:14–16; D&C 84:49–53.) It is more highly organized, more cleverly disguised, and more powerfully promoted than ever before. **Secret combinations lusting for power, gain, and glory are flourishing. A secret combination that seeks to overthrow the freedom of all lands, nations, and countries is increasing its evil influence and control over America and the entire world**. (See Ether 8:18–25.)

I testify that **the church and kingdom of God is increasing in strength. Its numbers are growing, as is the faithfulness of its faithful members. It has never been better organized or equipped to perform its divine mission**.

I testify that as **the forces of evil increase under Lucifer's leadership and as the forces of good increase under the leadership of Jesus Christ**, there will be growing battles between the two until the final confrontation. As the issues become clearer and more obvious, all mankind will eventually be required to align themselves either for the kingdom of God or for the kingdom of the devil. As these conflicts rage, either secretly or openly, the righteous will be tested. God's wrath will soon shake the nations of the earth and will be poured out on the wicked without measure. (See JS-H 1:45; D&C 1:9.) But **God will provide strength for the righteous and the means of escape; and eventually and finally truth will triumph** (See 1 Ne. 22:15–23). ("I Testify," *Ensign*, Nov. 1988, 86–87)

Several years ago, a colleague of mine was serving as a bishop in a ward in one of the western states. One of his counselors was with the FBI. As a result of one of the counselor's successful investigations into secret works of organized crime, a contract was put out on him that was to result in his death. The horror and reality of secret combinations in our day stared him directly in the face. Such contracts had a track record of complete success. Invoking the help of the Lord and soliciting the prayers of his friends, he "disappeared" for several weeks. When he finally returned, the contract had been cancelled and he was once again free to live a normal life with his family and serve openly in his Church calling and work responsibilities.

He told my friend, his bishop, what had transpired. He knew that the FBI and all other law enforcement agencies could not successfully protect him. As a result, he decided to risk all and go directly to the Mafia boss in the Chicago area who had issued the contract. Through a series of divine interventions, he found himself standing directly in front of this crime boss in his well-guarded office. The boss was incredulous that the FBI agent had made it to his office alive. Curiosity overrode his normal ego and killer instinct and he asked the bishop's counselor to explain to him what streak of insanity had inspired him to attempt to come directly to his headquarters. The counselor responded directly and simply, describing his love of his family and his certainty that, unless the contract were lifted, he faced imminent death. In a pure miracle, the heart of this hardened crime chief was softened. He informed the humble and courageous agent that the contract was cancelled as of that moment, instructed his guards to see that he got home safely, and dismissed him.

While the fulfillment of these prophecies that secret combinations and works of darkness, including active terrorism, subversion of democratic governments, and undermining of God-given individual freedoms, will indeed be an integral part of the world scene in the last days, we need to guard against becoming intimidated and depressed as a result. Indeed, we are reminded by our prophets, seers, and revelators that this is a wonderful time to be alive. Marvelous and encouraging signs of the times are all around us too. Nephi saw our day and assured us that the power of God will be wonderfully manifest in the lives of faithful members of the Church in the dispensation of the fulness of times (bold added for emphasis):

<u>1 Nephi 14:12–14</u>
12 And it came to pass that I beheld the church of the Lamb of God, and its numbers were few, because of the wickedness and abominations of the whore who sat upon many waters; nevertheless, I beheld that the church of the Lamb, who were the saints of God, were also upon all the face of the earth; and their dominions upon the face of the earth were small, because of the wickedness of the great whore whom I saw.

13 And it came to pass that I beheld that the great mother of abominations did gather together multitudes upon the face of all the earth, among all the nations of the Gentiles, to fight against the Lamb of God.

14 **And it came to pass that I, Nephi, beheld the power of the Lamb of God, that it descended upon the saints of the church of the Lamb, and upon the covenant people of the Lord, who were scattered upon all the face of the earth; and they were armed with righteousness and with the power of God in great glory.**

SIGN 60

PEOPLE WILL DENY THE POWER OF GOD

CATEGORY: BEING FULFILLED

Another sign closely tied in with the wickedness and spiritual emptiness prominent in the last days is the prophecy that large numbers will deny the power of God. This sign of the times was given by Moroni, as he finished the record of his father, Mormon, who had been killed in battle. Moroni prophesied of conditions in the last days that would clearly indicate that the coming of the Lord was drawing nigh (bold added for emphasis):

<u>Mormon 8:28</u>
28 Yea, it shall come **in a day when the power of God shall be denied**, and churches become defiled and be lifted up in the pride of their hearts; yea, even in a day when leaders of churches and teachers shall rise in the pride of their hearts, even to the envying of them who belong to their churches.

Paul alerted Timothy to this last days sign (bold added for emphasis):

<u>2 Timothy 3:1–5</u>
1 This know also, that in the last days perilous times shall come.

2 For men shall be lovers of their own selves, covetous, boasters, proud, blasphemers, disobedient to parents, unthankful, unholy,

3 Without natural affection, trucebreakers, false accusers, incontinent, fierce, despisers of those that are good,

4 Traitors, heady, highminded, lovers of pleasures more than lovers of God;

5 **Having a form of godliness, but denying the power thereof**: from such turn away.

There are many, many ways in which we can see the "power of God" being denied in our day. First, though, one of the ways in which it is clearly manifest to His people is that of continuing revelation to His chosen prophets upon the earth. Consider the power that radiates outward to the whole earth from the on-going revelation that attends general conferences. Think of the "power of God" felt by the children of Israel as Jehovah's own voice thundered the Ten Commandments down from Sinai for all to hear (Exodus 19:9). Consider the power of the preaching of Christ and His Apostles during New Testament times. The precedent for continuing revelation is clearly set in the Bible. Why should a loving God stop speaking to His children? Contrast the standard and precedent for continuing communication with His offspring (Acts 17:28–29) set by the Lord in the Bible to the prominent theme and doctrine among many Christian churches today that revelation has ceased, that the scriptures are complete, and that nothing can be added to the Bible. Nephi spoke of this (bold added for emphasis):

<u>2 Nephi 29:6–10</u>
6 Thou fool, that shall say: A Bible, we have got a Bible, and we need no more Bible. Have ye obtained a Bible save it were by the Jews?

7 Know ye not that there are more nations than one? Know ye not that I, the Lord your God, have created all men, and that I remember those who are upon the isles of the sea; and that I rule in the heavens above and in the earth beneath; and I bring forth my word unto the children of men, yea, even upon all the nations of the earth?

8 **Wherefore murmur ye, because that ye shall receive more of my word?** Know ye not that the testimony of two nations is a witness unto you that I am God, that I remember one nation like unto another? Wherefore, I speak the same words unto one nation like unto another. And when the two nations shall run together the testimony of the two nations shall run together also.

9 And I do this that I may prove unto many that I am the same yesterday, today, and forever; and that I speak forth my words according to mine own pleasure. And because that I have spoken one word ye need not suppose that I cannot speak another; for my work is not yet finished; neither shall it be until the end of man, neither from that time henceforth and forever.

10 Wherefore, **because that ye have a Bible ye need not suppose that it contains all my words; neither need ye suppose that I have not caused more to be written**.

Note the acknowledgments of the hand of God by the founding fathers of the United States as they hammered out the basic documents of our great nation under divine direction (see D&C 101:77–80). Contrast this with the mandates of our current laws of the land, which forbid mention of God and His laws and commandments in official public business. This is one of many prominent sad and significant ways of denying the power of God.

Another way of denying the power of God is to completely leave Him out of one's personal life. In our materialistic and self-centered societies today, it is all too common for the standards set forth in the scriptures to be totally ignored by men and women, families and companies, government entities, schools, universities, professors, media moguls, and public and private figures in general. In many cases, pressure is intentionally brought to bear to leave any mention of God and His word out of the picture. In other situations, tacit denying of God's power occurs by default, simply by leaving God and His influence completely out of conscious thought and actions.

You can no doubt think of many other ways in which this sign of the times is being literally fulfilled in our day.

SIGN 61
LEADERS OF CHURCHES AND TEACHERS RISE UP IN THE PRIDE OF THEIR HEARTS
CATEGORY: BEING FULFILLED

This is yet another facet of the gross wickedness that will engulf much of the world in the last days. Pride is indeed a root cause of much evil. It was the cause of the downfall of the people in the Book of Mormon (see D&C 20:9). It is the root cause of much of the evil we see in our day. It will lead the wicked to "burn as stubble" when the Savior comes in full glory (D&C 5:19; 2 Nephi 12:10, 19, and 21). It causes one to ignore or trample much that is good, in self and in others. It quickly opens the door wide for Satan's influence.

In the April 1989 general conference of the Church, President Ezra Taft Benson gave what has become known as a classic sermon on the topic of pride. Some excerpts from his talk follow:

> Most of us think of pride as self-centeredness, conceit, boastfulness, arrogance, or haughtiness. All of these are elements of the sin, but the heart, or core, is still missing.
>
> The central feature of pride is enmity—enmity toward God and enmity toward our fellowmen. Enmity means "hatred toward, hostility to, or a state of opposition." It is the power by which Satan wishes to reign over us.
>
> Pride is essentially competitive in nature. We pit our will against God's. When we direct our pride toward God, it is in the spirit of "my will and not thine be done." As Paul said, they "seek their own, not the things which are Jesus Christ's." (Philip. 2:21.)
>
> Our will in competition to God's will allows desires, appetites, and passions to go unbridled. (See Alma 38:12; 3 Ne. 12:30.) . . .
>
> Our enmity toward God takes on many labels, such as rebellion, hard-heartedness, stiff-neckedness, unrepentant, puffed up, easily offended, and sign seekers. . . .
>
> Another major portion of this very prevalent sin of pride is enmity toward our fellowmen. We are tempted daily to elevate ourselves above others and diminish them. (See Hel. 6:17; D&C 58:41.)
>
> The proud make every man their adversary by pitting their intellects, opinions, works, wealth, talents, or any other worldly measuring device against others. In the words of C. S. Lewis: "Pride gets no pleasure out of having something, only out of having more of it than the next man. . . . It is the comparison that makes you proud: the pleasure of being above the rest. Once the element of competition has gone, pride has gone" (*Mere Christianity*, New York: Macmillan, 1952, 109–10). ("Beware of Pride," *Ensign*, May 1989)

During my undergraduate years at a state university in Utah, I had a professor who couldn't quite resist the temptation to ridicule me for being a Mormon. It was a small class of just 13 or 14 students, and she was a good teacher. But one day she "rose up in the pride of her heart" as her disdain for Mormons and me as a recently returned missionary from the Austrian mission overcame her otherwise pleasant demeanor. Near the beginning of the quarter, she had had us all introduce ourselves, and she had asked questions to get better acquainted with each of us, so she knew somewhat about me. In the middle of this particular class discussion on classic literature, she suddenly looked directly at me and said, "David, I can't believe you spent all those months in Vienna pestering people rather than taking advantage of operas, museums, and all of the rich treasures available in that fabulous city!" I was somewhat taken aback by this sudden intense outburst of animosity, as were the other members of the class, some of whom were members of the Church and others who were not. I chose to simply smile and respond that I was sorry she felt that way but that was not the way I felt about it. The class continued and that seemed to be the end of it.

However, a few days later, she asked if I had time after class to visit with her. I did. She asked me to follow her downstairs to her office. I did. She sat me down in her office near her, at the rear of her desk, reached into the wide drawer in the center of the desk, took out a pack of cigarettes, extracted one, put it between her lips, and lit it. She then turned toward me and blew smoke directly in my face. I kept my composure and didn't react. She then leaned back in her chair and said she would like to ask me a question. I said that would be fine. She then asked me where our church came up with the name "Pearl of Great Price" for our small volume of scripture by that name. As it happened, I had been reading the New Testament in my personal scripture study just a few days before, so I was able to tell her it comes from the Savior's parable given in Matthew 13:45–46. She looked surprised, relaxed, smiled, and then said that she had asked a number of returned LDS missionaries the same question and I was the first who could answer it. Her animosity seemed to dissolve and the rest of the quarter went well.

This prophecy is no doubt also fulfilled in some measure as the Church gets considerable negative attention from various Christian churches whose ministers rise up in fiery sermons against us and our beliefs. Such negative attention is also heard often when LDS candidates run for political office. There are countless manifestations of the continuing and ongoing fulfillment of this prophecy. It will continue right up to the cleansing of the earth at the time of the Second Coming.

SIGN 62

MANY WILL OPENLY "APPROVE" GROSS SIN

CATEGORY: BEING FULFILLED

With the rapid dissemination of news by electronic media in our day, we are constantly appalled at the "approval" of gross sin, by example and word, especially by those in positions of power and influence. And many of the general public are quick to "jump on the bandwagon" and implement these perceived "permissions" for sin in their personal lives. We

see abortion on demand "approved." We see open acting out in homosexual relationships "approved" by celebrities, government legislative bodies, ministers in churches, and the media. Major Christian denominations have come out with public approval of premarital sex, as long as those involved are "in love."

By so doing, they have effectively "disapproved" the Bible, setting it aside as being less and less relevant in this last dispensation. Some years ago, during a summer school session for teachers in the Church Educational System, a presenter told us that he had recently come to the conclusion that, even though many Christian churches claim that we, as members of the Church, are not Christians and criticize us for saying that "We believe the Bible to be the word of God as far as it is translated correctly" (the eighth article of faith), in reality, we believe the Bible far better and more thoroughly than do our critics. His statement struck us as being wonderfully accurate and brought grins to our faces.

One way of "approving" sin is to simply say or believe that sin is not sin, or that sin is no longer sin. One of my students once asked if perhaps premarital sex is not that bad anymore since we have the means nowadays to prevent conception. The answer, of course, was that God's laws have not changed. Korihor taught his followers that there is no such thing as sin (bold added for emphasis):

Alma 30:17

17 And many more such things did he say unto them, telling them that there could be no atonement made for the sins of men, but every man fared in this life according to the management of the creature; therefore every man prospered according to his genius, and that every man conquered according to his strength; and **whatsoever a man did was no crime**.

As Moroni finished his father's record, he prophesied of the last days, saying that many will say that sin is not sin, that God will sustain them in their lifestyles, no matter what they do. He foretold (bold added for emphasis):

Mormon 8:31

31 Yea, it shall come in a day when there shall be great pollutions upon the face of the earth; there shall be murders, and robbing, and lying, and deceivings, and whoredoms, and all manner of abominations; when **there shall be many who will say, Do this, or do that, and it mattereth not, for the Lord will uphold such at the last day** [*judgment day*]. But wo unto such, for they are in the gall of bitterness and in the bonds of iniquity.

As the idea that there is really no such thing as sin or absolute right and wrong gains momentum, we see more and more looseness and fuzziness of boundaries in public and private behavior. We see breach of promise and corruption in public and private with seemingly little of shame and embarrassment or sorrow for wrong doing. Rather, we sense irritation at being caught and exposed. Isaiah prophesied of this redefining of right and wrong. He said (bold added for emphasis):

Isaiah 5:20–24

20 **Woe unto them that call evil good, and good evil; that put darkness for light, and light for darkness; that put bitter for sweet, and sweet for bitter!**

21 Woe unto them that are wise in their own eyes, and prudent in their own sight!

22 Woe unto them that are mighty to drink wine, and men of strength to mingle strong drink:

23 Which justify the wicked for reward, and take away the righteousness of the righteous from him!

24 **Therefore as the fire devoureth the stubble, and the flame consumeth the** chaff, so their root shall be as rottenness, and their blossom shall go up as dust: because they have cast away the law of the Lord of hosts, and despised the word of the Holy One of Israel.

SIGN 63

THE RIGHTEOUS WILL BE ALERTED BY THE SIGNS OF THE TIMES

CATEGORY: BEING FULFILLED

In the Pearl of Great Price, the Savior refers to the faithful Saints as "mine elect," and informs us that they will be alerted to the nearness of His coming by the signs of the times (bold added for emphasis):

Joseph Smith—Matthew 1:37–39

37 And whoso treasureth up my word, shall not be deceived, for the Son of Man shall come, and he shall send his angels before him with the great sound of a trumpet, and they shall gather together the remainder of his elect from the four winds, from one end of heaven to the other.

38 Now learn a parable of the fig tree— When its branches are yet tender, and it begins to put forth leaves, you know that summer is nigh at hand;

39 So likewise, **mine elect, when they shall see all these things, they shall know that he is near, even at the doors**;

This is one of the many good reasons for studying and becoming familiar with the signs of the times. Not only do they provide testimony that the scriptures are true, but they also provide strength and spiritual stamina for us against deception, discouragement, and despair as the prophesied punishments of God descend upon the inhabitants of the earth in an effort to encourage more to repent and come unto Christ before it is too late. Knowing that "he is near, even at the doors" can

100 SIGNS

provide hope and strength to endure, knowing that either as mortals (if He comes during our lifetimes), or as resurrected beings (if He comes after we have died), we can enjoy the blessings of the Millennium after He arrives.

Throughout my teaching career, one of the most popular discussion topics has been the signs of the times. It has been the focus of many questions from students. It has proven to be enjoyable and productive to provide students with a list of signs of the times (such as found in this book) and then go over them in class, entertaining questions and observations regarding them. Inevitably, the spirit of testimony has prevailed, as they have seen how many of these prophecies have been fulfilled or are currently underway. Testimonies have been increased and strengthened, and fears and concerns have been minimized. The Savior's counsel to "be not troubled" (Joseph Smith—Matthew 1:23) when discussing these signs has been read in class and followed.

SIGN 64

MATERIALISM WILL BE PRIORITY OVER SERVICE TO OTHERS

CATEGORY: BEING FULFILLED

Perhaps you are noticing, with this list of signs of the times, that the scriptures warn against many different kinds of wickedness that will be prevalent in the last days. We could easily just lump these together into one sweeping statement, namely, that there will be gross wickedness in the last days prior to the Second Coming. But that is not how the Lord has addressed this topic in the revelations. As we are seeing, He has given many specifics through His prophets, and we do well to look closely at each and be warned away from the numerous forms of these sins in modern society.

In yet another aspect of last days wickedness, Moroni saw our day and warned us that there would be many who are caught up in materialism to the point that they neglect the poor and the needy. This can happen to those of limited means as well as to those of great wealth. (Bold added for emphasis:)

Mormon 8:37
37 For behold, **ye do love money, and your substance, and your fine apparel, and the adorning of your churches, more than ye love the poor and the needy, the sick and the afflicted**.

This sign of the times, prophesied by Moroni as he finished his father's record, will become more and more apparent as the coming of the Savior in glory draws closer. There are obviously many ways in which it can be fulfilled.

There are probably many excuses that go through the minds of people who have the means to help the "poor and the needy, the sick and the afflicted" but choose not to.

King Benjamin addressed one of these (bold added for emphasis):

Mosiah 4:17–19
17 **Perhaps thou shalt say: The man has brought upon himself his misery**; therefore I will stay my hand, and will not give unto him of my food, nor impart unto him of my substance that he may not suffer, for his punishments are just—

18 But I say unto you, O man, whosoever doeth this the same hath great cause to repent; and except he repenteth of that which he hath done he perisheth forever, and hath no interest in the kingdom of God.

19 For behold, are we not all beggars? Do we not all depend upon the same Being, even God, for all the substance which we have, for both food and raiment, and for gold,

and for silver, and for all the riches which we have of every kind?

It is interesting that people of lesser means seem, by and large, to be more generous toward others than those of greater financial resources. On a positive note, Jacob pointed out a major avenue for avoiding getting caught up in fulfilling this sign. He explained that seeking wealth is not a sin if priorities are kept in the proper order. Said he (bold added for emphasis):

Jacob 2:17–19

17 Think of your brethren like unto yourselves, and be familiar with all and free with your substance, that they may be rich like unto you.

18 But **before ye seek for riches, seek ye for the kingdom of God**.

19 And after ye have obtained a hope in Christ ye shall obtain riches, if ye seek them; and **ye will seek them for the intent to do good—to clothe the naked, and to feed the hungry, and to liberate the captive, and administer relief to the sick and the afflicted**.

It is gratifying to know that many people of considerable means are indeed very generous. For many years, I had the fun and downright enjoyable privilege of being the "errand boy" for a wealthy friend. He was a faithful member of the Church and had thoroughly taken the passages of scripture listed above to heart. Upon hearing of someone in need, he would contact me. We would meet and he would tell me of the need and give me sufficient cash to provide immediate relief for that person or family. Wherever possible, he did not want the recipients to know the source of the money. Over time, I delivered thousands and thousands of dollars to the needy and had the satisfaction and joy of seeing their reactions.

One was an elderly widow in a neighboring community whose husband had just passed away. My friend did not know her but had heard that the husband did not have insurance and she, consequently, did not have sufficient funds nor help from family to bury him. He immediately contacted me and provided an envelope for me to deliver. The widow was overwhelmed to think that someone who did not know her was so generous and thoughtful. Several times he had me deliver money to widows who had encountered unexpected expenses far beyond their meager resources.

I remember well one of his own employees who had incurred massive medical bills for a family member, far beyond what the insurance paid for. I drove to the home, knocked on the door, and delivered a substantial sum in an envelope. He did not know me. He asked me to wait while he opened the envelope. He was speechless. Upon recovering his composure sufficiently, he did his best to find out who I was and who had provided the gift. My skills as a master of evasion in such settings had by now become finely honed and his efforts at the moment were unsuccessful. He did, however, follow me out where he could see my car in hopes that it would offer him a clue. It did, eventually, and he asked around enough to finally be led to my wealthy friend. Deep gratitude and sincere appreciation were then proffered.

As stated above, one does not have to be wealthy to get caught up in making selfish materialism a priority over helping the poor and the needy. But, on the other hand, it is gratifying to see so many who are generous, even with more limited means. As a bishop, I had many pleasant experiences with such kind individuals. Members of the ward who were struggling to pay

AND THEY SHALL
TURN AWAY
THEIR EARS FROM
THE TRUTH, AND
SHALL BE TURNED
UNTO FABLES.

2 TIMOTHY 4:4

their own bills, would hand me an envelope or stuff some cash in my pocket and say for me to give it to a young couple or someone they knew was struggling financially. On one occasion, an older member of the ward approached me after church one Sunday and asked me to come with him out to his car. I did so. He pointed to two bags of groceries in the backseat and asked me to deliver them to a particular young family living in an apartment in the ward. He threatened me with his cane, accompanied with a bit of a grin, pointing it to within an uncomfortable margin of safety of my nose, as he told me absolutely not to let them know who the giver was. I carried out his instructions with strict obedience, and again had the joy of seeing the fruits of generosity.

Being caught up in materialism, regardless of financial status, can be spiritually damaging and one way to avoid it is to be generous with whatever means we have.

SIGN 65

PEOPLE WILL REFUSE TO BELIEVE OBVIOUS TRUTH AND WILL INSTEAD ADHERE TO FABLES AND FALSEHOODS

CATEGORY: BEING FULFILLED

This prophecy of conditions shortly preceding the Second Coming of Christ needs little explanation. When people get sufficiently wicked and selfish, they no longer think rationally. Indeed, wickedness does not promote rational thought. In the face of social trends and political posturing that, to the rational mind, will obviously lead to the destruction of society as we know it, with its built-in safeguards for human freedom and use of agency, such people stand aghast at truth and moral principles. They flush in anger at those who advocate the standards of the Bible and the gospel of Christ

as the basis for the survival of society. Paul, the Apostle, prophesied this stance as follows (bold added for emphasis):

<u>2 Timothy 4:3–4</u>
3 For **the time will come when they will not endure sound doctrine**; but after their own lusts shall they heap to themselves teachers, having itching ears;
4 And **they shall turn away *their* ears from the truth, and shall be turned unto fables**.

We often apply these verses to the gospel and the tendency of the spiritually blind and deaf to reject its teachings and blessings. This is certainly the case. However, no doubt these verses can be applied also to common sense and rational thought processes in all matters relating to the governing of nations and communities as well as to standards to which the media and businesses should be held accountable.

The "teachers, having itching ears" and "fables" mentioned by Paul can certainly include the peers of those who would have the government pass unrighteous or unwise laws, as well as the peers and fans of Hollywood and other media production centers who insist on the "anything goes" philosophy for entertainment. It can likewise apply to leaders of companies, small and large, who counsel together in darkness to engage in dishonest business practices.

These things can and do also apply to individuals and families. The "sound doctrine" that family is "the fundamental unit of society" ("The Family, A Proclamation To The World," September 23, 1995), is being undermined and ignored, as more and more discount formal marriage and simply live together and have children. The "fables" that accompany the redefining of marriage and family trap many who fall into the web of walking in their own ways (D&C 1:16) and ring hollow in spiritually deaf ears as the disintegration of society accelerates.

The "sound doctrine" that we are literally offspring of God (Acts 17:28–29), that He has "a body of flesh and bones as tangible as man's" (D&C 130:22) is ridiculed and railed against by religionists with "itching ears" who fail to understand the Bible correctly and study to teach that which is popular and will increase their personal wealth. As stated many times in the true teachings of our church, until we understand who God is and what He is, we cannot understand ourselves.

It is obvious, even to the casual observer, that the rampant sexual immorality prevailing now throughout the world is undermining the stability of society and is devastating the future. Yet people in large numbers continue to adhere to fables and falsehoods that seem to give license to their irresponsible and sinful behaviors.

SIGN 66

MANY MANIFESTATIONS OF PRIDE WILL CAUSE GREAT DAMAGE TO SOCIETY

CATEGORY: BEING FULFILLED

As a root cause of evil, pride will wear many prominent faces in the last days. Moroni wrote of what he saw in vision about our day (bold added for emphasis):

Mormon 8:35–36
35 Behold, I speak unto you as if ye were present, and yet ye are not. But behold, Jesus Christ hath shown you unto me, and I know your doing.

36 And I know that **ye do walk in the pride of your hearts**; and there are none save a few only who do not lift themselves up in the pride of their hearts, unto the wearing

of very fine apparel, unto envying, and strifes, and malice, and persecutions, and all manner of iniquities; and your churches, yea, even every one, have become polluted because of the pride of your hearts.

If we are not careful, we too can become victims of this spiritual malady. Successfully following the constant injunction found in the scriptures and the words of our Church leaders to remain humble is good protection against falling into this trap set by the devil. Fasting, service to others, and constant self-evaluation can be helpful tools for us.

Pride is strongly manifest in the "natural man," as described by King Benjamin. Have you noticed that in the same verses in which King Benjamin warns against becoming a natural man, he gives the antidote against it?

Mosiah 3:17–19
17 And moreover, I say unto you, that there shall be no other name given nor any other way nor means whereby salvation can come unto the children of men, only in and through the name of Christ, the Lord Omnipotent.

18 For behold he judgeth, and his judgment is just; and the infant perisheth not that dieth in his infancy; but men drink damnation to their own souls except **they humble themselves and become as little children, and believe that salvation was, and is, and is to come, in and through the atoning blood of Christ, the Lord Omnipotent**.

19 For the natural man is an enemy to God, and has been from the fall of Adam, and will be, forever and ever, unless he **yields to the enticings of the Holy Spirit, and putteth off the natural man and becometh a saint through the atonement of Christ the Lord, and becometh as a child, submissive, meek, humble, patient, full of love, willing to submit to all things which the Lord seeth fit to inflict upon**

him, even as a child doth submit to his father.

We need to be vigilant and willing to acknowledge it when pride starts creeping into our thoughts and actions. A good friend of mine once purchased a very fine sports car. It was a thrill to ride in it with him. It was powerful, beautifully designed and sleek, and turned people's heads as we drove along. We both had a love of fine engineering and the car resonated deeply with us in our souls. He even had the portion of his garage carpeted in which he parked it. One family night, he brought the car over and gave each one of our children a ride in it. They were awed and impressed!

However, many months later, he sold it. When he told me, I was surprised and asked why. He said that one day when he was driving it, he was stopped at a traffic light and found himself looking at an older, somewhat beat-up car waiting next to him at the light. He then glanced at its driver and thought, "You poor soul, having to drive that piece of junk. I'm glad I'm not you. Eat your heart out as you look at me in mine." As he pulled rapidly away, when the light turned green, intentionally transmitting his disdain for the other driver and his wreck, it suddenly dawned on him what his fine car was doing to his soul. Startled, he faced the reality of what was coming over him, put the sports car up for sale, sold it quickly, and moved ahead with his life, working extra hard at avoiding pride.

SIGN 67

FALSE PROPHETS, FALSE CHURCHES, AND FALSE MIRACLES WILL ABOUND

CATEGORY: BEING FULFILLED

Speaking to His disciples about the last days, the Savior spoke of false Christs, false prophets, and the false miracles that would be performed by them (bold added for emphasis):

Joseph Smith—Matthew 1:22
22 For in those days there shall also arise **false Christs**, and **false prophets**, and **shall show great signs and wonders**, insomuch, that, if possible, they shall deceive the very elect, who are the elect according to the covenant.

John the Revelator likewise prophesied such things in the last days. He referred to the great power of Satan and his "front" organizations to do spectacular things to attract the foolish, the unwary, and the wicked in the last days (bold added for emphasis):

Revelation 13:13–15
13 And **he doeth great wonders**, so that **he maketh fire come down from heaven** on the earth **in the sight of men,** [*Making "fire come down from heaven" is a reference to Elijah's miracle recorded in 1 Kings, chapter 18, where he challenged 450 prophets of Baal to have their false god light the fire for their sacrifice. When they failed, God sent fire down from heaven to burn Elijah's offering. In other words, Satan and his followers can do spectacular things to woo their victims.*]

14 And **deceiveth them that dwell on the earth by *the means of* those miracles** which **he had power to do** in the sight of the beast; saying to them that dwell on the earth, that they should make an image to the beast, which had the wound by a sword, and did live.

15 And **he had power to give life unto the image of the beast** [*had power to make sin look very attractive*], that the image of the beast should both speak, and cause that as many as would not worship the image of the beast should be killed.

Sometimes we tend to think of these false Christs and false prophets as well as false miracles only in terms of strange people dressed in long robes, or some televangelists, or false healings, and so forth. On one occasion several years ago, during a break between sessions of general conference, my wife and I peacefully strolled out of the Salt Lake Temple grounds through the south gate, with pleasant thoughts of the conferences messages just heard in our minds and hearts. As we emerged from the Temple grounds, our thoughts were interrupted by a large man with a red Afro hairdo, dressed in a long white robe and standing on a small round three-foot-high table. His robe obscured the top of the table and almost made it appear as if he were standing in the air. He loudly claimed to be Moroni and was delivering anti-Mormon messages.

While such people and events can certainly fit this sign of the times, to limit our view of it to these would no doubt be too narrow of an interpretation. Certain media idols, liberal philosophers and teachers, corrupt politicians and business people, military tyrants and cruel dictators, along with a host of other public and private "heroes" who detract from gospel ideals and standards, could well fit into this category. In fact, any in positions of influence who lead others astray from the laws and counsels of God could be considered to be in the category of false prophets and false Christs.

From the same chapter of Revelation quoted above, we see a warning against admiring and "worshiping" public figures who represent the "beast" (symbolic of Satan's degenerate worldly kingdoms)—in other words, those who entice us away from the laws and commandments of God (bold added for emphasis):

> Revelation 13:3–4
> 3 And I saw one of his heads as it were wounded to death; and his deadly wound was healed: and **all the world wondered after the beast** [*the majority of the world will admire and desire wickedness in the last days*].

> 4 And they worshipped the dragon [*Satan*] which gave power unto the beast [*representing degenerate earthly kingdoms controlled by Satan; see heading to Revelation 13 in our Bible*]: and **they** [*the wicked*] **worshipped the beast, saying, Who is like unto the beast?** who is able to make war with him [*i.e., isn't he wonderful!*]?

Likewise, some verses in Alma remind us that people can become very susceptible to admiring and supporting such false prophets and false churches. In this case, the verse refers to Nehor and his false and spiritually damaging teachings (bold added for emphasis):

> Alma 1:4–5
> 4 And he also testified unto the people that all mankind should be saved at the last day, and that they need not fear nor tremble, but that they might lift up their heads and rejoice; for the Lord had created all men, and had also redeemed all men; and, in the end, all men should have eternal life.

> 5 And it came to pass that he did teach these things so much that many did believe on his words, even so many that **they began to support him and give him money**.

Perhaps one of the damaging "miracles" warned against for our day is the misuse of miraculous technology to create violent video games and rampant accessibility to pornography. "False miracles" could include Satan-sponsored use of the miracles of science and technology to miraculously make sin much more appealing and accessible. It can even include the frightening use of cell phones or the Internet (a "miracle" of communication) for bullying.

In summary, we need to be constantly vigilant to avoid becoming part of the fulfillment of this sign of the times. Using the scriptures to set our standards and carefully listening to and following the counsels and warnings of our living prophets, seers, and revelators, can dress us in "the whole armour of God." (Bold added for emphasis:)

Ephesians 6:11–13

11 **Put on the whole armour of God**, that ye may be able to stand against the wiles of the devil.

12 For we wrestle not against flesh and blood, but against principalities, against powers, against the rulers of the darkness of this world, against spiritual wickedness in high places.

13 Wherefore **take unto you the whole armour of God**, that ye may be able to withstand in the evil day, and having done all, to stand.

SIGN 68

PREACHERS WILL "TRANSFIGURE" GOD'S WORD FOR PERSONAL GAIN

CATEGORY: BEING FULFILLED

"Transfigure" is an interesting word. It means "to change," "to alter the outward appearance of," or "transform." In the case of this prophecy, it can include "changing or intentionally misinterpreting the word of God in order to gain popularity and personal wealth." This sign of the times is found in a strong warning and prophecy given by the Lord through Moroni concerning our day (bold added for emphasis):

Mormon 8:33

33 O ye wicked and perverse and stiffnecked people, why have ye built up churches unto yourselves to get gain? Why have ye **transfigured the holy word of God**, that ye might bring damnation upon your souls? Behold, look ye unto the revelations of God; for behold, the time cometh at that day when all these things must be fulfilled.

While we most definitely need to respect and appreciate the great amount of good done by other churches, we need to be alert also for the many fulfillments of this prophecy. The basic concern and problem regarding this was clearly pointed out to 14-year-old Joseph Smith during the First Vision (bold added for emphasis):

Joseph Smith—History 1:18–19

18 My object in going to inquire of the Lord was to know which of all the sects was right, that I might know which to join. No sooner, therefore, did I get possession of myself, so as to be able to speak, than I asked the Personages who stood above me in the light, which of all the sects was right (for at this time it had never entered into my heart that all were wrong)—and which I should join.

19 I was answered that I must join none of them, for they were all wrong; and the Personage who addressed me said that all **their creeds were an abomination in his sight; that those professors were all corrupt; that: "they draw near to me with their lips, but their hearts are far from me, they teach for doctrines the commandments of men, having a form of godliness, but they deny the power thereof."**

By the way, Elder Boyd K. Packer cautioned us about misinterpreting the phrase "for they were all wrong," in the above quote. He taught (bold added for emphasis):

Now this is not to say that the churches, all of them, are without some truth. **They have some truth—some of them very much of it.** They have a form of godliness. Often the clergy and adherents are not without dedication, and many of them practice remarkably well the virtues of Christianity. They are, nonetheless, **incomplete**. By his declaration, ". . . they teach for doctrines the commandments of men, having a form of godliness, but they deny the power thereof" (JS—H 1:19). (Packer, "The Only True and Living Church, *Ensign*, December 1971)

Now, back to this sign of the times. We see numerous examples of "transfiguring" God's word for personal gain. Some ministers intentionally study what their congregants want to hear and what they don't want to hear and then tailor their sermons accordingly, in order to build up a large base from which to derive income. Determining what will be popular among their members, some pastors and ministers look at social trends, and then bend their preaching and policies to match that for which the public is clamoring in their private lives. In so doing, they selectively neglect the clear teachings of the Bible. Examples include performing marriages for gay and lesbian couples, smiling upon couples who cohabitate without marriage, and approving premarital sex under certain conditions.

The Bible clearly teaches against homosexual relationships. Examples include (bold added for emphasis):

Leviticus 18:22
22 Thou shalt **not lie with mankind, as with womankind**: it is abomination.

Deuteronomy 23:17
17 There shall be no whore of the daughters of Israel, nor a **sodomite** of the sons of Israel [*homosexual behavior was the prominent sin of Sodom and Gomorrah that led to their destruction. See Genesis 19:5, 24–25*].

Romans 1:27
27 And likewise also the men, leaving the natural use of the woman, **burned in their lust one toward another; men with men** working that which is unseemly, and receiving in themselves that recompence of their error which was meet.

1 Corinthians 6:9
9 Know ye not that the unrighteous shall not inherit the kingdom of God? Be not deceived: neither fornicators, nor idolaters, nor adulterers, nor effeminate, nor **abusers of themselves with mankind,**

1 Timothy 1:10
10 For whoremongers, for **them that defile themselves with mankind**, for menstealers, for liars, for perjured persons, and if there be any other thing that is contrary to sound doctrine;

The Bible clearly teaches against sexual relations outside of marriage (bold added for emphasis):

Exodus 20:14
14 **Thou shalt not commit adultery.**

1 Timothy 4:1–3
1 Now the Spirit speaketh expressly, that in the latter times [*the last days*] some shall depart from the faith, giving heed to seducing spirits, and doctrines of devils;

2 Speaking lies in hypocrisy; having their conscience seared with a hot iron;

3 **Forbidding to marry** [*includes living together but refusing to marry*], and commanding to abstain from meats, which God hath created to be received with thanksgiving of them which believe and know the truth.

The Bible clearly teaches against premarital sex (bold added for emphasis):

Acts 15:20
20 But that we write unto them, that they **abstain** from pollutions of idols, and **from fornication**, and from things strangled, and from blood.

Yet another way of "transfiguring" God's word for personal gain is rationalizing circumstances to justify being unfaithful to one's spouse, thus going against His word, which forbids adultery, and engaging in illicit sexual relationships for perceived personal gain or satisfaction.

God's command to love one another is often ignored and certain passages of scripture taken out of context and twisted to justify so-called "holy wars" in which one denomination engages in battle against another. Religion is often used to stir people up to battle against one another, when the true motives are greed and desire to brutalize and bully others.

On an individual basis, there are numerous ways in which individuals might "transfigure" the word of the Lord in order to justify sin or sloppiness in living the gospel. Some might misinterpret the fact that family is so emphasized in the Church that they would opt to go picnicking in the mountains on Sunday, rather than attending their church meetings, supposedly in order to spend more quality time together. Because of a hectic schedule during the week, one might decide to go to a movie on Sunday because so many members recommend it. Tithe paying might be put off for a period of time in order to purchase more reliable transportation, rationalizing that providing for family takes precedence over tithing. The list is endless. King Benjamin said (bold added for emphasis):

> Mosiah 4:29
> 29 And finally, I cannot tell you all the things whereby ye may commit sin; for there are divers ways and means, even **so many that I cannot number them**.

SIGN 69

PEOPLE REFUSE TO BELIEVE THE SIGNS OF THE TIMES

CATEGORY: BEING FULFILLED

It is rather interesting to note that, according to Peter, one of the signs of the times is that people will refuse to even believe the signs of the times. People will be so far removed from God and His word in their lifestyles and in their thinking that they will pay no attention to the obvious fulfillment of prophecy all around them. In fact, they will scoff and say that things are just the

same as ever and there is no such thing as "the last days." In the Bible, we read the following (bold added for emphasis):

> 2 Peter 3:3–4
> 3 Knowing this first, that there shall come **in the last days scoffers**, walking after their own lusts,
>
> 4 And **saying, Where is the promise of his coming?** for since the fathers fell asleep, **all things continue as** *they were* **from the beginning of the creation**.

Occasionally, a prominent preacher or evangelist will be quoted in the media as having stated that the woes of our nation and the world are the result of God's punishments for the prevailing wickedness. They will quote scripture, citing prophecies that foretell the punishments of God that will be meted out in the last days because of large scale sinning. They quote from the Bible, including Isaiah (bold added for emphasis):

> Isaiah 13:9 and 11
> 9 Behold, the day of the Lord cometh, cruel both with wrath and fierce anger, to lay the land desolate: and he shall destroy the sinners thereof out of it.
>
> 11 And **I will punish the world for** *their* **evil**, and the wicked for their iniquity; and I will cause the arrogancy of the proud to cease, and will lay low the haughtiness of the terrible.

Prophecies about conditions in the last days are quoted from Revelation, chapters 8–9, 16–18. For example, chapter 8 foretells upheavals in nature as a result of extreme last days wickedness (bold added for emphasis):

> Revelation 8:5
> 5 And the angel took the censer, and filled it with fire of the altar, and cast it into the earth: and there were voices, and **thunderings**, and **lightnings**, and an **earthquake**.

The Doctrine and Covenants clearly confirms an increase in frequency and intensity of natural disasters as punishments and warnings because of widespread wickedness in the last days (bold added for emphasis):

D&C 88:88–91

88 And after your testimony cometh wrath and indignation upon the people.

89 For after your testimony cometh the testimony of **earthquakes**, that shall cause groanings in the midst of her, and men shall fall upon the ground and shall not be able to stand.

90 And also cometh the testimony of the voice of **thunderings**, and the voice of **lightnings**, and the voice of **tempests**, and the voice of the **waves of the sea heaving themselves beyond their bounds**.

91 And **all things shall be in commotion**; and surely, men's hearts shall fail them; for fear shall come upon all people.

Such pronouncements by people of faith are almost always met with outrage, scoffing, and indignant posturing by many of the very public figures who are promoting the downward spiral of morality in society. By so doing, these influential molders of public thinking and policy are unknowingly fulfilling this prophecy.

SIGN 70

NEW YORK, ALBANY, AND BOSTON DESTROYED, UNLESS . . .

CATEGORY: ?

Not long ago, an extended family member sent me an email asking whether or not they should heed sincere advice of LDS friends in the Boston area to move away because of a prophecy that Boston would be destroyed. He and his wife were told that one of the signs of the times was that New York, Albany, and Boston would be destroyed in the last days before the coming of the Lord. He hadn't heard of such a prophecy, but felt that I might be familiar with it and thus, able to advise them.

Likewise, some years ago, when I was serving as a stake president in Utah, a sincere member of one of our wards became concerned about relatives living in New England. She had been reading the Doctrine and Covenants and had run across these verses (bold added for emphasis):

D&C 84:114–115

114 Nevertheless, let the bishop [*Newel K. Whitney*] go unto the city of **New York**, also to the city of **Albany**, and also to the city of **Boston**, and warn the people of those cities with the sound of the gospel, with a loud voice, of the **desolation and utter abolishment** which await them **if** they do reject these things [*the gospel*].

115 For **if** they do reject these things the hour of their judgment is nigh, and their house shall be left unto them desolate.

In both cases, I was pleased to point out the "if's" in the prophecy. The good news is that a great number of faithful Saints live in these cities and the surrounding areas. They have not rejected "these things," which is the stated criterion for the fulfillment of the above prophecy. In fact, at the time of this writing, the Church has temples in New York and Boston. My wife and I recently had the pleasure and privilege to attend the Manhattan Temple. It was wonderful! An island of peace and spiritual renewal in the midst of a bustling city.

Furthermore, the Church has several successful missions, directing the work of numerous missionaries, who are finding, teaching, and baptizing in those areas. The Church Educational System has a large number of students who are furthering their testimonies in seminary and institute classes there.

AND THEY SHALL
SAY THAT CHRIST
DELAYETH HIS
COMING UNTIL
THE END OF
THE EARTH.

D & C   45:26

In short, this appears to be a "conditional" prophecy and we would do well to leave it as the Lord stated it.

SIGN 71

SOME WILL FEAR THAT CHRIST'S COMING IS BEING DELAYED TOO LONG

CATEGORY: ? (PERHAPS MOSTLY YET TO BE FULFILLED)

As the prophesied conditions of the last days continue to intensify, some people who believe in the Second Coming and the signs of the times will begin to fear that the Lord is waiting too long to come and, consequently, that few if any people will survive the extreme destructions brought about by warfare and environmental devastations in the last of the last days. The scripture reference for this sign is found in the Doctrine and Covenants (bold added for emphasis):

> D&C 45:26
> 26 And in that day shall be heard of wars and rumors of wars, and the whole earth shall be in commotion, and men's hearts shall fail them, and **they shall say that Christ delayeth his coming until the end of the earth**.

It would be absurd to believe that a mistake is being made and that heaven will be caught sleeping, with the dreadful result that most if not all are prematurely destroyed from the earth and few or none are left to greet the coming Lord. We know that there will be a great number of the righteous residing on earth at the time of the Second Coming. The Doctrine and Covenants tells us what will happen to them at that time (bold added for emphasis):

> D&C 88:96
> 6 And the saints that are upon the earth, who are alive, **shall be quickened and be caught up to meet him**.

Joseph Fielding Smith taught the following about those who will continue living on earth after the Second Coming as the Millennium commences:

> There will be millions of people, Catholics, Protestants, agnostics, Mohammedans, people of all classes and all beliefs, still permitted to remain upon the face of the earth, but they will be those who have lived clean lives, those who have been free from wickedness and corruption. All who belong, by virtue of their good lives, to [at least] the terrestrial order, . . . will remain upon the face of the earth during the millennium. (Smith, *Doctrines of Salvation*, Bookcraft, 1954, Vol. 1, 86–87)

With this in mind, it is clear that Christ will not delay His coming unreasonably, allowing destruction and devastation to go on unchecked. He will be right on time. In fulfillment of this sign, some will indeed fear that He is waiting too long to come. But He is not. It is certainly permissible for the righteous to wish that the Second Coming would get here right away and thus completely curtail the free fall of wickedness and debauchery now plaguing society. But to worry that the coming will be delayed too long would be a show of lack of faith in the Father's plan.

SIGN 72

THERE WILL BE SIGNS AND WONDERS ON EARTH AND IN THE HEAVENS

CATEGORY: BEING FULFILLED

Before the Savior's ascension into heaven, He spoke to His disciples about His Second

Coming. He related a parable to them that told how signs of the times on earth and in the heavens would alert the faithful in the last days that His coming was near. Among other places, we read these words in the Doctrine and Covenants (bold added for emphasis):

D&C 45:36–40

36 And when the light shall begin to break forth, it shall be with them like unto **a parable** which I will show you—

37 Ye look and behold the fig trees, and ye see them with your eyes, and ye say when they begin to shoot forth, and their leaves are yet tender, that summer is now nigh at hand;

38 Even so it shall be in that day **when they shall see all these things** (the signs of the times), **then shall they know that the hour is nigh.**

39 And it shall come to pass that he that feareth [*respects, trusts, has faith* in] me shall be looking forth for the great day of the Lord to come, even for **the signs of the coming of the Son of Man.**

40 And **they shall see signs and wonders**, for they shall be shown forth **in the heavens above**, and **in the earth beneath**.

Perhaps many of the things that we take for granted in our day, such as airplanes, trains, rocket ships, space stations, satellites, automobiles, busses, computers, and so forth, would serve as astonishing "signs and wonders" to all who have lived on the earth prior to these last days.

No doubt, optics such as the Hubble Telescope; personal electronic devices including cell phones, flash drives, solid state computer drives, and small cameras; and the sophisticated electronics onboard vehicles constitute "signs and wonders" on earth as well as in the heavens. Advances in medicine, prosthetic limbs, the microcosms being explored by scientists, manipulation of elements and subatomic particles for use in

information technology storage devices, and so on and so forth are all part of the ongoing fulfillment of this sign of the times.

SIGN 73

THE LAMANITES WILL BLOSSOM AS THE ROSE

CATEGORY: BEING FULFILLED

This much-anticipated sign of the times is certainly taking place on a broad scale right before our eyes. It is spoken of in the Doctrine and Covenants and reads as follows (bold added for emphasis):

D&C 49:24

24 But **before the great day of the Lord shall come** [*the Second Coming*], Jacob shall flourish in the wilderness, and **the Lamanites shall blossom as the rose**.

My wife and I have four sons, and all four of them served missions to South America where they witnessed firsthand the ongoing fulfilling of this prophecy. It is likewise being fulfilled in other parts of the world. On every hand we observe the continued rapid growth of the Church among our Lamanite brothers and sisters.

The Perpetual Education Fund, instituted by President Gordon B. Hinckley, is being implemented on a large scale among returned missionaries in Mexico, Central and South America, and elsewhere. This, no doubt, is helping also to fulfill this sign of the time, for it helps them not only to "blossom" in terms of membership in the Lord's true Church, but it also helps them to "blossom" and flourish in terms of economic well-being.

Nephi prophesied of the last days and the great gathering of Israel that is to take place. Among other things, he spoke of the conversion and

100 SIGNS

LAMANITES
BLOSSOMING AS A ROSE

gathering of the Book of Mormon peoples. It is a strong sign of the times (bold added for emphasis):

2 Nephi 30:4–6
4 And then shall the remnant of our seed know concerning us, how that we came out from Jerusalem, and that they are descendants of the Jews.

5 And **the gospel of Jesus Christ shall be declared among them**; wherefore, they shall be restored unto the knowledge of their fathers, and also to the knowledge of Jesus Christ, which was had among their fathers.

6 And **then shall they rejoice**; for they shall know that it is a blessing unto them from the hand of God; and their scales of darkness shall begin to fall from their eyes; and many generations shall not pass away among them, save **they shall be a pure and a delightsome people**.

SIGN 74

NEW JERUSALEM WILL BE BUILT

CATEGORY: YET TO BE FULFILLED

Before the Lord's Second Advent, the city of New Jerusalem will be built in Independence, Jackson County, Missouri (Moses 7:62). This "Holy City" is often referred to as the "city of Zion" (D&C 57:2) and will continue on into the Millennium, serving as one of two capital cities for the Savior during the Millennium. The other capital city will be Old Jerusalem.

The location of the city of Zion or New Jerusalem is given in the Doctrine and Covenants (bold added for emphasis):

D&C 57:1–3
1 Hearken, O ye elders of my church, saith the Lord your God, who have assembled yourselves together, according to my commandments, in this land, which is **the land of Missouri**, which is the land which I have

appointed and consecrated for the gathering of the saints.

2 Wherefore, **this is** the land of promise, and **the place for the city of Zion**.

3 And thus saith the Lord your God, if you will receive wisdom here is wisdom. Behold, the place which is now called **Independence is the center place**; and a spot for the temple is lying westward, upon a lot which is not far from the courthouse.

More details about New Jerusalem are given in section 45 (bold added for emphasis):

D&C 45:66–69
66 And **it shall be called the New Jerusalem**, a land of peace, a city of refuge, **a place of safety** for the saints of the Most High God;

67 And **the glory of the Lord shall be there**, and the terror of the Lord also shall be there, insomuch that **the wicked will not come unto it**, and it shall be called Zion.

68 And it shall come to pass among the wicked, that **every man that will not take his sword against his neighbor must needs flee unto Zion for safety**.

69 And **there shall be gathered unto it out of every nation under heaven**; and it shall be **the only people that shall not be at war one with another**.

We are given yet more information about this Holy City in the Pearl of Great Price, including the fact that the Savior will live there during the Millennium (bold added for emphasis):

Moses 7:62–64
62 And righteousness will I send down out of heaven; and truth will I send forth out of the earth, to bear testimony of mine Only Begotten; his resurrection from the dead; yea, and also the resurrection of all men; and righteousness and truth will I cause to sweep the earth as with a flood, to **gather out mine elect** from the four quarters of the earth, **unto a place which I shall prepare, an Holy City, that my people may** gird up

their loins, and **be looking forth for the time of my coming**; for there shall be my tabernacle, and **it shall be called Zion, a New Jerusalem**.

63 And the Lord said unto **Enoch**: Then shalt thou **and all thy city meet them there**, and we will receive them into our bosom, and they shall see us; and we will fall upon their necks, and they shall fall upon our necks, and we will kiss each other;

64 And there shall be **mine abode**, and it shall be Zion, which shall come forth out of all the creations which I have made; and **for the space of a thousand years** the earth shall rest.

We mentioned above that Old Jerusalem would also become a capital city for the Savior during the Millennium. Old Jerusalem will be built up again and will become "a holy city of the Lord" as prophesied in Ether as follows (bold added for emphasis):

Ether 13:5–6
5 And he spake also concerning the house of Israel, and **the Jerusalem from whence Lehi should come**—after it should be destroyed it **should be built up again**, **a holy city unto the Lord**; wherefore, it could not be a new Jerusalem for it had been in a time of old; but it should be built up again, and become a holy city of the Lord; and it should be built unto the house of Israel.

6 And that **a New Jerusalem should be built up upon this land**, unto the remnant of the seed of Joseph, for which things there has been a type.

Joseph Fielding Smith explained the above verses:

These two cities, one in the land of Zion and one in Palestine, are to become capitals for the kingdom of God during the Millennium. (Joseph Fielding Smith, *Doctrines of Salvation,* compiled by Bruce R. McConkie, 3 vols. [Salt Lake City: Bookcraft, 1954–56], 3:71)

In summary, while there is much more that could be said about New Jerusalem, suffice it to say that the building of New Jerusalem is yet to be fulfilled. It will be built, at least in part, before the Second Coming, and, according to Moses 7:62, as quoted above, the inhabitants of it will be "looking forth for the time of my coming" and will have a safe haven during the ravages of the last of the final days before the Lord's coming.

SIGN 75
MANY TEMPLES WILL BE BUILT
CATEGORY: BEING FULFILLED

In the last days, before the coming of the Lord, the inhabitants of the earth are to have numerous temples available to them. In the April 1980 general conference of the Church, Ezra Taft Benson prophesied that we would someday have temples in all the lands where the gospel has penetrated (bold added for emphasis):

But now—what of the future? We assuredly expect additional progress, growth, and increased spirituality. We will see our missionaries cover the earth with the message of the Restoration. **We will see temples in every land where the gospel has penetrated**, symbolizing the truth that families, living and deceased, may be joined together in love and eternal family associations. (Ezra Taft Benson, "A Marvelous Work and a Wonder," *Ensign*, May 1980, 33)

The word "mountain" is often used in the scriptures to symbolize "temple." Thus, the phrase "mountain of the Lord's house" in Isaiah's prophecy of the last days in Isaiah 2:2 can refer not only to the establishment of the Church in the tops of the mountains in the last days, but also to temples. The phrase "mountains (note that this is plural) of the Lord's house" in Doctrine and Covenants 133:13 can mean

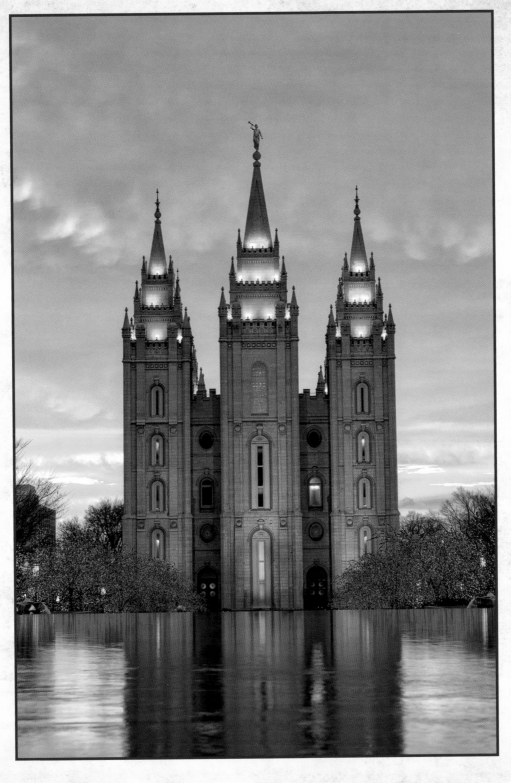

SALT LAKE TEMPLE

SALT LAKE CITY, UTAH

"temples." Both verses are given next, with bold added for emphasis:

Isaiah 2:2
2 And it shall come to pass in the last days, *that* **the mountain of the Lord's house shall be established in the top of the mountains**, and shall be exalted above the hills; and all nations shall flow unto it.

D&C 133:13
13 And let them who be of Judah flee unto Jerusalem, **unto the mountains of the Lord's house**.

Thus, it was prophesied by Isaiah and by the Prophet Joseph Smith that in the last days true temples of the Lord would once more be available on the earth. This interpretation of this phrase is summarized in the institute of religion's *Doctrine and Covenants Student Manual* (bold added for emphasis):

D&C 133:13: What Does the Phrase "Mountains of the Lord's House" Mean?

Other Church leaders have also taught about "the mountain of the Lord's house." Elder Erastus Snow said: " 'The mountain of the Lord's house'—this is a peculiar phrase, and was probably used by the Prophet because it was a common mode of expression in Israel in the days of David and many of the Prophets several hundred years after him, for, in **speaking of Mount Moriah**, **on which the Temple of Solomon was built**, they spoke of it as the mountain of the Lord's house. Moriah is a hill in the city of Jerusalem, on which David located the site of the Temple, and on which his son Solomon built it, and it was called the mountain of the house of the Lord." (In *Journal of Discourses*, 16:202.)

Elder Bruce R. McConkie explained that the phrase has more than one meaning: "The *mountain of the Lord's house* is the mountain where the temple of God is built. [Isaiah 2:2–3 quoted; see also Micah 4:1–2; 2 Nephi 12:2–3.] This great prophecy, as

is often the case, is subject to the law of multiple fulfillment. 1. In Salt Lake City and other mountain locations temples, in the full and true sense of the word, have been erected, and representatives of all nations are flowing unto them to learn of God and his ways. . . . 2. But the day is yet future when the Lord's house is to be built on that 'Mount Zion' which is 'the city of New Jerusalem' in Jackson County, Missouri (D&C 84:2–4). Mount Zion, itself, will be the mountain of the Lord's house in the day when that glorious temple is erected. 3. When the Jews flee unto Jerusalem, it will be 'unto the mountains of the Lord's house' (D&C 133:13), for a holy temple is to be built there also as part of the work of the great era of restoration." (Ezek. 37:24–28.) (*Doctrine and Covenants Student Manual*, 339)

Since President Gordon B. Hinckley announced the building of small temples, during the October 1997 general conference of the Church, there has been a dramatic increase in the number of temples throughout the world. The announcement of small temples was met with enthusiasm among faithful members throughout the world. Speaking of the construction of small temples, President Hinckley said:

We are planning such structures immediately in Anchorage, Alaska; in the LDS colonies in northern Mexico; and in Monticello, Utah. In areas of greater Church membership we will build more of the traditional temples, but we are developing plans that will reduce the costs without any reduction in terms of the work to be performed therein. We are determined, brethren, to take the temples to the people and afford them every opportunity for the very precious blessings that come of temple worship. (*Ensign*, November 1997)

On a personal note, during a time when the construction and dedication of small temples was in full swing, I was serving as a stake president in my hometown in Utah. We had been assigned a General Authority to preside at our upcoming stake conference, but he suffered a shoulder injury playing tennis and could not come. I was informed that, since all of the available General Authorities in Utah were involved in temple dedications throughout the world on that particular weekend, it was necessary to ask an Area Seventy serving in the Chicago area to change his plans for the weekend and fly in to preside at our stake conference. He was delightful and the conference went well, but the situation heightened in my mind the marvelous fulfillment of this prophecy that continues to take place.

SIGN 76

A TEMPLE WILL BE BUILT IN JERUSALEM

CATEGORY: YET TO BE FULFILLED

Members of the Church ask many questions about this temple that is yet to be built and that is a very prominent sign of the times. We will pose just a few questions and give answers:

Question: Will this temple be built on the site of the Dome of the Rock (a Muslim mosque in Jerusalem)?

Answer: This is a most unfortunate rumor because it causes additional animosity between Christians and Muslims. Nowhere in the scriptures does it state that the Jerusalem Temple has to be built on the exact site of the Dome of the Rock, a mosque that is so sacred to Muslims. There is actually plenty of room on the so-called "Temple Mount" for both.

Question: Is it possible that the BYU Jerusalem Center could be turned into a temple?

Answer: The Brethren are very concerned about this unfounded rumor and have actually asked seminary and institute of religion teachers to do everything they can to stop it from spreading. The Brethren gave their word to the Israeli government that the Jerusalem Center is an educational center, and so it is. To do otherwise with it would be a breach of promise.

Question: Will this temple be one in which temple ordinances will be performed?

Answer: Yes. Joseph Fielding Smith answers this question as follows:

Latter-day Temples Foretold. That temples and temple ordinances are essential to the Christian faith is well established in the Bible. Malachi predicted the coming of the Lord suddenly to his temple, in the day of vengeance, in the latter times, as a refiner and purifier. Ezekiel predicted the building of a **temple in Jerusalem which will be used for ordinance work** after the gathering of Israel from their long dispersion and when they are cleansed from their transgressions. (*Doctrines of Salvation*, 2: 244)

The Prophet Joseph Smith spoke of the temple that is to be built in Jerusalem (bold added for emphasis):

Judah must return, **Jerusalem must be rebuilt, and the temple**, and water come out from under the temple, and the waters of the Dead Sea be healed. It will take some time to rebuild the walls of the city and the temple, &c.; and **all this must be done before the Son of Man will make His appearance**. (April 6, 1843.) (Joseph Smith, *Teachings of the Prophet Joseph Smith,* selected by Joseph Fielding Smith [Salt Lake City: Deseret Book, 1976], 286)

100 SIGNS

SIGN 77

THE GOSPEL WILL FLOURISH IN EGYPT AND A TEMPLE WILL BE BUILT THERE

CATEGORY: YET TO BE FULFILLED

In a seldom-noticed, brief prophecy of Isaiah, we find a very encouraging statement by the Lord that our brothers and sisters in Egypt will someday accept the gospel and that there will be a temple in that land. As usual, we will use bold to point these things out. We will also add some explanatory notes to these verses.

Isaiah 19:18–22

18 In that day [*the last days*] shall five [*several*] cities in the land of Egypt speak the language of Canaan [*Israel; a prophecy of greatly improved relationship between Egypt and Judah in the last days*], **and swear to the Lord of Hosts** [*make covenants with Jesus Christ, implying that they will have the true gospel*]; one shall be called the city of destruction [*not a good translation; could be "city of the sun"*].

Verse 19, next, prophesies that in the last days there will be an altar to the Lord built in Egypt. Since the only altars that we have now in the true church are those found in the temples, we can conclude that a temple will be built in Egypt.

19 **In that day** [*the last days*] **shall there be an altar** [*a temple; in a temple*] **to the Lord in the midst of the land of Egypt**, and a pillar [*symbolic of a temple—see Revelation 3:12*] at the border thereof to the Lord.

20 **And it** [*the altar and the pillar*] **shall be for a sign and for a witness** [*reminder*] **unto** [*of*] **the Lord of hosts in the land of Egypt**: for **they** [*Egyptians*] **shall cry** [*pray*] **unto the Lord** because of the oppressors, and he shall send them a saviour, and a great one, and he shall deliver them.

21 **And the Lord shall be known to Egypt, and the Egyptians shall know the Lord in that day** [*the last days*], and shall do sacrifice [*3 Nephi 9:20; broken heart and contrite spirit*] and oblation [*D&C 59:12*]; yea, **they shall vow a vow** [*make covenants*] **unto the Lord, and perform it** [*and will be faithful to them*].

Often, the Lord has to first humble people, and then heal them. Otherwise they won't listen to Him. We see this in verse 22, next (bold added for emphasis):

22 And the Lord shall smite Egypt: he shall smite and heal it [*first humble it, then heal it*]: **and they shall return even to the Lord** [*the Egyptians will hear and live the gospel*], and he shall be intreated [*prayed to*] of [*by*] them, and shall heal them [*wonderful blessings are in store for Egypt*].

SIGN 78

THE RAINBOW IS WITHDRAWN

CATEGORY: ?

The Prophet Joseph Smith gave what has become known to some as "The Rainbow Prophecy." It is as follows (bold added for emphasis):

I have asked of the Lord concerning His coming; and while asking the Lord, He gave a sign and said, "In the days of Noah I set a bow in the heavens as a sign and token that **in any year that the bow should be seen the Lord would not come**; but there should be seed time and harvest during that year: but **whenever you see the bow withdrawn**, it shall be a token that there shall be famine, pestilence, and great distress among the nations, and that **the coming of the Messiah is not far distant**." (*History of The Church of Jesus Christ of Latter-day Saints*, 6:254)

THE RAINBOW
IS WITHDRAWN

Until we receive more information from an authorized source, we are left to wonder what category this prophecy should be placed in. Some people ask if it means that there would be absolutely no rainbows, not even in sprinkler systems or in small waterfalls. Most prophecies do not lend themselves to such extremes. We will simply have to wait for additional revelation on this one.

SIGN 79

SOME OF THE "VERY ELECT" WILL BE DECEIVED

CATEGORY: BEING FULFILLED

One of the important signs of the times that should serve as a strong caution to active members of the Church is found in Matthew 24 in the Bible and in Joseph Smith—Matthew in the Pearl of Great Price. Both of these chapters serve as major resources for studying a number of prophecies that are to be fulfilled in the last days prior to the Second Coming. By way of background, the Prophet Joseph Smith, in his inspired translation of the Bible (The Joseph Smith Translation of the Bible or "JST"), added about 450 words to Matthew 24, and rearranged the order of some verses. For this particular sign, we will use Matthew 24:24 and JS—Matthew 1:22.

> Matthew 24:24
> 24 For there shall arise false Christs, and false prophets, and shall shew great signs and wonders; insomuch that, **if it *were* possible, they shall deceive the very elect**.
>
> Joseph Smith—Matthew 1:22
> 22 For in those days there shall also arise false Christs, and false prophets, and shall show great signs and wonders, insomuch, that, **if possible, they shall deceive the very elect, who are the elect according to the covenant**.

As you can see, among other changes, the Prophet added "according to the covenant" to the final phrase of Matthew 24:24. The warning is clear. Even faithful members of the Church with long years of diligence in living the gospel who have made covenants in the temple can be deceived. This is a threat of sufficient import in our day that it becomes a notable sign of the times.

This type of deception can appear to be very subtle on the surface, but when examined in the light of pure doctrine, it shows up clearly. Over the years, there have been a number of seemingly well meaning, active members who have advocated change in the position of the Church on various matters. They have come across, initially, as sincere and desiring the best interests of the Church and its members.

For example, many years ago (before the 1978 revelation which gave the priesthood to all worthy males) as I was pursuing an advanced degree at a large university in Utah, I met a fellow who looked vaguely familiar. We were working in the same room in one of the large buildings on campus and were the only ones in that laboratory at the time. In the course of just a few minutes, we struck up a conversation and shortly discovered that we had been in the same group of young missionaries at the Mission Home in Salt Lake City as we prepared for our missions in various parts of Europe. As we conversed, it brought back to my mind memories of his fervent and sincere testimony and strong commitment to the Church.

Before long, he guardedly brought up the topic of the blacks and the priesthood, and soon told me that if more members of the Church would petition the First Presidency on this matter, there was no doubt in his mind that its then-current position could be changed. Because of his strong feelings on the matter, he had relinquished his membership privileges and was quite caught up in his campaign to change the Church's stand. Attempts on my part to counter his thinking were painfully unsuccessful.

It left me in deep thought, wondering how a person who once had a strong testimony could have lost it so. It left a hollow place in my soul, mourning for his loss to the gospel. As I later analyzed his position in my mind, it came down to a simple conclusion. The Prophet and First Presidency are not the head of the Church. The Savior is! Therefore, those who seek to "lobby" for change in doctrine, position, policy, or whatever, by pressuring Church leaders through petitions, media, and other means either do not understand that this is the Lord's church or do not actually believe it. Thus, they look at the leadership of the Church as being men who can be pressured into changing things, just as is the case with man-made organizations. Thus, some members who are "the elect according to the covenant" can be deceived. They are reduced by the subtleties of Satan to becoming "social Mormons" who treat the Church as human-made and led, rather than members with deep and abiding faith and testimony, who know the Church is led by direct revelation.

In the late 1970s, when popular pressure to pass the Equal Rights Amendment was sweeping the nation, and the Church had spoken out strongly against it, a self-proclaimed feminist who was then a member of the Church gained considerable notoriety and fame by publicly denouncing the position of the Church on the ERA and lobbying for its passage. She brought great media and political pressure against the leadership of the Church, striving to bring about the desired change in position. The Church did not yield to the pressure and she persisted, eventually losing her membership and her husband. She went on to lead out in many feminist initiatives, bitterly railing publicly against God, and becoming increasingly radical in her views. Again, in this case, it appears that a steady, faithful, endowed member fell into the trap of deception, failing to realize that the Lord is at the helm of the Church and His will and wisdom for His children are reflected in its doctrines, programs, and policies.

Joseph Smith clearly defined what happens in such cases.

> That man who rises up to condemn others, finding fault with the Church, saying that they are out of the way, while he himself is righteous, then know assuredly, that that man is in the high road to apostasy; and if he does not repent, will apostatize, as God lives. (Joseph Smith, *Teachings of the Prophet Joseph Smith, Deseret Book, 1959*, 156–57)

We continue to see such fulfillments of this prophecy as, from time to time, great pressure is brought to bear on the Church by endowed, active members as they "lobby" for support of other members and engage the media in trying to secure the priesthood for women, the acceptance of practicing homosexuals and lesbians, the endorsement of gay marriage, the approval of abortion, and so forth.

Again, the simple eternal truth, not to be altered by the misguided thinking of men and women, nor by the sincere but erroneous thinking of honest men and women, is that God is in charge and does what He knows is best for the growth and development of His children here on earth. He wants us to become like Him. Those with deep testimony appreciate that He ultimately leads the Church and go forward with humble, peace-bringing faith, while those whose faith falters continue to "kick against the pricks" (Acts 9:5). A verse from the Doctrine and Covenants provides a concise summary for us:

100
SIGNS

D&C 121:38
38 Behold, ere he is aware, he is left unto himself, to kick against the pricks, to persecute the saints, and to fight against God.

Another way in which the "very elect" can be and sometimes are deceived is through feeling that they have been given special insights by the Spirit that go beyond the teachings of the First Presidency and Quorum of the Twelve Apostles. They often give talks and write books in which they share their "special insights." Over time, they begin giving their personal thoughts the status of revelation for the Church. Some members of the Church who listen to them are excited about the new things they, themselves, are learning and begin spreading the teachings they have inhaled. Thus, the speaker or author gains a following which encourages him or her to share their insights in ever widening circles.

There usually comes a time when such individuals start wondering why the Brethren don't preach these things themselves to the Church. Impatience begins to set in along with a subtle sense that Church leaders are out of touch with the Lord and the original Church established by Joseph Smith and the early Brethren. When counseled to cease their teaching and "gathering" activities by their local Church leaders, they refuse, feeling and saying that they are enlightened and their leaders are under the same apostasy and cloud of spiritual darkness that is over the general Church leadership. Long story short, they apostatize and lose their membership in God's kingdom. Thus, some of the very elect are skillfully extracted from the Lord's true Church by the wiles of the devil.

Just in passing, it is important to realize that the Spirit can sometimes give insights and personal revelation that are not yet preached by the Brethren to the Church or the world at large. Such inspiration is to be kept to the individual and not shared or taught publicly until if and when authorized Church leaders teach it. An example of this would be Lorenzo Snow. We will quote from the priesthood and Relief Society study manual for 2013:

> In the spring of 1840, Lorenzo Snow was in Nauvoo, Illinois, preparing to leave for a mission in England. He visited the home of his friend Henry G. Sherwood, and he asked Brother Sherwood to explain a passage of scripture. "While attentively listening to his explanation," President Snow later recalled, "the Spirit of the Lord rested mightily upon me—the eyes of my understanding were opened, and I saw as clear as the sun at noonday, with wonder and astonishment, the pathway of God and man. I formed the following couplet which expresses the revelation, as it was shown me. . . .
> "As man now is, God once was:
> "As God now is, man may be."
> Feeling that he had received "a sacred communication" that he should guard carefully, Lorenzo Snow did not teach the doctrine publicly until he knew that the Prophet Joseph Smith had taught it. Once he knew the doctrine was public knowledge, he testified of it frequently. (*Teachings of the Presidents of the Church, Lorenzo Snow*, 2012, 83.)

My mother had an experience with personal revelation that was to be kept private. Three years before my father was called as a patriarch, she was wondering one day what he would be doing in his retirement years. As she thought about it, a vision was opened up to her and she saw that he would be called to serve as a patriarch. At the same time that she received her answer, she was strictly instructed to tell no one what she now knew about him until after he was called. She complied absolutely and not until three years later, after Dad was called by a visiting Apostle attending their stake conference, sustained and

SIGNING OF THE CONSTITUTION OF THE UNITED STATES

BY HOWARD CHANDLER CHRISTY

ordained, did she disclose what she had received as very personal revelation.

SIGN 80

THE CONSTITUTION WILL HANG BY A THREAD

CATEGORY: BEING FULFILLED

In our day, it seems that we are watching the Constitution being unraveled. But it is not that the actual wording of the Constitution is being changed. Rather, the intent and meaning of the Founding Fathers is being reinterpreted by the courts of our land, thus rendering their inspired intent and wording ineffective.

The Lord established the Constitution of the United States of America by the hands of the Founding Fathers. These were wise and inspired men who were sent to earth and positioned by the Lord for this exact purpose. We read in the Doctrine and Covenants (bold added for emphasis):

D&C 101:77–80

77 According to **the** laws and **constitution** of the people, **which I have suffered to be established**, and should be maintained for the rights and protection of all flesh, according to just and holy principles;

78 **That every man may act** in doctrine and principle pertaining to futurity, **according to** the **moral agency** which I have given unto him, **that every man may be accountable for his own sins** in the day of judgment.

79 Therefore, it is not right that any man should be in bondage one to another.

80 And for this purpose have **I established the Constitution of this land**, **by the hands of wise men whom I raised up unto this very purpose**, and redeemed the land by the shedding of blood.

Brigham Young was one of a number who prophesied that the day would come that the Constitution would hang by a thread. But he also said that it would not be destroyed. Members of the Church will save it. We will include two statements from Brigham Young here (bold added for emphasis):

> **Will the Constitution be destroyed: No**: it will be held inviolate by this people; and, as Joseph Smith said, "The time will come when the destiny of the nation will hang upon a single thread. At that critical juncture, this people will step forth and save it from the threatened destruction." It will be so. (*Journal of Discourses*, Vol. 7, 15)

> When the Constitution of the United States hangs, as it were, upon a single thread, **they will have to call for the "Mormon" elders to save it** from utter destruction; **and they will step forth and do it**. (*Journal of Discourses*, Vol. 2, 182)

President Ezra Taft Benson spoke of this when taught us (bold added for emphasis):

> Unfortunately, we as a nation have apostatized in various degrees from different Constitutional principles as proclaimed by the inspired founders. **We are fast approaching that moment prophesied by Joseph Smith** when he said: "Even this nation will be on the very verge of crumbling to pieces and tumbling to the ground, and **when the Constitution is upon the brink of ruin, this people will be the staff upon which the nation shall lean, and they shall bear the Constitution away from the very verge of destruction**" (19 July 1840, as recorded by Martha Jane Knowlton Coray; ms. in Church Historian's Office, Salt Lake City). (President Ezra Taft Benson, *Ensign*, November 1987, 4)

100 SIGNS

SIGN 81

DESTROYING ANGELS WILL BE ALLOWED TO GO FORTH UPON THE EARTH

CATEGORY: BEING FULFILLED

In the Doctrine and Covenants, the Lord told the early Saints of this dispensation that angels even at that time were asking for permission to go forth and begin to harvest the tares (the wicked). We read the following (bold added for emphasis):

D&C 86:5–6

5 Behold, verily I say unto you, **the angels are crying unto the Lord day and night**, who are ready and waiting **to be sent forth to reap down the fields**;

6 **But the Lord saith** unto them, **pluck not up the tares** while the blade is yet tender (for verily your faith is weak), **lest you destroy the wheat also**.

President Wilford Woodruff told members of the Church that these angels have now been loosed and are going forth upon the earth:

What is the matter with the world today? What has created this change that we see coming over the world? Why these terrible earthquakes, tornados, and judgments? What is the meaning of all these mighty events that are taking place? The meaning is, these angels that have been held for many years in the temple of our God [in heaven] have got their liberty to go out and commence their mission and their work in the earth, and they are here today in the earth. (*The Young Woman's Journal*, Vol. 56, 643, October 8, 1894)

SIGN 82

THERE WILL BE AN EXTRAORDINARY INCREASE IN BLATANT LYING AND DECEIVING

CATEGORY: BEING FULFILLED

The Apostle Paul prophesied about conditions that will exist in the last days prior to the coming of the Savior. Among other things, he saw that there would be widespread lying and attempts to deceive in our day. He described conditions as being as if people had intentionally destroyed their consciences, such that they no longer work.

1 Timothy 4:1–2

1 Now the Spirit speaketh expressly, that in the latter times [*the last days*] some shall depart from the faith, giving heed to seducing spirits, and doctrines of devils;

2 Speaking lies in hypocrisy; having their conscience seared with a hot iron;

The phrase "conscience seared with a hot iron," in verse 2, above, means that a person has deliberately ignored or gone against his or her conscience to the point that it no longer is an effective deterrent against wrong doing. Such people get to the point that they can lie and deceive with no qualms. There is no question but what we are seeing the fulfillment of this prophecy today. In private circles as well as in large public settings such as politics and business, honesty and integrity have eroded away to an alarming degree. It has already come to the point that few trust people in positions of power and influence to be reliable in telling the truth, including politicians, entertainers, business people, and other high-profile individuals.

Moroni also prophesied of this as he finished his father, Mormon's, letter, foreseeing that there

100 SIGNS

would be much of lying and deceiving as part of the great "pollutions" upon the earth in the last days, both physical and spiritual.

Joseph Smith—Matthew 1:32
31 Yea, it shall come in a day when there shall be great pollutions upon the face of the earth; there shall be murders, and robbing, and lying, and deceivings, and whoredoms, and all manner of abominations; when there shall be many who will say, Do this, or do that, and it mattereth not, for the Lord will uphold such at the last day. But wo unto such, for they are in the gall of bitterness and in the bonds of iniquity.

No doubt, you have noticed greatly increasing attempts to lie and deceive without getting caught, both in public as well as private settings. This prophecy is clearly being fulfilled and can serve to strengthen our testimony that the gospel is true and that God's word is completely reliable.

SIGN 83

THERE WILL BE MUCH OF TRUCE-BREAKING

CATEGORY: BEING FULFILLED

Paul spoke of dangerous and unstable times to come in the last days leading up to the Second Coming of the Lord. One of the things he pointed out prophetically was that a prominent aspect of dysfunctional society would be that of truce-breaking.

2 Timothy 3:1–3
1 This know also, that in the last days perilous times shall come.

2 For men shall be lovers of their own selves, covetous, boasters, proud, blasphemers, disobedient to parents, unthankful, unholy,

3 Without natural affection, trucebreakers, false accusers, incontinent, fierce, despisers of those that are good,

The ongoing fulfillment of this prophecy makes up a significant portion of the news we hear almost every day. Nations make treaties and truces and then with impunity ignore and break them, generally without consequences from other nations. There is much of public chastisement but little of action. Even the United Nations is often seen condemning truce-breaking by constituent nations or others but, it seldom, if ever, votes to take actions against those nations who violate agreements.

SIGN 84

THERE WILL BE MORE AND MORE MEMBERS OF THE CHURCH WHO REMAIN STRONG AND FAITHFUL AS THE TIME OF THE SECOND COMING DRAWS NEAR

CATEGORY: BEING FULFILLED

This sign of the times is implied by a number of prophecies in combination with each other. For example, we know that in the last days, the gospel will go forth to all the world with the result that the Church will grow tremendously.

Matthew 24:14
14 And this gospel of the kingdom shall be preached in all the world for a witness unto all nations; and then shall the end come.

Joseph Smith made it very clear that the Church will continue to grow and expand dramatically now that it has been restored in the last days. He wrote this clearly in a letter to Mr. John Wentworth, editor and proprietor of the *Chicago Democrat*, on March 1, 1842. This letter has become known as "The Wentworth Letter," and, among other things, contains the Articles of Faith. The following excerpt from that letter prophesies that the Church will indeed go into every nation and reach all people as the coming of Christ draws near.

THE WENTWORTH LETTER

The Standard of Truth has been erected; no unhallowed hand can stop the work from progressing; persecutions may rage, mobs may combine, armies may assemble, calumny may defame, but the truth of God will go forth boldly, nobly, and independent, till it has penetrated every continent, visited every clime, swept every country, and sounded in every ear; till the purposes of God shall be accomplished, and the Great Jehovah shall say the work is done.

With this spreading forth of the gospel to all the world, it follows that there will be a rapidly increasing number of strong and faithful members who will anchor the Church wherever they are throughout the world. Our Apostles and General Authorities are constantly meeting these faithful Saints in their widespread travels as reported in the *Church News* and elsewhere.

Nephi saw these faithful Saints of our day and saw that the power of God would be upon them.

1 Nephi 14:12
12 And it came to pass that I beheld the church of the Lamb of God, and its numbers were few, because of the wickedness and abominations of the whore who sat upon many waters; nevertheless, I beheld that the church of the Lamb, who were the saints of God, were also upon all the face of the earth; and their dominions upon the face of the earth were small, because of the wickedness of the great whore whom I saw.

1 Nephi 14:14
14 And it came to pass that I, Nephi, beheld the power of the Lamb of God, that it descended upon the saints of the church of the Lamb, and upon the covenant people of the Lord, who were scattered upon all the face of the earth; and they were armed with

righteousness and with the power of God in great glory.

In the Pearl of Great Price, we are told how such faithful Saints will achieve such steadfastness and avoid being deceived in the last days. They will stay close to the scriptures and the words of our modern apostles and prophets.

Joseph Smith—Matthew 1:37
37 And whoso treasureth up my word, shall not be deceived, for the Son of Man shall come, and he shall send his angels before him with the great sound of a trumpet, and they shall gather together the remainder of his elect from the four winds, from one end of heaven to the other.

Also, they will use the signs of the times to shore up and strengthen their testimonies.

Joseph Smith—Matthew 1:39
39 So likewise, mine elect, when they shall see all these things [the signs of the times], they shall know that he is near, even at the doors;

SIGN 85

SPIRITS OF DEVILS WILL WORK MANY MIRACLES, DECEIVING MANY

CATEGORY: BEING FULFILLED

This is an interesting prophecy, especially in a day when fewer and fewer people even believe in God or the devil. Nevertheless, it is prophesied that evil spirits will be much involved in causing the turmoil and wickedness that will be rampant leading up to the Second Coming. It is indeed one of the signs of the times.

The Apostle John saw these evil spirits working miracles designed to deceive in the last days as recorded in the Bible.

Revelation 16:14

14 For they are the spirits of devils, working miracles, which go forth unto the kings of the earth and of the whole world, to gather them to the battle of that great day of God Almighty.

We might be wise to not be too narrow in our definition and thinking regarding the "miracles" performed by these "spirits of devils." For example, in addition to personal miracles of healing, fortune-telling, wizardry, and so forth, we might want to include behind-the-scenes inciting of riots, mob actions, inspiration to cyberbully, evil inspiration to be uncivil in public forums and gatherings, promoting hatred and the holding of grudges, encouraging infidelity and contention in families, and all other thoughts and actions that promote unrest and evil throughout the world in fulfillment of last days prophecies.

You may ask how we can tell the difference between miracles from evil spirits and miracles from God. The answer is actually very simple, and very important. We have the gift of the Holy Ghost, and if we live worthily and pay attention to its promptings, we will be able to tell the difference. One of the major functions of the Holy Ghost is to help us discern between right and wrong, between that which is of God and that which is of the devil. For example, if the source of a miracle is of evil, we will have an uncomfortable feeling, even if those around us are marveling and expressing positive feelings about the event. However, if the source is of God, we will have a feeling of peace and comfort. The gift of the Holy Ghost is a vital resource for us if we are to avoid deception of any kind.

SIGN 86

THE "ABOMINATION OF DESOLATION" WILL TAKE PLACE AGAIN

CATEGORY: BEING FULFILLED

The reason I suggest this prophecy is being fulfilled is that, in the Bible Dictionary, under "Abomination of Desolation," it explains this sign, as far as the last days are concerned (bold added for emphasis):

> **Speaking of the last days**, of the days following the restoration of the gospel and its declaration "for a witness unto all nations," our Lord said: "And again shall the abomination of desolation, spoken of by Daniel the prophet, be fulfilled" (Joseph Smith—Matthew 1:31–32). That is, **Jerusalem again will be under siege.** (Bible Dictionary, 601)

Jerusalem is certainly "under siege" today and has been for years. This is one of the signs of the times spoken of, among other places, in the Pearl of Great Price, wherein we are told that this prophecy will be fulfilled in the last days before the Savior Comes (bold added for emphasis):

Joseph Smith—Matthew 1:32

32 And **again** shall the **abomination of desolation**, spoken of by Daniel the prophet, be fulfilled.

It is also mentioned in the Bible as follows (bold added for emphasis):

Matthew 24:15

15 When ye therefore shall see the **abomination of desolation**, spoken of by Daniel the prophet, stand in the holy place, (whoso readeth, let him understand:)

For additional explanation of the phrase "abomination of desolation," and the fact that

BEHOLD, I WILL HASTEN MY WORK IN ITS TIME.

D & C   88:73

it was prophesied to occur twice (once in New Testament times and once in the last days), we will include a quote from the institute of religion New Testament Student Manual, entitled, *The Life and Teachings of Jesus and His Apostles*, page 152, as follows (bold added for emphasis):

Matthew 24:15–22, 29, 34, 35. What Is the Abomination of Desolation Spoken of by Daniel the Prophet and the Savior?
There were to be **two times** when this great tragedy would occur:

1. To the Jews at Jerusalem
"And now the ax was laid at the root of the rotted tree. Jerusalem was to pay the price. Daniel had foretold this hour when desolation, **born of abomination and wickedness**, would sweep the city. (Dan. 9:27; 11:31; 12:11.) Moses had said the siege would be so severe women would eat their own children. (Deut. 28.) Jesus specified the destruction would come in the days of the disciples.

"And come it did, in vengeance, without restraint. Hunger exceeded human endurance; blood flowed in the streets; destruction made desolate the temple; 1,100,000 Jews were slaughtered; Jerusalem was ploughed as a field; and a remnant of a once mighty nation was scattered to the ends of the earth. The Jewish nation died, impaled on Roman spears, at the hands of Gentile overlords.

"**But what of the saints who dwelt in Jerusalem in that gloomy day? They heeded Jesus' warning and fled in haste. Guided by revelation, as true saints always are, they fled to Pella in Perea and were spared.**" (Bruce R. McConkie, *Doctrinal New Testament Commentary*, 3 vols. [Salt Lake City: Bookcraft, 1980] 1:644–45.)

2. At the Time of the Second Coming
"All the desolation and waste which attended the former destruction of Jerusalem is but prelude to the coming siege. Titus and his legions slaughtered 1,100,000 Jews, destroyed the temple, and ploughed the city. **In the coming reenactment of this 'abomination of desolation,' the whole world will be at war**, **Jerusalem will be the center of the conflict**, every modern weapon will be used, and in the midst of the siege the Son of Man shall come, setting his foot upon the mount of Olives and fighting the battle of his Saints. (Zech. 12:1–9.)

"Speaking of these final battles which shall accompany his return, the Lord says: 'I will gather all nations against Jerusalem to battle; and the city shall be taken, and the houses rifled, and the women ravished; and half of the city shall go forth into captivity, and the residue of the people shall not be cut off from the city.' However, the final end of the conflict shall be different this time than it was anciently. 'Then shall the Lord go forth,' the prophetic record says, 'and fight against those nations, as when he fought in the day of battle. And his feet shall stand in that day upon the mount of Olives, . . . and the Lord shall be king over all the earth.' (Zech. 14.)" (*Doctrinal New Testament Commentary*, 1:659–60.)

SIGN 87

THE LORD "WILL HASTEN [HIS] WORK IN ITS TIME"

CATEGORY: BEING FULFILLED

Members of the Church were thrilled when President Thomas S. Monson announced the lowering of ages for young missionaries, in the October 2012 general conference. Young men could serve at age 18, after graduating from high school or its equivalent. Young sisters could serve at age 19. He said:

I am pleased to announce that effective immediately all worthy and able young men who have graduated from high school or its equivalent, regardless of where they live, will have the option of being recommended for missionary service beginning at the age of 18, instead of age 19. . . .

Today I am pleased to announce that able, worthy young women who have the desire to serve may be recommended for missionary service beginning at age 19, instead of age 21. ("Welcome to Conference," *Ensign*, November 2012)

This is no doubt a major facet of the prophecy given in the Doctrine and Covenants wherein the Lord stated (bold added for emphasis):

D&C 88:73
73 Behold, **I will hasten my work in its time**.

The resulting surge in applications for missionary service on the part of both young men and young women was amazing. Six months later, in the April 2013 general conference of the Church, Elder Neil L. Andersen spoke of the increasing growth of the Church and the surge in young men and women serving missions. It is exciting! He said:

Our day is no different. When Elder David A. Bednar and I were missionaries approximately 40 years ago (and I can assure you that we are not the oldest of the returned missionaries sitting in the red chairs), there were 16,000 missionaries. As President Thomas S. Monson reported yesterday, we now have 65,000—more than ever before. There were then 562 stakes. Today there are more than 3,000. At that time, our wards and branches were in 59 countries. Today we have congregations in 189 of the 224 nations and territories of the world. We are few in number, just as Nephi foretold. But at the same time, you and I are eyewitnesses of Daniel's prophetic words: the "stone . . . cut . . . without hands . . . [is filling] the whole earth."

Our day is a remarkable time of miracles. Six months ago as President Monson announced the age change for young men and young women desiring to serve missions, there was an undeniable spiritual outpouring. Faith overcame doubt,

and young men and women moved forward. The Thursday following conference, I was assigned to recommend missionary calls to the First Presidency. I was amazed to see the applications of 18-year-old men and 19-year-old women who had already adjusted their plans, visited their doctors, been interviewed by their bishops and stake presidents, and submitted their missionary applications— all in just five days. Thousands more have now joined them. It's a miracle.

We are watching this sign of the times being fulfilled in many ways, and, no doubt, there are yet fulfillments that we haven't even begun to imagine. We see unprecedented building of temples throughout the world. We see the translation of the scriptures in more and more languages. The development and publication of *Preach My Gospel* had a major impact on the missionary work of the Church. Not only has it fostered much more capable missionary efforts in the field, but it is leading to much better prepared young men and women to teach and assume leadership roles when they are released and return home from their missions.

Surely, the development of modern transportation, electronic media, computers, cell phones, flash drives, electronic readers, personal electronic note pads, communication satellites, and so forth, are all evidences of the amazing and accelerating "hastening" of the Lord's work in our day. In the context of this prophecy, all of these things and much more to come, yet unimagined, provide increasingly strong evidence that the gospel is true. Accompanied by the witness of the Spirit, our testimonies are fortified and our hearts are lifted up in gratitude for being alive in these marvelous last days.

100 SIGNS

SIGN 88

WICKEDNESS WILL BE RAMPANT

CATEGORY: BEING FULFILLED

While this sign of the times may be considered a summary of several of the signs of the times discussed elsewhere in this book, it merits being discussed as a sign in and of itself. It appears that wickedness in the last days prior to the second advent of Christ won't just "happen" as a matter of natural deterioration of morals and values. Rather, if we understand this prophecy correctly, it will be the direct result of wickedness spread intentionally by use of mass media, which will cause an unprecedented acceleration of evil and virtual "free fall" of society. Satan will be at the helm of this "desolating scourge" of wickedness. Nephi warns of Satan's devastating power in the last days (bold added for emphasis):

2 Nephi 28:20
20 For behold, **at that day** [*in the last days*] **shall he rage in the hearts of the children of men**, and stir them up to anger against that which is good.

This intentional spread of wickedness by Lucifer and his "front organizations" is spoken of in the Bible. In the great vision given to John the Apostle, known in the Bible as "The Revelation of St John the Divine," and which we usually refer to as the book of Revelation, one of the things that John was shown was that great masses of people would admire and basically worship wicked heroes in the last days. Thus, the mass admiration and virtual "worship" of unworthy media personalities and political figures is a significant contributor to the rampant wickedness of the last days.

We find this prophecy in Revelation 13:3–4. The context is that of Satan's control of many "beasts" representing "degenerate earthly kingdoms" (see

heading to Revelation 13 in our LDS Bible). (Bold added for emphasis:)

Revelation 13:3–4
3 And I saw one of his heads as it were wounded to death; and his deadly wound was healed: and **all the world wondered after** [*admired*] **the beast**.

4 And they worshipped the dragon which gave power unto the beast: and they **worshipped** [*admired*] **the beast, saying, Who** *is* **like unto the beast?** who is able to make war with him?

Yet another scripture which reflects the rampant wickedness of the last days is found in Isaiah (bold added for emphasis):

Isaiah 5:20
20 Woe unto them that **call evil good, and good evil**; that put darkness for light, and light for darkness; that put bitter for sweet, and sweet for bitter!

In the Lord's preface to the Doctrine and Covenants, known as section one, He pointed out some of the wickedness that was then upon the earth and that will continue to increase, explaining that the restored gospel is designed to help sincere, righteous people avoid the last days pitfalls of evil and have light and spirituality in their lives. Some of the wickedness He delineated is found in the following verses (bold added for emphasis):

D&C 1:11–16
11 Wherefore the voice of the Lord is unto the ends of the earth, that all that will hear may hear:

12 Prepare ye, prepare ye for that which is to come, for the Lord is nigh;

13 And the anger of the Lord is kindled, and his sword is bathed in heaven, and it shall fall upon the inhabitants of the earth.

14 And the arm of the Lord shall be revealed; and the day cometh that they who will not

hear the voice of the Lord, neither the voice of his servants, neither give heed to the words of the prophets and apostles, shall be cut off from among the people;

15 For **they have strayed from mine ordinances, and have broken mine everlasting covenant;**

16 **They seek not the Lord** to establish his righteousness, but **every man walketh in his own way, and after the image of his own god**, whose image is in the likeness of the world, and whose substance is that of an idol, which waxeth old and shall perish in Babylon, even Babylon the great, which shall fall.

Moroni saw our day and described it thus as he finished the record of his father, Mormon (bold added for emphasis):

Mormon 8:35–36
35 Behold, I speak unto you as if ye were present, and yet ye are not. But behold, Jesus Christ hath shown you unto me, and I know your doing.

36 And I know that ye do walk in the **pride** of your hearts; and there are none save a few only who do not lift themselves up in the **pride** of their hearts, unto **the wearing of very fine apparel**, unto **envying**, and **strifes**, and **malice**, and **persecutions**, and **all manner of iniquities**; and your churches, yea, even every one, have become **polluted** because of the pride of your hearts.

The same types of wickedness that led to the downfall of the Nephite nation at the time Moroni's son, Moronihah was leading the Nephite armies, are seen throughout our world today. They were described by Mormon (bold added for emphasis):

Helaman 4:12–13
12 And it was because of the **pride** of their hearts, because of their exceeding riches, yea, it was because of their **oppression to the poor**, withholding their food from the hungry, withholding their clothing from the naked, and smiting their humble brethren upon the cheek, **making a mock of that which was sacred, denying the spirit of prophecy and of revelation, murdering, plundering, lying, stealing, committing adultery**, rising up in **great contentions**, and deserting away into the land of Nephi, among the Lamanites—

13 And because of this their **great wickedness**, and their boastings in their own strength, they were left in their own strength; therefore they did not prosper, but were afflicted and smitten, and driven before the Lamanites, until they had lost possession of almost all their lands.

SIGN 89
BABYLON WILL FALL
CATEGORY: BEING FULFILLED

"Babylon" may be basically defined as "Satan's kingdom." All who follow his wicked and evil ways are "citizens" of Babylon. Obviously, Babylon has not yet fallen. Therefore, this sign is yet to be fulfilled. This prophecy seems to be divided into two categories. First, many of the wicked in the last days will fall before the actual coming of Christ. The carnage and destruction among the wicked is depicted as a great "feast" for carrion birds such as vultures. Second, those who remain will be destroyed by the glory of the Lord when He actually comes. We read about this in Revelation 19:17–21. In verse 21, we see that the wicked who survived the terrible battles among the wicked in the final stages of the earth are destroyed "with the sword of him that sat upon the horse," in other words, Christ (see Revelation 19:11). These verses read as follows (bold added for emphasis):

Revelation 19:17–21
17 And I saw an angel standing in the sun; and he cried with a loud voice, saying to

100 SIGNS

AND THERE SHALL
BE A GREAT
HAILSTORM
SENT FORTH TO
DESTROY THE
CROPS OF
THE EARTH.

D & C 29:16

all the fowls that fly in the midst of heaven, Come and gather yourselves together unto the supper of the great God;

18 That ye may eat the flesh of kings, and the flesh of captains, and the flesh of mighty men, and the flesh of horses, and of them that sit on them, and the flesh of all men, both free and bond, both small and great.

19 And I saw the beast, and the **kings of the earth, and their armies, gathered together to make war against him that sat on the horse** [*the Savior—see Revelation 19:11–13*]**, and against his army**.

20 And the beast was taken, and with him the false prophet that wrought miracles before him, with which he deceived them that had received the mark of the beast, and them that worshipped his image. These both were cast alive into a lake of fire burning with brimstone.

21 And the **remnant** were **slain with the sword of him that sat upon the horse**, which sword proceeded out of his mouth: and all the fowls were filled with their flesh.

"Babylon" has many names in the scriptures. Two of these names are used in Doctrine and Covenants 29:21 in referring to the fall of Satan's kingdom at the time of the Second Coming. They are "the great and abominable church" and "the whore of all the earth." These are very strong terms and are a reminder of how evil Lucifer and his wicked hosts are. This verse reads as follows:

D&C 29:21
21 And **the great and abominable church**, which is **the whore of all the earth**, **shall be cast down** by devouring fire, according as it is spoken by the mouth of Ezekiel the prophet, who spoke of these things, which have not come to pass but surely must, as I live, for abominations shall not reign.

I mentioned above that the remaining wicked will be destroyed by the glory of the Lord when He comes. This fact is found in the following

Isaiah chapter in the Book of Mormon (bold added for emphasis):

2 Nephi 12:10, 19, and 21
10 O ye wicked ones, enter into the rock, and hide thee in the dust, for the fear of the Lord and **the glory of his majesty shall smite thee**.

19 And they shall go into the holes of the rocks, and into the caves of the earth, for the fear of the Lord shall come upon them and **the glory of his majesty shall smite them**, when he ariseth to shake terribly the earth.

21 To go into the clefts of the rocks, and into the tops of the ragged rocks, for the fear of the Lord shall come upon them and the majesty of his glory shall smite them, when he ariseth to shake terribly the earth.

Thus, the fall and destruction of the large and mighty kingdom of the devil, known as Babylon, will be finalized (for a thousand years) as the remaining wicked are literally burned "as stubble" (Isaiah 47:14) and Satan is bound for a thousand years (D&C 88:110), unable to tempt or cause trouble on earth at all (D&C 101:28.) The ultimate and final permanent destruction of his kingdom will take place at the end of the Millennium, when he and his evil followers will be released and the battle of Gog and Magog will take place, at the end of which he and his like-thinking, completely evil followers will be banished to perdition, which is often referred to in gospel discussions as "outer darkness." (Bold added for emphasis:)

D&C 88:111–114
111 And then he shall be loosed for a little season, that he may gather together his armies.

112 And Michael, the seventh angel, even the archangel, shall gather together his armies, even the hosts of heaven.

113 And the devil shall gather together his armies; even the hosts of hell, and shall come up to battle against Michael and his armies.

114 And then cometh the battle of the great God [*the battle of Gog and Magog*]; and **the devil and his armies shall be cast away into their own place, that they shall not have power over the saints any more at all**.

At this point, the prophesied fall of Babylon will have been finally and completely fulfilled.

SIGN 90

A GREAT HAILSTORM WILL DESTROY THE CROPS OF THE EARTH

CATEGORY: YET TO BE FULFILLED

All we know about this sign of the times is that the Lord said that it would happen in the last days before His coming. We read in the Doctrine and Covenants (bold added for emphasis):

> D&C 29:16
> 16 And there shall be **a great hailstorm sent forth to destroy the crops of the earth**.

We find another reference to hail as a sign of the times in the book of Revelation. In this reference, it indicates that there will be damage to people as a result (bold added for emphasis):

> Revelation 16:21
> 21 And **there fell upon men a great hail** out of heaven, every stone about the weight of a talent: and men blasphemed God because of the plague of the hail; for the plague thereof was exceeding great.

It is interesting to wonder how heavy a "talent" is, as used in verse 21, above. We really don't know (see Bible Dictionary, under "Talent"). On occasions someone will use the Old Testament system of weights in which a talent would be the

equivalent of about 75 pounds, and thus they describe these hailstones which "fell upon men" as being in the neighborhood of 75 pounds each. The problem with this is that the New Testament system of weights is not the same as the Old Testament system. Therefore, we are left to understand simply that a devastating hailstorm will be one of the signs of the times when gross wickedness dominates the earth.

SIGN 91

THERE WILL BE A GREAT EARTHQUAKE SUCH AS NEVER BEFORE

CATEGORY: YET TO BE FULFILLED

This too is a sign of the times for which we have little information. We read in the book of Revelation (bold added for emphasis):

> Revelation 16:18
> 18 And there were voices, and thunders, and lightnings; and there was **a great earthquake, such as was not since men were upon the earth**, so mighty an earthquake, and so great.

Another reference to this monumental event is also found in Revelation (bold added for emphasis):

> Revelation 6:12
> 12 And I beheld when he had opened the sixth seal, and, lo, there was **a great earthquake**; and the sun became black as sackcloth of hair [*black fabric made from the hair of black goats*], and the moon became as blood;

From these references, we understand that this earthquake will be unprecedented in the history of the earth since the fall of Adam. With that in mind, it appears that this earthquake will exceed the earthquakes on the American continent at the time of the Savior's crucifixion. Looking again at Revelation 6:12, quoted above, one possibility for the darkening of the sun and the moon becoming "as blood" (not blood but, rather, appearing blood red) might be the tremendous dust clouds and air pollution stirred up by such an earthquake. Thus, this future sign of the times will be a very strong indicator to those who are familiar with the signs of the times that the coming of the Lord is near.

SIGN 92

WATERS WILL FLOW FROM THE TEMPLE IN JERUSALEM AND HEAL THE DEAD SEA

CATEGORY: YET TO BE FULFILLED

After giving a rather lengthy prophecy about the future temple to be built in Jerusalem in the last days (Ezekiel 40–46), the prophet Ezekiel foretold that water would flow "out from under the threshold of the house [*the temple*] eastward" (Ezekiel 47:1) and "into the sea [*the Dead Sea*] . . . the waters shall be healed" (Ezekiel 47:8). We will give the complete prophecy by Ezekiel and then quote the Prophet Joseph Smith regarding it.

Ezekiel 47:1–10
1 Afterward he brought me again unto the door of the house; and, behold, waters issued out from under the threshold of the house eastward: for the forefront of the house stood toward the east, and the waters came down from under from the right side of the house, at the south side of the altar.

2 Then brought he me out of the way of the gate northward, and led me about the way without unto the utter gate by the way that looketh eastward; and, behold, there ran out waters on the right side.

3 And when the man that had the line in his hand went forth eastward, he measured a

thousand cubits, and he brought me through the waters; the waters were to the ankles.

4 Again he measured a thousand, and brought me through the waters; the waters were to the knees. Again he measured a thousand, and brought me through; the waters were to the loins.

5 Afterward he measured a thousand; and it was a river that I could not pass over: for the waters were risen, waters to swim in, a river that could not be passed over.

6 And he said unto me, Son of man, hast thou seen this? Then he brought me, and caused me to return to the brink of the river.

7 Now when I had returned, behold, at the bank of the river were very many trees on the one side and on the other.

8 Then said he unto me, These waters issue out toward the east country, and go down into the desert, and go into the sea: which being brought forth into the sea, the waters shall be healed.

9 And it shall come to pass, that every thing that liveth, which moveth, whithersoever the rivers shall come, shall live: and there shall be a very great multitude of fish, because these waters shall come thither: for they shall be healed; and every thing shall live whither the river cometh.

10 And it shall come to pass, that the fishers shall stand upon it from En-gedi even unto En-eglaim; they shall be a place to spread forth nets; their fish shall be according to their kinds, as the fish of the great sea, exceeding many.

Joseph Smith spoke of this as follows (bold added for emphasis):

Judah must return, Jerusalem must be rebuilt, and the temple, and **water come out from under the temple, and the waters of the Dead Sea be healed**. It will take some time to rebuild the walls of the city and the temple, &c.; and all this must be done before the Son of Man will make

His appearance. (*Teachings of the Prophet Joseph Smith*, 286)

This prophecy could be literal, and it seems, based on the above quote, that Joseph Smith considered it to be literal. It could be figurative in the sense that the water could symbolize the "living water" from the Savior, which heals and refreshes (John 4:14), including healing the spiritually dead (symbolized by the Dead Sea). And it could be both.

The institute of religion's *Old Testament Student Manual, 1 Kings through Malachi* (Religion 302, 1981), suggests a possibility for the fulfilling of this prophecy.

> The waters issuing forth from under the temple and the healing of the Dead Sea may occur when the Lord himself sets foot upon the Mount of Olives, causing this mountain to divide in two and create a large valley. (See Zechariah 14:4; D&C 133:20–24.)

SIGN 93

THE BATTLE OF ARMAGEDDON
CATEGORY: YET TO BE FULFILLED

This will be a tremendous battle, focused against the Jews in the Holy Land and signaled by an unprecedented siege against Jerusalem. All nations of the earth will be involved in it, whether fighting against the Jews or fighting for them. Sometimes this battle is also called the battle of Gog and Magog. Joseph Fielding Smith clarified these terms as follows (bold added for emphasis):

> **Before the coming of Christ**, the great war, sometimes called **Armageddon**, will take place as spoken of by Ezekiel, chapters 38 and 39. Another war of **Gog and Magog will be after the millennium**. (*Doctrines of Salvation*, 3:45)

Speaking of the final scenes before the coming of the Lord, John the Revelator describes what he saw in vision, including a reference to the final great battle before the Second Coming in a place called "Armageddon." This is recorded as follows (bold added for emphasis):

> Revelation 16:14–16
> 14 For they are the spirits of devils, working miracles, which go forth unto the kings of the earth and of the whole world, **to gather them to the battle of that great day of God Almighty.**
>
> 15 Behold, I come as a thief. Blessed is he that watcheth, and keepeth his garments [*is prepared; keeps covenants made with the Lord*], lest he walk naked [*the wicked will have no excuses left to cover their sinful lifestyle*], and they see his shame.
>
> 16 And **he gathered them together into a place called** in the Hebrew tongue **Armageddon.**

You may wish to read a bit more about Armageddon in the Bible Dictionary in the LDS Bible, under "Armageddon." It refers to Zechariah, chapters 11 to 14, which have considerable prophecy about these final scenes. For instance, Zechariah speaks of the Savior as He saves the Jews from all nations who choose to fight against them (bold added for emphasis):

> Zechariah 12:2–9
> 2 Behold, I will make Jerusalem a cup of trembling unto all the people round about, **when they shall be in the siege both against Judah *and* against Jerusalem.**
>
> 3 And in that day will I make Jerusalem a burdensome stone for all people: **all that burden themselves with it shall be cut in pieces**, though all the people of the earth be gathered together against it [*even if all nations were to gather against it*].
>
> 4 In that day, saith the Lord, I will smite every horse [*symbolic of military power*] with astonishment, and his rider with madness:

LOOKING OVER
ADAM-ONDI-AHMAN

ADAM-ONDI-AHMAN, MISSOURI

and I will open mine eyes upon the house of Judah, and will smite every horse of the people with blindness.

5 And the governors of Judah shall say in their heart, The inhabitants of Jerusalem shall be my strength in the Lord of hosts their God [*there will be a great conversion among the Jews*].

6 In that day will I make the governors of Judah like an hearth of fire among the wood, and like a torch of fire in a sheaf; and they shall devour all the people round about, on the right hand and on the left: and **Jerusalem shall be inhabited again in her own place,** *even* **in Jerusalem.**

7 **The Lord also shall save the tents of Judah** first, that the glory of the house of David and the glory of the inhabitants of Jerusalem do not magnify themselves against Judah.

8 **In that day shall the Lord defend the inhabitants of Jerusalem**; and he that is feeble among them at that day shall be as David; and the house of David shall be as God, as the angel of the Lord before them.

9 And it shall come to pass **in that day,** *that* **I will seek to destroy all the nations that come against Jerusalem.**

One caution, as counseled by several of the Brethren. We would do well not to make each of the battles in the Holy Land in these last days into *the* Battle of Armageddon in our minds. Certainly they are leading up to it and we would be wise to look at them with a knowing eye, being aware of the prophecies about Armageddon. But we should leave it to our prophets to alert us when the actual Battle of Armageddon begins taking place.

Just one last note now regarding the location of the valley of Armageddon, which is known today as the valley of Megiddo. This quote is taken from the Bible Dictionary under "Armageddon":

The valley of Megiddo is in the western portion of the plain of Esdraelon, 50 miles north of Jerusalem.

SIGN 94
THE MEETING AT ADAM-ONDI-AHMAN
CATEGORY: YET TO BE FULFILLED

Prior to the actual Second Coming of the Savior, a large meeting will be held in Adam-ondi-Ahman, which is located in the state of Missouri, about 70 miles north-northeast of Independence. (See map of "The Missouri-Illinois Area" in the back of your Doctrine and Covenants.) We will discuss who will attend in a moment, but first, some background as to the historic and sacred nature of this beautiful area. Adam died when he was 930 years old. When Adam was 927 years old, he gathered his posterity together for a final meeting with them at Adam-ondi-Ahman. We read of this in the Doctrine and Covenants as follows (bold added for emphasis):

D&C 107:53–57

53 **Three years previous to the death of Adam, he called** Seth, Enos, Cainan, Mahalaleel, Jared, Enoch, and Methuselah, who were all high priests, with the residue of **his posterity who were righteous, into the valley of Adam-ondi-Ahman**, and there bestowed upon them his last blessing.

54 **And the Lord appeared** unto them, and they rose up and blessed Adam, and called him Michael, the prince, the archangel.

55 And **the Lord administered comfort unto Adam**, and said unto him: I have set thee to be at the head; a multitude of nations shall come of thee, and thou art a prince over them forever.

56 And **Adam stood up** in the midst of the congregation; **and**, notwithstanding he was bowed down with age, being full of the Holy

Ghost, **predicted whatsoever should befall his posterity unto the latest generation**.

57 These things were **all written in the book of Enoch**, and are to be testified of in due time.

We are told in the Doctrine and Covenants, section 116, as well as in Daniel 7:9–14, that Adam will once again meet with his righteous posterity who will honor him prior to the Second Coming. The Savior will also attend this gathering:

D&C 116
Spring Hill [*HC 3:34–35*] is named by the Lord Adam-ondi-Ahman, because, said he, it is the place where Adam shall come to visit his people, or the Ancient of Days shall sit, as spoken of by Daniel the prophet.

According to Daniel, this will be a rather large gathering, as you will see in the following quote (bold added for emphasis plus some explanatory notes in brackets).

Daniel 7:9–14
9 I [*Daniel*] beheld till the thrones were cast down [*in the last days*], and **the Ancient of days** [*Adam*] did sit, whose garment *was* white as snow, and the hair of his head like the pure wool: his throne *was like* the fiery flame, *and* his wheels *as* burning fire.

10 A fiery stream issued and came forth from before him: **thousand thousands** [*millions*] ministered unto him, and **ten thousand times ten thousand** [*a hundred million*] stood before him: the judgment was set, and the books were opened.

11 I beheld then because of the voice of the great words which the horn spake: I beheld *even* till the beast was slain, and his body destroyed, and given to the burning flame.

12 As concerning the rest of the beasts, they had their dominion taken away: yet their lives were prolonged for a season and time.

13 I [*Daniel*] saw in the night visions, and, behold, *one* like **the Son of man** [*Christ*]

came with the clouds of heaven, and **came to the Ancient of days** [*Adam*], and they brought him [*Christ*] near before him [*Adam—see TPJS, 157*].

14 And **there was given him** [*Christ*] **dominion, and glory, and a kingdom, that all people, nations, and languages, should serve him** [*the Millennium*]: his dominion *is* an everlasting dominion, which shall not pass away, and his kingdom *that* which shall not be destroyed.

We learn from the above quote that the meeting at Adam-ondi-Ahman, before the actual Second Coming, will be a rather large gathering, where Adam will gather his righteous posterity together. Christ will come also, and those present, who are or have been in authority, will turn their keys of power over to Him to use as He ushers in the Millennium and governs the world during the Millennium as "King of Kings, and Lord of Lords" (D&C 29:11; Revelation 19:16).

Bruce R. McConkie gives additional explanation about what takes place at this gathering:

Before the Lord Jesus descends openly and publicly in the clouds of glory, attended by all the hosts of heaven; before the great and dreadful day of the Lord sends terror and destruction from one end of the earth to the other; before he stands on Mount Zion, or sets his feet on Olivet, or utters his voice from an American Zion or a Jewish Jerusalem; before all flesh shall see him together; before any of his appearances, which taken together comprise the second coming of the Son of God—before all these, there is to be a secret appearance to selected members of his Church. He will come in private to his prophet and to the apostles then living. Those who have held keys and powers and authorities in all ages from Adam to the present will also be present. And further, all the faithful members of the Church then living and all the faithful saints of all the ages past will be present. It

100 SIGNS

will be the greatest congregation of faithful saints ever assembled on planet earth. It will be a sacrament meeting. It will be a day of judgment for the faithful of all the ages. And it will take place in Daviess County, Missouri, at a place called Adam-ondi-Ahman. (Bruce R. McConkie, *The Millennial Messiah: The Second Coming of the Son of Man* [Salt Lake City: Deseret Book, 1982], 578)

Also from Bruce R. McConkie on this subject:

With reference to the use of sacramental wine in our day, the Lord said to Joseph Smith: "You shall partake of none except it is made new among you; yea, in this my Father's kingdom which shall be built up on the earth." In so stating, he is picking up the language he used in the upper room. Then he says: "The hour cometh that I will drink of the fruit of the vine with you on the earth." Jesus is going to partake of the sacrament again with his mortal disciples on earth. But it will not be with mortals only. He names others who will be present and who will participate in the sacred ordinance. These include Moroni, Elias, John the Baptist, Elijah, Abraham, Isaac, Jacob, Joseph (who was sold into Egypt), Peter, James, and John, "and also with Michael, or Adam, the father of all, the prince of all, the ancient of days." Each of these is named simply by way of illustration. The grand summation of the whole matter comes in these words: "And also with all those whom my Father hath given me out of the world." (D&C 27:4–14.) The sacrament is to be administered in a future day, on this earth, when the Lord Jesus is present, and when all the righteous of all ages are present. This, of course, will be a part of the grand council at Adam-ondi-Ahman.

Adam-ondi-Ahman—meaning the place or land of God where Adam dwelt—is at a place called Spring Hill, Daviess County, Missouri. This site is named by the Lord "Adam-ondi-Ahman, because, said he, it is the place where Adam shall come to visit his people, or the Ancient of Days shall sit, as

spoken of by Daniel the prophet." (D&C 116.) There is a great valley there in which the righteous will assemble; and where there are valleys, the surrounding elevations are called mountains. Thus our revelations speak of "the mountains of Adam-ondi-Ahman" and of "the plains of Olaha Shinehah, or the land where Adam dwelt." (D&C 117:8.) Sacred indeed is the whole region for what has taken place and what will take place in its environs. (*The Millennial Messiah*, 587–88)

We will use a quote from the Prophet Joseph Smith as a final summary for this particular sign of the times:

Daniel, in his seventh chapter speaks of the Ancient of Days; he means the oldest man, our Father Adam, Michael, he will call his children together and hold a council with them to prepare them for the coming of the Son of Man. He (Adam) is the father of the human family, and presides over the spirits of all men, and all that have had the keys must stand before him in this grand council. This may take place before some of us leave this stage of action. The Son of Man stands before him, and there is given him glory and dominion. Adam delivers up his stewardship to Christ, that which was delivered to him as holding the keys of the universe, but retains his standing as head of the human family. (*Teachings of the Prophet Joseph Smith*, 157; punctuation as in the original)

SIGN 95

TWO PROPHETS WILL BE KILLED IN JERUSALEM

CATEGORY: YET TO BE FULFILLED

This is one of the signs of the times in which many of our Christian friends in other churches also strongly believe. During the last days, before the Savior's coming, two latter-day prophets will minister to the Jews in Jerusalem for a period of

42 months, that is, 3½ years, after which time they will be killed. Their bodies will be left lying in the streets of Jerusalem for 3½ days, during which people in Jerusalem and throughout the world will celebrate their deaths and will send gifts one to another as part of their celebration. After the 3½ days have passed, the two prophets will be resurrected and the party will be "very over." It would be difficult for those who know the scriptures to miss this sign of the times.

It is found in Revelation, chapter eleven. We will quote some of the verses here and bold some words and phrases for emphasis. But first, a note about a significant change made here by the Prophet Joseph Smith. In Revelation 11:3, it uses the phrase "two witnesses." This could mean any two people, including two missionaries or whoever. It reads in the Bible as follows (bold added for emphasis):

Revelation 11:3
3 And I will give *power* unto **my two witnesses**, and they shall prophesy a thousand two hundred *and* threescore days, clothed in sackcloth.

However, in the Doctrine and Covenants, Joseph Smith changed the word from "witnesses" to "prophets" (bold added for emphasis):

D&C 77:15
15 Q. What is to be understood by the **two witnesses**, in the eleventh chapter of Revelation?

A. **They are two prophets** that are to be raised up to the Jewish nation in the last days, at the time of the restoration, and to prophesy to the Jews after they are gathered and have built the city of Jerusalem in the land of their fathers.

Thus, we understand that these martyrs will necessarily be members of our First Presidency or of the Quorum of the Twelve Apostles. These men are all sustained as "prophets, seers, and revelators" and as such are all prophets. One of my colleagues who was serving as a stake president at the same time I was, told me that one of our Apostles mentioned this in a conversation with him. The Apostle told him that it was a very sobering thing to realize that two of them or their successors in the First Presidency and the Twelve would fulfill this prophecy.

Quoting now from Revelation, chapter eleven, we will consider the following verses (bold added for emphasis) and add a few explanatory notes in brackets:

Revelation 11:3–13
3 And I will give power unto my **two witnesses** [*two prophets to the Jews in the last days; D&C 77:15*], and they shall prophesy [*serve, minister, prophesy, etc.*] a thousand two hundred and threescore days [*42 months or 3½ years, about the same length as Christ's ministry*], clothed in sackcloth [*in humility*].

4 These are the two olive trees [*olive trees provide olive oil for lamps so people can be prepared to meet Christ; compare with the parable of the ten virgins in Matthew 25:1–13*], and the two candlesticks [*they hold light so people can see clearly*] standing before the God of the earth.

5 And if any man will hurt them [*the two prophets*], fire [*the power of God to destroy*] proceedeth out of their mouth, and devoureth their enemies [***the two prophets will be protected during their mission***]: and if any man will hurt them, he must in this manner be killed [*he will be killed by the power of God; Strong's #1163*].

6 **These** [***two prophets***] **have power to shut heaven** [*have the power of God; compare with the Prophet Nephi in Helaman 10:5–10 and 11:1–6*], that it rain not in the days of their prophecy: and have power over waters to turn them to blood, and to smite the earth with all plagues [***to encourage people to***

repent; *to deliver from evil, bondage, as with the plagues in Egypt*], as often as they will.

7 And **when they shall have finished their testimony** [*ministry*], the beast [*Satan*] that ascendeth out of the bottomless pit [*Revelation 9:1–2*] shall make war against them [*the two prophets*], and shall overcome them, and **kill them.**

8 And **their dead bodies shall lie in the street** of the great city [*Jerusalem*], which spiritually is called Sodom and Egypt [*i.e., is very wicked*], where also our Lord was crucified.

9 And **they** [*the wicked*] of the people and kindreds and tongues and nations shall see their dead bodies three days and an half [*perhaps symbolically tying in with their 3½-year ministry as well as the Savior's 3 days in the tomb; the Savior was killed, too, by the wicked for trying to save them*], and **shall not suffer** [*allow*] **their dead bodies to be put in graves** [*many in Eastern cultures believed that if the body is not buried, the spirit is bound to wander the earth in misery forever*].

10 And **they that dwell upon the earth** [*not just people in Jerusalem; implies that knowledge of the death of the two prophets will be known worldwide*] **shall rejoice** over them, and **make merry**, and shall **send gifts one to another** [*people all over the world will cheer and send gifts to one another* **to celebrate** *the deaths of these two prophets*]; because these two prophets tormented them [*the wicked*] that dwelt on the earth [*implies that these prophets' influence was felt and irritated the wicked far beyond Jerusalem*].

11 And **after three days and an half** the Spirit of life from God entered into them [***they are resurrected** at this time—see heading to this chapter in your LDS English Bible*], and they stood upon their feet; and great fear fell upon them which saw them.

12 And they [*the wicked who were celebrating*] heard a great voice from heaven saying unto them [*the two slain prophets*], Come up hither. And they **ascended up to heaven**

in a cloud; and their enemies beheld [*saw*] them.

13 And the same hour [*immediately*] was there a great earthquake, and the tenth part of the city fell, and in the earthquake were slain of men seven thousand: and the remnant were affrighted, and gave glory to the God of heaven [*perhaps implying that* **some of the wicked are converted** *at this time, as was the case with the Savior's resurrection and also when Lazarus was brought back from the dead; if so, the deaths of the two prophets bore immediate fruit in helping some begin returning to God*].

As mentioned above, this is a well-known sign of the times, looked forward to by many good people in many different faiths. It will be one that the faithful will not miss.

SIGN 96

THE MOUNT OF OLIVES WILL SPLIT IN TWO

CATEGORY: YET TO BE FULFILLED

In the last days, when the Jews are engaged in an unprecedented battle for survival as many wicked nations of the world lay siege to Jerusalem and the people of Judah, and it looks like they will be destroyed, the Savior will set foot on the Mount of Olives, which is located just outside Jerusalem. It will split in two from east to west. Part of the mountain will move to the north and part to the south. The remaining Jews will flee into the newly created rift or valley in the mountain where they will meet their Savior. Charles W. Penrose described this sign of the times:

> His [*Christ's*] next appearance [*after his appearance in the New Jerusalem*] will be among the distressed and nearly vanquished sons of Judah. At the crisis of their fate, when the hostile troops of several nations are ravaging the city and all the horrors of war

AND THEN SHALL
APPEAR THE SIGN
OF THE SON OF MAN
IN HEAVEN.

MATTHEW 24:30

are overwhelming the people of Jerusalem, he will set his feet upon the Mount of Olives, which will cleave and part asunder at his touch. Attended by a host from heaven, he will overthrow and destroy the combined armies of the Gentiles, and appear to the worshipping Jews as the mighty Deliverer and Conqueror so long expected by their race; and while love, gratitude, awe, and admiration swell their bosoms, the Deliverer will show them the tokens of his crucifixion and disclose himself as Jesus of Nazareth, whom they had reviled and whom their fathers put to death. Then will unbelief depart from their souls, and "the blindness in part which has happened unto Israel" be removed. (Charles W. Penrose, "The Second Advent," *Millennial Star*, 10 Sept. 1859, 583)

It is not likely that anyone who is familiar with the signs of the times and is alive at that time will miss the fulfillment of this prophecy. The Doctrine and Covenants tells us that the entire world will feel the earthquake, which is caused by the splitting of the Mount of Olives (bold added for emphasis):

D&C 45:48
48 And then shall the Lord set his foot upon **this mount**, and **it shall cleave in twain**, and **the earth shall tremble, and reel to and fro**, and **the heavens also shall shake**.

Another account of this great event is given by Zechariah (bold added for emphasis):

Zechariah 14:1–5
1 Behold, **the day of the Lord cometh**, and thy spoil shall be divided in the midst of thee.

2 For I will gather all **nations** [*all the wicked*] **against Jerusalem** to battle; and the city shall be taken, and the houses rifled, and the women ravished; and half of the city shall go forth into captivity, and the residue of the people shall not be cut off from the city.

3 **Then shall the Lord go forth, and fight against those nations**, as when he fought in the day of battle.

4 And **his feet shall stand in that day upon the mount of Olives**, which is before Jerusalem on the east, and **the mount of Olives shall cleave** in the midst thereof toward the east and toward the west, and *there shall be a very great valley*; and half of the mountain shall remove toward the north, and half of it toward the south.

5 And **ye shall flee *to* the valley** of the mountains; for the valley of the mountains shall reach unto Azal: yea, ye shall flee, like as ye fled from before the earthquake in the days of Uzziah king of Judah: and **the Lord my God shall come, *and* all the saints with thee**.

Perhaps someday it will be reported on the news that a major earthquake has been recorded near Jerusalem, and seismologists believe that it is the cause for the strange earthquake felt throughout the world. Furthermore, the news may well report that numerous Jews were seen fleeing into the valley created by the earthquake. The faithful who are aware of the signs of the times will know what is going on and their testimonies will be strengthened. In fact, they will be excited to know that at that very moment the Savior is appearing to the Jews, their fellow Israelites, according to prophecy, and that a great conversion among the Jews is about to take place.

SIGN 97
THE SIGN OF THE COMING OF THE SON OF MAN
CATEGORY: YET TO BE FULFILLED

This sign is mentioned in Matthew 24:30. We will include a verse before and a verse after for context (bold added for emphasis):

Matthew 24:29–31

29 Immediately after the tribulation of those days shall the sun be darkened, and the moon shall not give her light, and the stars shall fall from heaven, and the powers of the heavens shall be shaken:

30 And then shall appear **the sign of the Son of man** in heaven: and then shall all the tribes of the earth mourn, and they shall see the Son of man coming in the clouds of heaven with power and great glory.

31 And he shall send his angels with a great sound of a trumpet, and they shall gather together his elect from the four winds, from one end of heaven to the other.

This sign is also mentioned in the Pearl of Great Price. We will include several verses here from Joseph Smith—Matthew for context (bold added for emphasis). As you can see, the Savior is mentioning several signs of the times to His disciples in answer to their question asked near the end of verse 4 in this chapter. "What is the sign of thy coming, and of the end of the world, or the destruction of the wicked, which is the end of the world?"

Joseph Smith—Matthew 1:31–36

31 And again, this Gospel of the Kingdom shall be preached in all the world, for a witness unto all nations, and then shall the end come, or the destruction of the wicked;

32 And again shall the abomination of desolation, spoken of by Daniel the prophet, be fulfilled.

33 And immediately after the tribulation of those days, the sun shall be darkened, and the moon shall not give her light, and the stars shall fall from heaven, and the powers of heaven shall be shaken.

34 Verily, I say unto you, this generation, in which these things shall be shown forth, shall not pass away until all I have told you shall be fulfilled.

35 Although, the days will come, that heaven and earth shall pass away; yet my words shall not pass away, but all shall be fulfilled.

36 And, as I said before, after the tribulation of those days, and the powers of the heavens shall be shaken, **then shall appear the sign of the Son of Man in heaven**, and then shall all the tribes of the earth mourn; and they shall see the Son of Man coming in the clouds of heaven, with power and great glory;

It appears that the "sign of the Son of Man in heaven" is one of the signs that precede the actual Second Coming, but there is no specific indication as to what the sign is or how much time goes by between it and His coming.

According to footnote 30a, for Matthew 24:30 in our LDS Bible, Doctrine and Covenants 88:93 is another mention of this sign. We will quote this verse from section 88 with other verses provided for context. Speaking of the last days, the Lord says the following (bold added for emphasis):

D&C 88:90–93

90 And also cometh the testimony of the voice of thunderings, and the voice of lightnings, and the voice of tempests, and the voice of the waves of the sea heaving themselves beyond their bounds.

91 And all things shall be in commotion; and surely, men's hearts shall fail them; for fear shall come upon all people.

92 And angels shall fly through the midst of heaven, crying with a loud voice, sounding the trump of God, saying: Prepare ye, prepare ye, O inhabitants of the earth; for the judgment of our God is come. Behold, and lo, the Bridegroom cometh; go ye out to meet him.

93 And immediately there shall appear **a great sign in heaven**, and all people shall see it together.

The Prophet Joseph Smith spoke of this sign also (bold added for emphasis):

There will be wars and rumors of wars, signs in the heavens above and on the earth beneath, the sun turned into darkness and the moon to blood, earthquakes in divers places, the seas heaving beyond their bounds; then will appear **one grand sign of the Son of Man in heaven**. But what will the world do? They will say it is a planet, a comet, etc. But the Son of man will come as **the sign of the coming of the Son of Man**, which will be as the light of the morning cometh out of the east. (*Teachings of the Prophet Joseph Smith*, 286–87)

Joseph Smith also gave the following clarification regarding seeing this sign: namely, that no one would see "the sign of the Son of Man, as foretold by Jesus; neither has any man, nor will any man, until after the sun shall have been darkened and the moon bathed in blood" (ibid., 280). The Prophet also taught that the devil does not know what this sign is. Said he, "The devil knows many signs, but does not know the sign of the Son of Man, or Jesus" (*History of The Church of Jesus Christ of Latter-day Saints*, 4:608).

As you can see, based on the above information, we are still left without much understanding of this sign of the times. It is one of the signs for which we must await additional clarification and revelation from the Lord through His living prophet. In the meantime, we understand that it will be impossible to miss, since "all people shall see it together" (D&C 88:93).

SIGN 98

THE RIGHTEOUS WILL BE TAKEN UP TO MEET THE COMING LORD

CATEGORY: YET TO BE FULFILLED

When the time comes for the Savior to actually come, the righteous will be caught up to meet Him. We understand the "righteous" to mean those who are living a celestial quality life at that time. Many in the Christian world believe that the righteous will be taken up. However, many of them are not sure whether it is literal or not. Many who believe it is literal believe incorrectly that it will begin happening to the righteous some years before the actual Second Coming and that the worthy will gradually disappear from the earth until there are none but the wicked left to be burned when He comes.

From modern revelation, we understand that it is indeed literal and that the righteous will be taken up as a group to meet the Master at the time of His coming. Since they will still be mortal, and since the Lord will come in full power and full glory, these Saints will have to be "quickened" or "transfigured" in order to be in the direct presence of Christ without being burned by His glory. We also are told that these Saints, along with the resurrected righteous, after they have been caught up to meet Him, will accompany Him as He descends to the earth to begin His millennial reign. These facts are summarized in the Doctrine and Covenants as follows (bold added for emphasis):

D&C 88:96–98

96 And **the saints that are upon the earth, who are alive**, shall be **quickened** and be **caught up to meet him**.

97 And **they** [*who are celestial quality*] **who have slept in their graves shall come forth**, for their graves shall be opened; and they **also** shall be **caught up to meet him** in the midst of the pillar of heaven—

98 **They are Christ's**, the **first fruits** [*those who are celestial quality*], they who **shall descend with him** first, and they who are on the earth and in their graves, who are first caught up to meet him; and all this by the voice of the sounding of the trump of the angel of God.

As stated above, it will be those who are living worthy of the celestial glory who are taken up, and those dead who are worthy of a celestial resurrection who rise from the grave and go up to meet the coming Lord. Those who are to be burned are those who are living a telestial lifestyle or a sons of perdition lifestyle. All this is found by reading Doctrine and Covenants 88:96–102 as a block of related scripture. The question that remains in some people's minds is, "What happens to those who are living a terrestrial lifestyle at the time?" Answer: They will not be destroyed when the Savior comes, but we have no scriptural detail as to how they are preserved from being destroyed. We will have to wait for further revelation on this matter. In the meantime, Joseph Fielding Smith verified that it is celestials who will be caught up to meet Him:

> In modern revelation given to the Church, the Lord has made known more in relation to this glorious event. There shall be at least two classes which shall have the privilege of the resurrection at this time: First, those who "shall dwell in the presence of God and his Christ forever and ever;" and second, honorable men, those who belong to the terrestrial kingdom as well as those of the celestial kingdom.
>
> At the time of the coming of Christ, "They who have slept in their graves shall come forth, for their graves shall be opened; and they also shall be caught up to meet him in the midst of the pillar of heaven—They are Christ's, the first fruits, they who shall descend with him first, and they who are on the earth and in their graves, who are first caught up to meet him; and all this by the voice of the sounding of the trump of the angel of God." These are the just, "whose names are written in heaven, where God and Christ are the judge of all. These are they who are just men made perfect through Jesus the mediator of the new covenant, who wrought out this perfect atonement through

the shedding of his own blood." (*Doctrines of Salvation*, 2:296)

According to the Parable of the Wheat and the Tares, as explained in the Doctrine and Covenants, the righteous will be taken up first, and then the wicked will be burned (bold added for emphasis):

> D&C 86:7
> 7 Therefore, let the wheat and the tares grow together until the harvest is fully ripe; then ye shall **first gather out the wheat** from among the tares, and **after the gathering of the wheat, behold and lo, the tares are bound in bundles, and the field remaineth to be burned**.

By the way, the correct order of the gathering of the wheat and the tares is that first the righteous are gathered and taken up (D&C 88:96) and then the wicked are burned. The Bible has the tares being gathered first, but the JST corrects it (bold added for emphasis):

> Matthew 13:30
> 30 Let both grow together until the harvest: and in the time of harvest I will say to the reapers, Gather ye together **first the tares**, and bind them in bundles to burn them: but gather the wheat into my barn.

> JST Matthew 13:29
> 29 Let both grow together until the harvest, and in the time of harvest, I will say to the reapers, Gather ye together **first the wheat** into my barn; and the tares are bound in bundles to be burned.

Just a note regarding the JST. The verses in the Joseph Smith Translation of the Bible do not always coincide with the versification of the Bible. Quite often, the JST adds more verses or combines verses.

100 SIGNS

HOPE IN THE SECOND COMING

BY DEL PARSON

SIGN 99

THE WICKED WILL BE BURNED

CATEGORY: YET TO BE FULFILLED

The wicked are those who are living a telestial lifestyle (see D&C 76:103 for a description) or the lifestyle of sons of perdition (see D&C 76:31–35 for a description). They will be destroyed at the Second Coming. There are numerous scripture references to this effect. One of the best known is at the end of the Old Testament (bold added for emphasis):

> Malachi 4:1
> 1 For, behold, the day cometh, that shall burn as an oven; and all the proud, yea, and all that do wickedly, shall be stubble: and **the day that cometh shall burn them up**, saith the Lord of hosts, that it shall leave them neither root nor branch.

Many wonder how the wicked will be burned. There seem to be a number of opinions and theories about this. The scriptures, however, if carefully read, clearly say that the wicked will be burned by the glory of the coming Lord. Since they are not worthy to be "quickened" or transfigured with the righteous (see D&C 88:96), they will be consumed by the glory of the resurrected and glorified Christ. Among other places in scripture, we read the following in the Doctrine and Covenants (bold added for emphasis):

> D&C 5:19
> 19 For a desolating scourge shall go forth among the inhabitants of the earth, and shall continue to be poured out from time to time, if they repent not, until the earth is empty, and the inhabitants thereof are consumed away and **utterly destroyed by the brightness of my coming**.

It is helpful to have other verses in the scriptures on this subject. We read the same message in the New Testament (bold added for emphasis):

> 2 Thessalonians 2:8
> 8 And then shall that Wicked be revealed, whom the Lord shall consume with the spirit of his mouth, and **shall destroy with the brightness of his coming**:

We read it also in the Book of Mormon (bold added for emphasis):

> 2 Nephi 12:10, 19, and 21
> 10 O ye wicked ones, enter into the rock, and hide thee in the dust, for the fear of the Lord and **the glory of his majesty shall smite thee**.
>
> 19 And they shall go into the holes of the rocks, and into the caves of the earth, for the fear of the Lord shall come upon them and **the glory of his majesty shall smite them**, when he ariseth to shake terribly the earth.
>
> 21 To go into the clefts of the rocks, and into the tops of the ragged rocks, for the fear of the Lord shall come upon them and **the majesty of his glory shall smite them**, when he ariseth to shake terribly the earth.

Since this will be a selective destruction, only those people and those things that do not belong on earth during the Millennium will be destroyed. This answers the concern that some people have who wonder if the temples will survive the burning at the Second Coming. Some have also wondered about the status of animals and other creatures when He comes. We understand that they are not judged, and that they will revert to the peaceful creatures they were before the fall of Adam (Isaiah 11:6–9). Thus, it appears that they will not be destroyed.

Also, as mentioned in sign 63, above, the question comes up as to how those living a terrestrial lifestyle (good and honorable people—see D&C 76:75) will survive the Second

Coming. They are not "Saints" (D&C 88:96), in other words, faithful, covenant-keeping members of the Church, and thus apparently do not qualify to be taken up to meet the coming Christ. Neither are they wicked, so they do not qualify to be burned at His coming. Micah 4:3–5 —especially verse 5—teaches that, at the beginning of the Millennium, there will be peace and that there will still be peaceable people who do not believe in the true God. Jeremiah 31:31–34 and Doctrine and Covenants 84:98 teach that eventually during the Millennium, virtually all will join the Church. Thus, even though we don't know how these people will be spared from the destruction that awaits the wicked at the time of the Second Coming, we do know that they will survive and be on the earth as the Millennium commences.

Modern prophets have spoken about the fact that large numbers of good and honorable nonmembers will still inhabit the earth as the thousand years get underway. Joseph Fielding Smith taught us:

> There will be millions of people, Catholics, Protestants, agnostics, Mohammedans, people of all classes and all beliefs, still permitted to remain upon the face of the earth, but they will be those who have lived clean lives, those who have been free from wickedness and corruption. All who belong, by virtue of their good lives, to [at least] the terrestrial order, . . . will remain upon the face of the earth during the millennium. (*Doctrines of Salvation*, 2:86–87)

It will be a wonderful and very successful missionary undertaking to teach these good people the gospel during the Millennium.

SIGN 100

EVERYONE WILL SEE CHRIST WHEN HE COMES

CATEGORY: YET TO BE FULFILLED

In Revelation, we read that everyone will see the coming of the Savior, including those involved in His crucifixion (bold added for emphasis):

Revelation 1:7
7 Behold, he cometh with clouds; and **every eye shall see him**, and **they** *also* **which pierced him**: and all kindreds of the earth shall wail because of him. Even so, Amen.

For some, this will be a wonderful day, for they will be transfigured and caught up to meet him (see D&C 88:96). For others, it will be a time of great terror, for there is no escaping the accountability for their intentional wickedness. Speaking of the plight of the wicked at the Second Coming, the Bible teaches us (bold added for emphasis):

Revelation 6:14–16
14 And the heaven departed as a scroll when it is rolled together; and every mountain and island were moved out of their places.

15 And [*speaking of the wicked*] **the kings of the earth, and the great men, and the rich men, and the chief captains, and the mighty men, and every bondman, and every free man, hid themselves** in the dens and in the rocks of the mountains;

16 And **said to the mountains and rocks, Fall on us, and hide us from the face of him that sitteth on the throne, and from the wrath of the Lamb**:

On the other hand, the righteous will have great cause to rejoice, for they will humbly greet the Savior and will be at peace in His presence. They will dwell with Him on earth as the Millennium begins. They will have the pleasure of associating with resurrected loved ones who visit the earth as needed to carry on with the work of the Lord. They will be in a society of true saints and others who will gradually accept the gospel and who will uphold righteousness on every side. They will enjoy the privilege of living in peace at the time spoken of in scripture when (bold added for emphasis):

> Isaiah 11:6–9
> 6 **The wolf also shall dwell with the lamb** and **the leopard shall lie down with the kid** [*young goat*]; and **the calf and the young lion** and the fatling together; **and a little child shall lead** [*herd*] **them** [*Millennial conditions*].
>
> 7 And **the cow and the bear shall feed** [*graze*]; their young ones shall lie down together: and **the lion shall eat straw like the ox**.
>
> 8 And **the sucking** [*nursing*] **child shall play on the hole of the asp** [*viper*], and the weaned child shall put his hand on the cockatrice' [*venomous serpent's*] den.
>
> 9 **They shall not hurt nor destroy in all my holy mountain** [*throughout the earth*]: for **the earth shall be full of the knowledge of** [*Hebrew: devotion to*] **the Lord**, as the waters cover the sea.

SUMMARY

These and other signs of the times are strong and obvious witnesses that the gospel is true. They strengthen testimonies and assure that all the promises of the Lord will be fulfilled, including the wonderful promise that He will cleanse us from all sin if we keep His commandments

and thus come unto Him. The fulfillment and approaching fulfillment of these prophecies come at a time in the history of the world when there is much skepticism and unbelief in God. It is as if the Lord were saying that in the last days, He will provide such absolutely clear evidence that He exists that anyone who honestly considers these signs would have to conclude that the scriptures are true and God lives.

As stated at the beginning of this book, if we use these signs of the times as intended by the Savior, we will not use them to spread fear and panic. Rather we will adhere to the Master's counsel regarding them and not become troubled by them. We will use them to strengthen our knowledge that all His promises will be fulfilled. He told His disciples (bold added for emphasis):

> D&C 45:35
> 35 And I said unto them: **Be not troubled**, for, when all these things shall come to pass, ye may know that the promises which have been made unto you shall be fulfilled.

AND EVERY EYE SHALL SEE HIM, AND THEY *ALSO* WHICH PIERCED HIM.

REVELATION 1:7

CHAPTER 5

CONDITIONS PRECEDING CHRIST'S APPEARANCE TO THE NEPHITES COMPARED TO CONDITIONS LEADING UP TO THE SECOND COMING

THERE ARE MANY interesting parallels between the "signs of the times" for their day among the Nephites and the signs of the times for our day. The conditions in their "last days" before the destruction of the wicked at the coming of the resurrected Christ to them (recorded, beginning in 3 Nephi 8), and the conditions in our day that are leading up to the Second Coming of the Lord in our dispensation, are surprisingly similar. We will note just a few of these parallels.

We will start in the book of Helaman in the Book of Mormon. The date at the beginning of Helaman is 85 years before the appearance of the resurrected Christ to the Nephites. Therefore, it is 85 years before the destruction of the wicked in the Americas and 85 years before the deliverance of the "more righteous" (3 Nephi 9:13) from their wicked oppressors. The righteous in the Book of Mormon had 200 years of peace after the coming of the resurrected Lord to them. The "more righteous" (meaning those who are living a terrestrial quality life or a celestial quality life, as described in D&C 76) who are spared at the Second Coming will be with Christ as the 1000 years of peace begin.

BEFORE APPEARANCE OF RESURRECTED CHRIST TO THE NEPHITES	BEFORE THE SECOND COMING
Helaman 1:1–13. Political turmoil and overthrow of governmants, including political assassinations.	Same thing going on all over the world in our day.
Helaman 1:14; 3 Nephi 3:26. Wars and rumors of wars.	D&C 45:26; Matt. 24:6. Wars and rumors of wars.
Helaman 4:4. Many dissenters and apostates abandon personal righteousnedss and join the enemies of the righteous.	Many dissenters abandoning the Bible and God's commandments and seeking to undermine laws and governments which strive to preserve righteous principles.
Helaman 4:12. Widespread personal wickedness and corruption.	Widespread personal wickedness and corruption.

BEFORE APPEARANCE OF RESURRECTED CHRIST TO THE NEPHITES	BEFORE THE SECOND COMING
Helaman 5:14–19. Great success in reactivating members, plus large numbers of converts to the Church.	Activation efforts are leading to increased activity and retention rates, plus large numbers of converts to the Church.
Helaman 6:12–14. Members of the Church prosper as a whole and have great joy and much revelation from God, in spite of such gross wickedness all around them.	Same thing happening among faithful members today.
Helaman 6:15–16. Increasing wickedness and more political assassinations.	Same thing happening throughout the world today.
Helaman 6:17. Materialism and pride take over the majority of society.	Same things happening throughout the world today.
Helaman 6:22–23. Secret combinations are formed to commit acts of terrorism against society.	Same things happening throughout the world today.
Helaman 6:31. The majority of society turns away from God and to wickedness.	Same things happening throughout the world today.
Helaman 6:35. The Spirit of the Lord begins to withdraw from the Nephites.	D&C 63:32. "I am holding my Spirit from the inhabitants of the earth."
Helaman 6:38. Government policies and laws, etc., are changed to support personal wickedness.	Laws are passed that support abortion, adultery, homosexuality, etc., remove God from public meetings, prohibit prayers in government, and so forth.
Helaman 7:4–6. Rapid takeover of government by unprincipled leaders who set aside God's commandments, and so forth.	Same things happening throughout the world today.
Helaman 11:1. Wars everywhere.	Same thing happening throughout the world today.

CONDITIONS LEADING TO THE SECOND COMING

BEFORE APPEARANCE OF RESURRECTED CHRIST TO THE NEPHITES	BEFORE THE SECOND COMING
Helaman 11:4–6. People have ignored the gospel preaching, so famine is sent to humble them and reclaim as many as possible back to God.	D&C 88:88–90. Natural disasters happening throughout the world today for the same purpose.
Helaman 13:27–28. Many teach that there is no such thing as right and wrong. They gain popularity and large followings.	Same thing happening throughout the world today.
Helaman 14:6. Many signs and wonders in heaven.	D&C 45:40. Many signs and wonders in heaven and on the earth.
3 Nephi 1:22. Satan tries to get people to refuse to believe obvious signs and wonders.	2 Peter 3:3–4. Many people refuse to believe obvious signs and wonders in the last days.
3 Nephi 1:23. Much peace among faithful members of the Church.	Much peace and happiness among faithful members of the Church.
3 Nephi 2:14–16. Many Lamanites join the Church.	D&C 49:24. Lamanites "blossom as the rose." Large numbers are joining the Church.
3 Nephi 3:9–10. The wicked claim that their evil works are good works.	Isaiah 5:20. Same things happening throughout the world today.
3 Nephi 6:11. Many lawyers were employed in the land.	Same thing happening throughout the world today.
3 Nephi 7:2. Society divided up into ethnic groups who were against each other.	Same thing happening throughout the world today.
3 Nephi 7:16. Nephi testified boldly to the people.	Church leaders today testify boldly to the world as well as to members.

CONDITIONS
LEADING TO
THE SECOND
COMING

BEFORE APPEARANCE OF RESURRECTED CHRIST TO THE NEPHITES	BEFORE THE SECOND COMING
3 Nephi 17–20. People got so wicked that they became angry at Nephi for doing miracles.	The wicked get very angry at the leaders and members of the Church as the Church continues its miraculous growth and service.
3 Nephi 7:22. Many miracles and great outpourings of the Spirit among the faithful.	The righteous today experience many miracles and great outpourings of the Spirit.
3 Nephi 7:26. Many baptisms just before the coming of the Lord (recorded in 3 Nephi 8).	Convert baptisms continue to increase in unprecedented numbers.

CONDITIONS LEADING TO THE SECOND COMING

CHAPTER 6
THE ACTUAL SECOND COMING OF CHRIST

BEFORE WE BRIEFLY consider what will happen at the time of the actual Second Coming, we will mention that there are some major appearances of Christ before *the* Second Coming that are often confused with His appearance to all the world. We will mention three of these appearances here, not necessarily in sequence:

1. To those in the New Jerusalem in America (3 Nephi 21:23–25; D&C 45:66–67)

Before the Lord's Second Coming, the city of New Jerusalem will be built in Independence, Jackson County, Missouri. This "Holy City" (Moses 7:62) is often referred to as the "city of Zion" (D&C 57:2) and will continue on into the Millennium, serving as one of two capital cities for the Savior during the Millennium. The other capital city will be Old Jerusalem. The Savior will be in their midst.

2. To the Jews in Jerusalem (D&C 45:48; 51–53; Zechariah 12:10; 14:2–5)

When the Jews are being destroyed in an unprecedented siege against Jerusalem, they will be rescued by the appearance of the Savior upon the Mount of Olives. The Mount will split in two and the nearly vanquished Jews will flee into the valley that is formed. There, they will see the Savior and will ask Him to explain what happened to Him that caused such wounds in His hands and feet. He will then fight their battle for them and win.

3. To those assembled at Adam-ondi-Ahman (Daniel 7:9–10, 13–14; D&C 116)

> Adam-ondi-Ahman is located in Missouri, roughly 70 miles north, northeast of Independence. Joseph Fielding Smith taught about this meeting at Adam-ondi-Ahman, before the Second Coming. He said, "All who have held keys will make their reports and deliver their stewardships, as they shall be required. Adam will . . . then . . . make his report, as the one holding the keys for this earth, to his superior officer, Jesus Christ. Our Lord will then assume the reins of government; directions will be given to the Priesthood; and He, whose right it is to rule, will be installed officially by the voice of the Priesthood there assembled. This grand council of Priesthood will be composed, not only of those who are faithful who now dwell on this earth, but also of the prophets and apostles of old, who have had directing authority. (Joseph Fielding Smith, *Way to Perfection*, [Salt Lake City: Deseret Book, 1984], 290–91)

Bruce R. McConkie described this assembly at Adam-ondi-Ahman as follows:

We now come to the least known and least understood thing connected with the second coming . . . It is a doctrine that has scarcely dawned on most of the Latter-day Saints themselves; . . . Before the Lord Jesus descends openly . . . there is to be a secret appearance to selected members of His Church. He will come in private to his prophet and to the apostles then living . . . and further, all the faithful members of the church then living and all the faithful saints of all the ages past will be present . . . and it will take place in Daviess County, Missouri, at a place called Adam-ondi-Ahman. . . . The grand summation of the whole matter comes in these words: 'and also with all those whom my Father hath given me out of the world' (D&C 27:14). The sacrament is to be administered . . . this, of course, will be a part of the Grand Council at Adam-ondi-Ahman. (*The Millennial Messiah*, 578–79, 587)

THE ACTUAL SECOND COMING

We will now use the scriptures to briefly describe what will happen when the Savior actually comes to all the world; in other words, the actual Second Coming, which has been prophesied repeatedly throughout the earth's history. In order to keep it simple and to the point, we will present a few commonly asked questions associated with this long-awaited event and provide brief answers from the scriptures (as has been the case throughout this book, we will add **bold** for emphasis along with some explanatory notes in brackets for teaching purposes).

ACTUAL SECOND COMING

QUESTION: What will happen to the faithful Saints who are alive on earth when He comes?

ANSWER: They will be "quickened" (transfigured) and taken up alive, to meet the coming Lord.

D&C 88:96

96 And **the saints** that are upon the earth, **who are alive**, shall be **quickened** and be **caught up to meet him**.

Note: the reason they will be "quickened" or transfigured is that these righteous members of the Church will still have mortal bodies and, otherwise, the glory of the coming Lord would consume them (see 2 Nephi 12:10, 19, and 21). Their situation will be like that of Moses who had to be transfigured in order to survive the direct presence of Jehovah. Moses explained:

Moses 1:11

11 But now mine own eyes have beheld God; but not my natural, but my spiritual eyes, for my natural eyes could not have beheld; for **I should have withered and died in his presence; but** his glory was upon me; and I beheld his face, for **I was transfigured before him**.

QUESTION: Who is resurrected at His coming?

ANSWER: Those in their graves who are worthy of celestial glory.

D&C 88:97

97 And they who have slept in their graves shall come forth, for their graves shall be opened; and they also shall be caught up to meet him in the midst of the pillar of heaven—

AND THE SAINTS THAT ARE UPON THE EARTH, WHO ARE ALIVE, SHALL BE QUICKENED AND BE CAUGHT UP TO MEET HIM.

D & C   88:96

QUESTION: What color will Christ be wearing? Why will He wear that color?

ANSWER: Red, symbolizing the blood of the unrepentant wicked, who now must answer to the law of justice, having refused the law of mercy (the Atonement of Christ). Whether the Savior's clothing is red literally, or red symbolically, the imagery is the same. The color represents the blood of the wicked who are destroyed at His coming.

D&C 133:46–51

46 And it shall be said: Who is this that cometh down from God in heaven **with dyed garments** [*with dyed clothing*]; yea, from the regions which are not known, clothed in his glorious apparel, traveling in the greatness of his strength?

47 And he shall say: I am he who spake in righteousness, mighty to save.

48 **And the Lord shall be red in his apparel** [*clothing*], and his garments like him that treadeth in the wine–vat [*like one who has been treading grapes in the wine tub*].

49 And so great shall be the glory of his presence that the sun shall hide his face in shame, and the moon shall withhold its light, and the stars shall be hurled from their places.

50 And his voice shall be heard: I have trodden the wine–press alone, and have brought judgment upon all people; and none were with me [*Jesus had to do the Atonement alone*];

51 And **I have trampled them** [*the wicked*] in my fury, and I did tread upon them in mine anger, and **their blood have I sprinkled upon my garments** [*clothing*]**, and stained all my raiment** [*clothing*]; for this was the day of vengeance [*the law of justice is being satisfied*] which was in my heart [*which is part of the plan of salvation, which*

the Savior is carrying out for the Father, along with the law of mercy*].

QUESTION: From what direction will He come?

ANSWER: From the east.

Joseph Smith—Matthew 1:26

26 For **as the light of the morning cometh out of the east**, and shineth even unto the west, and covereth the whole earth, **so shall also the coming of the Son of Man be.**

QUESTION: How will the wicked be destroyed?

ANSWER: By the glory of the Lord as He comes to earth.

2 Thessalonians 2:8

8 And then shall that Wicked be revealed, whom the Lord shall consume with the spirit of his mouth, and **shall destroy with the brightness of his coming:**

D&C 5:19

19 For a desolating scourge shall go forth among the inhabitants of the earth, and shall continue to be poured out from time to time, if they repent not, until the earth is empty, and the inhabitants thereof are consumed away and **utterly destroyed by the brightness of my coming**.

2 Nephi 12:10, 19, and 21

10 O ye wicked ones, enter into the rock, and hide thee in the dust, for the fear of the Lord and **the glory of his majesty shall smite thee**.

19 And they shall go into the holes of the rocks, and into the caves of the earth, for the fear of the Lord shall come upon them **and**

the glory of his majesty shall smite them, when he ariseth to shake terribly the earth.

21 To go into the clefts of the rocks, and into the tops of the ragged rocks, for the fear of the Lord shall come upon them and **the majesty of his glory shall smite them**, when he ariseth to shake terribly the earth [*perhaps referring to the moving of the continents back together, in conjunction with His Second Coming*].

QUESTION: What will happen to the earth?

ANSWER: The continents will be moved back together and the earth will be restored to a Garden of Eden like condition [see footnote 10f for the tenth Article of Faith]. In other words, it will receive its "paradisiacal glory" in preparation for the Millennium.

D&C 133:23
23 He shall command the great deep, and it shall be driven back into the north countries, and **the islands shall become one land**;

Article of Faith 10
10 We believe in the literal gathering of Israel and in the restoration of the Ten Tribes; that Zion (the New Jerusalem) will be built upon the American continent; that Christ will reign personally upon the earth; and, that **the earth will be renewed and receive its paradisiacal glory**.

QUESTION: Who will actually come with Him?

ANSWER: The hosts of heaven, including the previously resurrected righteous (D&C 133:54–55), plus the righteous who have just been resurrected and the righteous

mortals who have just been caught up to meet Him.

D&C 88:96–98
96 And **the saints** that are **upon the earth, who are alive**, shall be quickened [*made capable of being in the presence of the Lord, with their mortal bodies*] and be caught up to meet him.

97 And **they** [*the righteous*] **who have slept in their graves** shall come forth, for their graves shall be opened; and they also shall be caught up to meet him in the midst of the pillar of heaven—

98 **They are Christ's**, the first fruits, **they who shall descend with him** first, and they who are on the earth [*the righteous saints who are still alive*] and in their graves [*the righteous dead, who have just been resurrected*], who are first caught up to meet him; and all this by the voice of the sounding of the trump of the angel of God.

QUESTION: Will everyone be caught off guard (like a "thief in the night")?

ANSWER: No. The righteous will be ready and will know that His coming is getting close. However, the wicked will be caught off guard.

D&C 106:4–5
4 And again, verily I say unto you, **the coming of the Lord draweth nigh** [*is getting close*], and **it overtaketh the world** [*the wicked*] **as a thief in the night**—

5 Therefore, gird up your loins [*get ready*], that you may be the children of light [*that you may be counted among the righteous*], and **that day** [*the Second Coming*] **shall not overtake you as a thief**.

ACTUAL SECOND COMING

QUESTION: How will the wicked feel at the time of the Second Coming?

ANSWER: They will wish they could die and somehow avoid facing the Savior.

Revelation 6:16–17
16 And said to the mountains and rocks, **Fall on us, and hide us** from the face of him that sitteth on the throne, and from the wrath of the Lamb:

17 For the great day of his wrath is come; and who shall be able to stand?

QUESTION: Will our prophets tell us the exact time of His coming?

ANSWER: No.

Matthew 24:36
36 But **of that day and hour knoweth no man**, no, **not the angels** of heaven, but my Father only.

Mark 13:32
32 But of that day and that hour knoweth **no man**, no, **not the angels** which are in heaven, **neither the Son**, but the Father.

D&C 49:7
7 I, the Lord God, have spoken it; but the hour and the day no man knoweth, neither the angels in heaven, **nor shall they know until he comes**.

ACTUAL SECOND COMING

Elder M. Russell Ballard

"**I do not know when He is going to come again**. **As far as I know, none of my brethren in the Council of the Twelve or even in the First Presidency knows**. And I would humbly suggest to you, my young brothers and sisters, that **if we do not know, then nobody knows**, no matter how compelling their arguments or how reasonable their calculations." (Address given March 12, 1996, BYU Marriott Center)

QUESTION: Will things get better between now and the Second Coming?

ANSWER: No.

D&C 84:97
97 And plagues shall go forth, and **they shall not be taken from the earth until I have completed my work**, which shall be cut short in righteousness—

D&C 97:23
23 The Lord's scourge shall pass over by night and by day, and the report thereof shall vex all people; yea, **it shall not be stayed** [*restrained, stopped*] **until the Lord come**;

QUESTION: As we see the "signs of the times" being fulfilled all around us, should we panic?

ANSWER: No. The Savior made it clear to his disciples that the purpose of the "signs of the times" was not to promote panic. Rather, these signs are given to strengthen the testimonies of the faithful, as they see these prophecies fulfilled. We will quote the Master as He taught His disciples on this matter:

Joseph Smith—Matthew 1:23, 37, and 39
23 Behold, I speak these things [*the signs of the times*] unto you for the elect's sake; and you also shall hear of wars, and rumors of wars; **see that ye be not troubled**, for all I

WHEN THEY SHALL SEE ALL THESE THINGS, THEY SHALL KNOW THAT HE is NEAR.

JOSEPH SMITH— MATTHEW 1:39

have told you must come to pass; but the end is not yet.

37 And **whoso treasureth up my word, shall not be deceived**, for the Son of Man shall come, and he shall send his angels before him with the great sound of a trumpet, and they shall gather together the remainder of his elect from the four winds, from one end of heaven to the other.

39 So likewise, **mine elect, when they shall see all these things, they shall know that he is near, even at the doors**;

QUESTION: Who is resurrected when the Savior comes?

ANSWER: The righteous from Adam to Christ, meaning those who were worthy of celestial glory, were resurrected with the Savior three days after His crucifixion (D&C 133:54–55). The righteous who have died since then (except for those who have already been resurrected, such as Peter, James, and Moroni) will be resurrected at the beginning of the Millennium.

D&C 88:97–98
97 And they who have slept in their graves shall come forth, for their graves shall be opened; and they also shall be caught up to meet him in the midst of the pillar of heaven—

98 **They are Christ's** [*are worthy of celestial glory*], the first fruits, they who shall descend with him first, and they who are on the earth and in their graves, who are first caught up to meet him; and all this by the voice of the sounding of the trump of the angel of God.

ACTUAL SECOND COMING

Next, still near the beginning of the Millennium, the dead who lived terrestrial quality lives will be resurrected.

D&C 88:99
99 And after this another angel shall sound, which is the second trump; and then cometh the redemption of those who are Christ's at his coming; who have received their part in that prison which is prepared for them, that they might receive the gospel, and be judged according to men in the flesh [*terrestrials, see D&C 76:71, 73–74*].

Then, at the end of the Millennium, all who have earned telestial glory will be resurrected.

D&C 88:100–101
100 And again, another trump shall sound, which is the third trump; and then come **the spirits of men who are to be judged, and are found under condemnation** [*telestials*];

101 And these are the rest of the dead; and they live not again [*are not resurrected*] until the thousand years are ended, neither again, until the end of the earth.

And finally, sons of perdition—not the ones who were the wicked spirits who followed Lucifer in the war in heaven and were cast down to earth with him (Revelation 12:4), rather, those individuals who came to earth, received mortal bodies, and afterward rebelled completely and became sons of perdition (D&C 76:31–35, 44).

D&C 88:102
102 And another trump shall sound, which is the fourth trump, saying: There are found among those who are to remain until that great and last day, even the end, who shall remain filthy still.

CHAPTER 7
HOW GOOD DO YOU HAVE TO BE IN ORDER TO HAVE A PLEASANT SECOND COMING?

WHILE WE DON'T know if we will be around when the Second Coming takes place, nevertheless, the question posed as the title of this chapter is relevant to all of us. If we are dead already, we will want to be worthy to be resurrected and join Him as He descends upon the earth to start the Millennium. If we are still alive, we will want to be worthy to be taken up off the earth to meet Him and then, likewise, descend with Him.

Over many years of teaching and hearing students ask and answer this question in class discussions, it seems that a second question can be asked that will help lead to the answer to the first. The question is this. "In order to be in the presence of God, do you need to be **perfect**, or do you need to be **spotless**?"

Before we answer this second question, perhaps we should ask which of the following statements is correct:

1. "No imperfect thing can dwell in the presence of God."

or,

2. "No unclean thing can dwell in the presence of God."

There are many scriptural references that will provide the correct answer for us, for example:

1 Nephi 10:21
21 Wherefore, if ye have sought to do wickedly in the days of your probation, then ye are found unclean before the judgment-seat of God; and **no unclean thing can dwell with God**; wherefore, ye must be cast off forever.

Helaman 8:25
25 But behold, ye have rejected the truth, and rebelled against your holy God; and even at this time, instead of laying up for yourselves treasures **in heaven**, where nothing doth corrupt, and **where nothing can come which is unclean**, ye are heaping up for yourselves wrath against the day of judgment.

3 Nephi 27:19
19 And **no unclean thing can enter into his kingdom**; therefore nothing entereth into his rest save it be those who have washed their garments in my blood, because of their faith, and the repentance of all their sins, and their faithfulness unto the end.

The answer, repeated over and over again in the scriptures is that no **"unclean"** thing can return into the presence of God. In other words, we must be **"spotless," not "perfect."** This is very good news! It is summarized by Nephi as follows:

2 Nephi 33:7
7 I have charity for my people, and great faith in Christ that I shall meet **many souls spotless** at his judgment-seat.

If we get mixed up in our thinking between "spotless" and "perfect," and decide that we have to be perfect, it can lead to much discouragement and can lead some members to the point where they quit trying to live the gospel. With the help of the Savior and the Atonement, we can all get to the point where we can be made clean, or spotless, and thus qualify to enter back into the presence of God. Perfection will come along in due time after we have passed through the veil, but Christ was the only one who was perfect during mortality.

Elder Dallin H. Oaks, of the Quorum of the Twelve Apostles, gave some powerful advice, which helps us understand that we are not expected to become perfect in all things in this life:

> Another idea that is powerful to lift us from discouragement is that the work of the Church . . . is an eternal work. Not all problems . . . are fixed in mortality. The work of salvation goes on beyond the veil of death, and we should not be too apprehensive about incompleteness within the limits of mortality. ("Powerful Ideas," *Ensign*, November 1995, 25)

The Prophet Joseph Smith taught that there is much progress to be made after we pass through the veil:

> When you climb up a ladder, you must begin at the bottom, and ascend step by step, until you arrive at the top; and so it is with the principles of the Gospel—you must begin with the first, and go on until you learn all the principles of exaltation. But it will be a great while after you have passed through the veil before you will have learned them. It is not all to be comprehended in this world; it will be a great work to learn our salvation and exaltation even beyond the grave. (*Teachings of the Prophet Joseph Smith*, 348)

PLEASANT SECOND COMING?

Now, having been taught by the scriptures and the living prophets that we do not have to be perfect, but rather, spotless or clean, one major question remains: What must we do to enable the Savior to make us clean?

We could go on for some time giving many correct answers, including, "keep the commandments," "follow the Brethren," "read the scriptures," "say our prayers," "serve one another," "keep the Sabbath Day holy," and on and on. And each answer would be correct as a part of a wonderful body of commandments and teachings designed to lead us back into the presence of God. Since all faithful Saints and all who desire to become faithful are striving constantly to do these and many other good things, there must be some simple, basic answer that provides encouragement for the honest in heart, without being overwhelming. There must be some simple principle that gives us confidence that we can qualify to have the Savior make us clean. There is. It is found in the Book of Mormon as follows (bold added for emphasis):

> Alma 34:33 and 36
> 33 And now, as I said unto you before, as ye have had so many witnesses, therefore, I beseech of you that ye do not procrastinate the day of your repentance until the end; for after this day of life, which is given us to prepare for eternity, behold, if we do not **improve** our time while in this life, then cometh the night of darkness wherein there can be no labor performed.
>
> 36 And this I know, because the Lord hath said he dwelleth not in unholy temples, but in the hearts of the righteous doth he dwell; yea, and he has also said that **the righteous** shall sit down in his kingdom, to go no more out; but their garments should be **made white through the blood of the Lamb.**

The word "improve" in verse 33, above, becomes a key word. If we "do not improve," we are in

HAPPY FAMILY

trouble. On the other hand, if we do **improve**, sincerely, we enable the Savior to make us clean through His Atonement (verse 36). Being made clean, we are spotless. Being spotless, we are allowed to be in the presence of God, where, as Joseph Smith pointed out in the previous quote, we can continue to progress until we become perfect.

Elder Marvin J. Ashton of the Quorum of the Twelve taught that the emphasis in the gospel of Christ is on direction and diligence, not necessarily on speed. He taught the importance of continuing improvement. In an address in general conference of April 1989, he said the following:

> I am also convinced of the fact that the speed with which we head along the straight and narrow path isn't as important as the direction in which we are traveling. That direction, if it is leading toward eternal goals, is the all-important factor.

In Summary

How good do we have to be in order to have a pleasant Second Coming? Or a pleasant Judgment Day? Or a pleasant meeting of the Savior when we die? Answer: We have to be honestly striving to be righteous. No matter where we are along the path that leads to the presence of the Father, if we desire to be good, and we are sincerely improving, then we enable the Savior to make us clean. And thus, we can meet Christ humbly and comfortably, and be welcomed into the presence of the Father (D&C 45:3–5).

I HAVE CHARITY FOR MY PEOPLE, AND GREAT FAITH IN CHRIST THAT I SHALL MEET MANY SOULS SPOTLESS AT HIS JUDGMENT-SEAT.

2 NEPHI 33:7

ARTWORK

JOSE MARIA VELASCO
Inspiration of Christopher Columbus

SCOTT JARVIE
Kirtland Temple

DEL PARSON
Hope in the Second Coming

HOWARD CHANDLER CHRISTY
Signing of the Constitution of the United States

ABOUT THE
AUTHOR

DAVID J. RIDGES taught for the Church Educational System for thirty-five years and has taught for several years at BYU Campus Education Week. He taught adult religion classes and Know Your Religion classes for BYU Continuing Education for many years. He has also served as a curriculum writer for Sunday School, seminary, and institute of religion manuals.

He has served in many callings in the Church, including Gospel Doctrine teacher, bishop, stake president, and patriarch. He and Sister Ridges served a full-time eighteen-month mission, training senior CES missionaries and helping coordinate their assignments throughout the world.

Brother Ridges and his wife, Janette, are the parents of six children and make their home in Springville, Utah.

ISBN 978-1-4621-2129-8   USA $36.99 CAN $42.99

53699

9 781462 121298

CFI
AN IMPRINT OF
CEDAR FORT, INC.

CEDAR FORT
Publishing & Media

WWW.CEDARFORT.COM   WWW.DAVIDJRIDGES.COM